LITERARY REPRESENTATIONS OF PANDEMICS, EPIDEMICS AND PESTILENCE

Disease, pestilence and contagion have been an integral component of human lives and stories. This book explores the articulations and representations of the vulnerability of life or the trauma of death in literature about epidemics both from India and around the world.

This book critically engages with stories and narratives that have dealt with pandemics or epidemics in the past and in contemporary times to see how these texts present human life coming to terms with upheaval, fear and uncertainty. Set in various places and times, the literature examined in this book explores the themes of human suffering and resilience, inequality, corruption, the ruin of civilizations and the rituals of grief and remembrance. The chapters in this volume cover a wide spatio-temporal trajectory analysing the writings of Fakir Mohan Senapati and Suryakant Tripathi Nirala, Jack London, Albert Camus, Margaret Atwood, Sarat Chandra, Pandita Ramabai and Christina Sweeney-Baird, among others. It gives readers a glimpse into both grounded and fantastical realities where disease and death clash with human psychology and where philosophy, politics and social values are critiqued and problematized.

This book will be of interest to students of English literature, social science, gender studies, cultural studies, psychology, society, politics and philosophy. General readers too will find this exciting as it covers authors from across the world.

Nishi Pulugurtha is Associate Professor at the Department of English, Brahmananda Keshab Chandra College, Kolkata, India.

LITERARY REPRESENTATIONS OF PANDEMICS, EPIDEMICS AND PESTILENCE

Edited by Nishi Pulugurtha

Routledge
Taylor & Francis Group

LONDON AND NEW YORK

Designed cover image: Aditya Banerjee

First published 2023
by Routledge
4 Park Square, Milton Park, Abingdon, Oxon OX14 4RN

and by Routledge
605 Third Avenue, New York, NY 10158

Routledge is an imprint of the Taylor & Francis Group, an informa business

British Library Cataloguing-in-Publication Data
A catalogue record for this book is available from the British Library

ISBN: 978-1-032-21091-9 (hbk)
ISBN: 978-1-032-27856-8 (pbk)
ISBN: 978-1-003-29443-6 (ebk)

DOI: 10.4324/9781003294436

Typeset in Bembo
by Apex CoVantage, LLC

CONTENTS

CONTRIBUTORS

Riti Agarwala is Senior Research Fellow pursuing her Ph.D. in the Department of Comparative Literature, Jadavpur University. As a part of her M.Phil. project, she had studied the representation of nature and its forms by the Pardhan Gonds (a Central India based tribal community) in her thesis: "Indigeneity and its Discontents: In conversation with Pardhan Gond nature-culture". As a part of her Ph.D. thesis, she is studying various forms of body representation in visual art. She was also a part of the Global Initiative for Academic Network (GIAN) project at Jadavpur University. She has presented papers at the University of Perpignan, France; IIT Patna; Jadavpur University; Ramakrishna Mission; Burdwan University; and Serampore College.

Amit R. Baishya is Associate Professor in the Department of English at the University of Oklahoma. His first monograph *Contemporary Literature from Northeast India: Deathworlds, Terror and Survival* was published by Routledge in 2018. He is also the co-editor of three collections: *Northeast India: A Place of Relations* (co-editor Yasmin Saikia, Cambridge University Press, 2017), *Postcolonial Animalities* (co-editor Suvadip Sinha, Routledge, 2019) and a special issue of the journal *Postcolonial Studies* titled "Planetary Solidarities: Postcolonial Theory, the Anthropocene and the Nonhuman" (co-editor Priya Kumar, 2021). He is currently co-editing a special issue titled "Insides-Outsides: Anglophone Literatures from Northeast India" for *South Asian Review* with Rakhee Kalita Moral, and also writing his second monograph on species extinction, deep time and multispecies cohabitation in contemporary postcolonial literature. Baishya translates short stories and novels from Assamese to English. His translation of Debendranath Acharya's Assamese novel, *Jangam* (The Movement, Vitasta Press), on the "forgotten long march" of Indians from Burma during WWII was released in 2018.

Sumantra Baral is currently pursuing M.Phil. from the Department of English, Jadavpur University, Kolkata. Interested in the areas of nineteenth-century Bengal, Book History, Modernism and Disaster Studies, he has presented papers in universities like the University of Oxford, Johns Hopkins University, University of Rochester and more. Some of his recent writings have been published in Muse India, Café Dissensus, among others. As a SUISS Alumnus, his poems have frequently appeared in the University of Edinburgh Journal.

Subarna Bhattacharya is Assistant Professor in the Department of English, Symbiosis College of Arts and Commerce, Pune. Her research interests are travel writing studies, women's writing and feminist studies. She is currently working on a minor research project on "Women's travel writings of 19th century colonial India" as co-investigator. She has published research papers on travel writing studies. Her recent academic publication is "Beyond Postcoloniality: Female Subjectivity and Travel in Jamaica Kincaid's Among Flowers" in *Rupkatha Journal on Interdisciplinary Studies in Humanities*. She has authored a chapter on travel writing in an edited volume titled *Modern Indian Literature. Diaspora, Travel and Culture*, published by Prestige Books International. She has co-edited two anthologies, *We and Our World* and *Soft Skills Through Literature*, published by Pearson India.

Sayan Aich Bhowmik is currently Assistant Professor in the Department of English, Shirakole College. He is the co-editor of *Plato's Caves Online*, a semi-academic space of poetry, politics and culture. He has recently brought out his debut collection of poems, *I Will Come With A Lighthouse*, from Hawakal Publishers, New Delhi. He is currently co-editing an anthology of critical essays on Popular Culture to be brought out by Orient Blackswan in 2022.

Tania Chakravertty is the Dean of Students' Welfare, Diamond Harbour Women's University, West Bengal. Educated at Presidency College and Calcutta University, Chakravertty has a Ph.D. on Ernest Hemingway. Chakravertty was part of a US state-aided academic group project in 2010, as part of the prestigious International Visitor Leadership Program. She has authored *Rhapsodies and Musings: poets in the mirrors of other eyes*. Her monographs have appeared in National and International journals. Her areas of academic interest include Gender Studies, American Literature and Literature of the Diaspora. She is the Joint Assistant Secretary, Executive Council, of the Inter-Cultural Poetry and Performance Library.

Paramita Dutta, OCELT, is currently based in Toronto, Canada, where she is an ESL Instructor at Halton District School Board. Previously, she taught as English lecturer at Ryerson University, Toronto and effectively contributed as a research assistant in the "Lexicons of Early Modern English" research project of the English Department at the University of Toronto. She was Assistant Professor of English in India for over 9 years. She completed her doctoral thesis from Jadavpur University, India, on early modern drama and her research and teaching interests include

Shakespeare and early modern drama, Shakespeare and film, English as a Second Language and modern fiction. She has presented papers widely at conferences held in India, Canada, the United Kingdom and the United States. Her publications include an article on *Shakespeare Wallah* in Shormishtha Panja and Babli Moitra Saraf Ed. *Performing Shakespeare in India* published by Sage (2016), Tagore's *Bidaay Abhishaap* in Bhattacharya and Renganathan ed. *The Politics and Reception of Rabindranath Tagore's Drama* published by Routledge (New York, 2015) and a short story titled "The First Time" in the collection *Emanations 2 + 2 = 5* edited by Carter Kaplan and published by International Authors (Massachusetts, 2015).

Subham Dutta is Assistant Professor at the Department of English, Gokhale Memorial Girls' College, Kolkata. He completed his Ph.D. on Sri Aurobindo's Mingled Drama from the Department of English, Visva-Bharati in December 2021. He has presented papers at various National and International symposiums. He co-edited "Popular Narratives: Texts and Contexts" with Dr. Ankur Konar. He has published paper in several national journals and also written some book chapters too.

Yash Gupta is Documentation and Research Assistant at Chhatrapati Shivaji Maharaj Vastu Sangrahalaya (Formerly Prince of Wales Museum of Western India). A Graduate in Literary and Cultural Studies from FLAME University, Pune, his prior publications include "Remembering Online: Reinscribing Normative Autobiographies in the Pandemic Era Digital Obituary" at *Café Dissensus* and "Paranormal Patriarchy and Vengeful Women: Tracing Misogyny in the Cultural Constructions of Vindictive Spirits" at *Supernatural and Spirituality*, organized by Progressive Connections, along with other forthcoming academic negotiations. His research interests focus on the intersections of digital cultures and mourning behaviour, with a specific focus on mortuary discourses. His other research works have engaged with culinary discourses of the Sindhi experience of the Indian Partition, culinary narratives of resistance within the Dalit community, feminist critiques of mythological texts and intersectional analysis of asexuality in media, among others.

Sacaria Joseph is an assistant professor of English at St. Xavier's College, Kolkata. A student of St. Xavier's College during his graduation, he did his MA in English Literature from Pune University, M.Phil. from Jadavpur University, Kolkata and Doctorate from Visva-Bharati University, West Bengal. As a visiting faculty at Jnana-Deepa Vidyapeeth, Pune, he teaches courses related to literature and philosophy in the department of philosophy. His area of special interest and research is cinema and literature. He writes on issues related to literature, philosophy, cinema, culture, politics, etc.

Goutam Karmakar is an NRF Postdoctoral Fellow at the University of the Western Cape, South Africa. He is also an Assistant Professor of English at Barabazar

Bikram Tudu Memorial College, Sidho-Kanho-Birsha University, Purulia, West Bengal, India. His forthcoming and recently published edited books are *Nation and Narration: Hindi Cinema and the Making and Remaking of National Consciousness* (Routledge, forthcoming), *The Poetry of Jibanananda Das: Aesthetics, Poetics, and Narratives* (Routledge, forthcoming), *Narratives of Trauma in South Asian Literature* (Routledge, 2022), *The City Speaks: Urban Spaces in Indian Literature* (Routledge, 2022) and *Religion in South Asian Anglophone Literature: Traversing Resistance, Margins and Extremism* (Routledge, 2021). He has been published in journals, including *Visual Anthropology, Quarterly Review of Film and Video, Intersections, MELUS, Interdisciplinary Literary Studies, Journal of Environmental Planning and Management, Comparative Literature: East & West, Journal of International Women's Studies, IUP Journal of English Studies, South Asia Research, Journal of Graphic Novels and Comics, South Asian Review, Journal of Gender Studies, Journal of Postcolonial Writing, National Identities, Nationalism and Ethnic Politics, Asian Journal of Women's Studies* and *Asiatic* among others.

Tabish Khair is the author of critically acclaimed books, including the novels *Filming: A Love Story, The Thing About Thugs, How to Fight Islamist Terror from the Missionary Position, Just Another Jihadi Jane,* and the poetry collections *Where Parallel Lines Meet* and *Man of Glass.* His studies include *The Gothic, Postcolonialism and Otherness* and *The New Xenophobia.* Winner of the All India Poetry Prize, his novels have been shortlisted for more than a dozen major prizes, including the Man Asian, the DSC Prize, the Sahitya Academy Award and the Encore. An associate professor at Aarhus University, Denmark, he has been a Leverhulme Guest Professor at Leeds University, UK, and has held fellowships at JNU, Delhi University, Hong Kong City University and Hong Kong Baptist University (China), York University and Cambridge University (UK), etc. He recently published a poetry pamphlet, *Quarantined Sonnets* (Kitaab, Singapore), on the pandemic, with profits being donated to a migrant worker charity. He is currently finishing a speculative post-pandemic novel, titled *The Body by the Shore.*

Sarottama Majumdar is Associate Professor of English at a college affiliated with the University of Calcutta. She has been a fellow at the School of Cultural Texts and Records at Jadavpur University and is a member of other literary associations in the city and country. Her research interests include culture and identity formation in nineteenth-century British India on which she has published and presented papers and articles in national and international journals, books and conferences.

Ishan Mehandru is a graduate student in the Comparative Literary Studies programme at Northwestern University, USA. In the past, he has worked at the Centre for Studies in Gender and Sexuality at Ashoka University, conducting workshops for students across colleges, and facilitating research on feminist media studies. He is interested in women's writings in Hindi-Urdu literature, masculinity studies and intellectual histories of emancipation in South Asia.

Sipra Mukherjee is Professor, Department of English, West Bengal State University, India. Her research interests are religion, caste and modern literatures.

Nishi Pulugurtha is Associate Professor, Department of English, Brahmananda Keshab Chandra College, Kolkata. Her areas of interest are British Romantic literature, Indian writing in English, the diaspora and Shakespeare adaptations in film. She has a monograph on *Derozio* and a collection of travel essays, *Out in the Open*, an edited volume of essays on travel, *Across and Beyond* (2020), a volume of poems *The Real and The Unreal and Other Poems* (2020) and a collection of short stories *The Window Sill* (2021). She has edited a special feature issue of *Muse India* on "Shakespeare in Indian Cinema" (July–August 2021). A volume of poems is forthcoming from Writers Workshop, Kolkata. She also writes about Alzheimer's Disease.

Sanghita Sanyal is Assistant Professor in the Departments of English and B.Ed., Loreto College. Gender and Sexuality Studies are her special areas of interest and function, besides Culture Studies and Translations. She is also one of the Executive Council Members of the Intercultural Poetry and Performance Library, Kolkata.

INTRODUCTION

Nishi Pulugurtha

"... The plague –"

"That's enough, keep your mouth shut! In a house full of people you shouldn't mention the name of that ruinous disease." ...

Pustules came out on Jagdish, then on Pandit Dayaram, then on Misra-ji. Then they kept coming out on other people. Funeral processions left from one house, then another house, then house after house. Bi Amma and Sharifan together kept count of them, up to ten. Then they lost count. In a single day, such a number of houses sent out funeral processions!

– Basti *by Intizar Husain*[1]

Living in COVID-19 times, certain words have now become commonplace. The 2-year-old who comes visiting her maternal grandmother, my neighbour, refuses to budge outdoors without a mask. On social media, I see a video that has little children press a pole, a bottle, a jar, a fence, whatever they see and emulate the act of hand sanitization. Several months since the lockdown and we still are unsure of how things are going to be. The pandemic has wrecked lives and destroyed livelihoods. Vast changes in all aspects of life are already clearly visible, in economic systems and various institutional processes.

Etymologically, the word pandemic has its roots in Greek and is a combination of two words – "pan" meaning "all" and "demos" meaning "people". The word has often been used interchangeably with the word epidemic. Chinmay Tumbe in *The Age of Pandemic* notes,

For a disease to become an epidemic, it must suddenly affect many members of a community at the same time. Time, that is, simultaneity, matters more than space, or geographic coverage.

DOI: 10.4324/9781003294436-1

> But for an epidemic to become a pandemic, both time and space are equally important, that is, the disease has to spread across a sufficiently wide geographical region to be declared a pandemic.[2]

As Tumbe notes,

> An English language dictionary in 1775 defined "pandemic" as an adjective derived from Greek that meant "incident to a whole people". The word was rarely used in the way it is used today, and "pandemic love" was a phrase used to describe forms of vulgar love.

Tumbe writes that "The words *mari* or *maari* have been used for epidemics for many centuries now, in large parts of India. *Mahamaari*, now used for the word 'pandemic', is clearly mentioned in the 19th century to describe plague in northern India". Tumbe's work published in 2020, the year of the pandemic, focuses on India in the period between 1817 and 1920, a time when India had to deal with three pandemics – cholera, plague and influenza.

As we have been living through a pandemic, we have become more conscious of texts that deal with them, often re-reading and re-evaluating them as the resonances are uncannily similar, so very real now. Literary texts which deal with pandemics hold up before us examples of how things have been managed before in times of similar crises, as well as ideas about how we might restructure our societies in their aftermath. They reveal to us life in times of crises and aspects of human behaviour. There has always been literature on pandemic because there have always been pandemics and epidemics. What is characteristic of literary works in which epidemics feature is an attempt to try and make some sense of meaning out of the experiences of life in pandemic times, of the panic, fear and hopelessness that characterizes the times. Pandemic literature does not seek to analyse the reasons for the pestilence, rather the narratives and stories work as a reminder, that in spite of everything, there is a sense in things around us, in spite of the quarantine, the physical distancing, the isolation and all the fear – if not anywhere else, at least in the stories we tell and write.

As we try to hold on and deal with the immense changes that are happening all around us, in a world where the virus controls much of our lives, it is definitely interesting to examine the way pandemics/epidemics have been presented in literature. Virginia Woolf, who dealt with so much illness and whose health suffered due to the 1918 virus, writes in her essay "On Being Ill" how illness and the body are left out of our art and conscious experiences.[3] It is yet to be seen whether COVID-19 changes this. Disease, death and mortality are issues that face us on a regular basis and we talk about death rates, mortality percentages, statistics and the like much more now.

Literary texts that deal with pandemics/epidemics are many – Giovanni Boccaccio's *The Decameron* (1353), Daniel Defoe's *A Journal of the Plague Year* (1722), Katherine Anne Porter's short story "Pale Horse, Pale Rider" (1939), Ahmed

Ali's *Twilight in Delhi* (1940), Albert Camus' *The Plague* (1947), Kenzaburo Oe's *Nip the Buds, Shoot the Kids* (1958), Octavia E. Butler's *Survivor* (1978), Philip Roth's *Nemesis* (2010) and Edgar Allan Poe's short story "The Masque of Red Death" (1842), to name just a few. Indian literature too has texts that deal with epidemics and pandemics that reveal life affected, turbulent times, fear and anxiety that rupture life in terrible ways. Some of these texts have been recently translated into English, the times make us go back to them, to try to make some sense of the turbulence that had been a part of society sometime in the historical past. *Pahighar*, a Hindi novel by Kamalkant Tripathi is set in 1857, the time of the first uprising against the British in India, a time when floods and epidemics ravaged lives. George Verghese Kakkananan's novel *Vasoori* (1968) depicts the outbreak of smallpox in a hamlet in Kerala, while *Plague ki Chudail* (1902) by Master Bhagwan Das explores the fear and anxiety that become a part of the lives of people in Allahabad in northern India during the plague pandemic in the late nineteenth and early twentieth centuries. Sarat Candra Chattopadhay's novels *Palli Samaj*, *Pandit Mashai* and *Srikanta* all have epidemics as a major part of the narrative. Munshi Premchand's short story "Idgah", and "Doodh Ka Daam", Fakir Mohan Senapati's "Rebati", Thakazhi Sivasankara Pillai's novel *Thottiyude Makan* are other works where epidemics feature. It is interesting to see the kind of literary works that COVID-19 pandemic will result in. Already one notices a lot of poetry, short fiction and essays where life in the present pandemic times is reflected – the *Decameron 2020* project, *Quarantined Sonnets* (2020) by Tabish Khair, *Intimations* (2020) by Zadie Smith and *And We Came Outside and Saw the Stars Again* (2020) edited by Ilan Stavans, among other works. I would here like to refer to what Tabish Khair notes,

> It is obvious that the profusion of pandemic writing is not simply the index of a world fighting a virus. It is also an index of the capacity to be secluded and indulge in creative activities in relative safety. In that sense, it is an index of privilege.[4]

A pertinent idea since vulnerability will possibly make such writing difficult. Many of the writers who have written of pandemics and epidemics have written about ones located in the distant past or the distant future; this sense of distancing is important to fictionalizing as the trauma associated with it, with one who has been through all, might overpower and inhibit artistic creation.

One of the oldest works of literature that works in the plague as part of the narrative is Boccaccio's *The Decameron*. Published in Italy in around 1353, this work about a small group of people who flee Florence to escape the Black Death and spend two weeks telling each other stories to distract from the horror around them is possibly one of the first works that come to mind when we think of literature and epidemics. The stories in *The Decameron* are not about the plague. They are tales of love, sadness, life, politics and fun – stories that reveal a sense of community, a sense of meaning in times that are terrifying and beyond control. The work reveals the idea that one of our first responses to crisis, to the helplessness that the crisis entails is to find a way to tell stories about it. Storytelling, after all, has always been a community enterprise. It is this community space, that shared experience of living that is most disturbed as the need of the times demands physical isolation, quarantine, distancing to survive and to be away from the virus that wreaks havoc. Living through such times, we are more than aware now of mental health issues that result because of this isolation, the break in community spaces and the disruption in shared experiences, a disruption in shared memories that result in anxiety and depression and many other maladies.

The very idea of storytelling and shared experiences bring into contention the idea of memories. It is these memories, both individual and shared that find their way into texts. Jan Assman explains in "Collective Memory and Cultural Identity" that shared memories are essential to the formation and preservation of social identity, without a collective memory to connect the survivors to one another because of the regulations that the pandemic entails individual experiences of pandemics and epidemics become isolated and individualized.[5] This is noticed in narratives as they work to foreground pandemics and epidemics, bringing in memory and experiences, both shared and individual, to create a kind of connection that weaves the past and present, which links the two together.

Narratives are essential, not only because they tell stories but also since they, at times, serve, as a means of recovery, of trying to deal with trauma and suffering. Jose Saramago's novel *Blindness* (1995) shows how a mass epidemic of blindness afflicts a city and how the society and people react and behave as a result. There is panic as no one knows why things are happening and the authorities use repressive measures to control the spread. All this leads to a break in social order, and then the epidemic vanishes almost as suddenly as it had appeared. In *Unclaimed Experience: Trauma, Narrative and History*, Cathy Caruth describes trauma as a

> wound of the mind – the breach in the mind's experience of time, self and the world – [that is] not like a wound of the body, simple and healable vent, but rather an event that . . . is experienced too soon, too unexpectedly, to be fully known and is therefore not avoidable to consciousness until it imposes itself again, repeatedly, in the nightmares and repetitive actions of the survivor.
>
> *(4)*

Dominik La Capra notes in *Writing History, Writing Trauma* that "some of the most powerful forms of modern art and writing . . . often seem to be traumatic writing or post-traumatic writing" (23).

Human illness has often been explained as retribution for wrongs done, a punishment by the gods. *The Iliad* begins with a plague on the Greek camp at Troy, a punishment for Agamemnon's enslavement of Chryseis. *Oedipus the King* also begins with the city and its people troubled by the plague. The worship of the goddesses Sitala and Ola Bibi to cure someone of plague and pestilence is commonly seen in various parts of India and in Indian literature as well. The Athenian historian Thucydides, an eyewitness of the epidemic that struck Athens early in the Peloponnesian War (the war began in 431 BC), describes its effects vividly, mentioning each stage and its effects leading to a painful death:

there was no ostensible cause; but people in good health were all of a sudden attacked by violent heats in the head, and redness and inflammation in the eyes, the inward parts, such as the throat or tongue, becoming bloody and emitting an unnatural and fetid breath. These symptoms were followed by sneezing and hoarseness, after which the pain soon reached the chest, and produced a hard cough. When it fixed in the stomach, it upset it; and discharges of bile of every kind named by physicians ensued, accompanied by very great distress. In most cases also an ineffectual retching followed, producing violent spasms, which in some cases ceased soon after, in others much later. Externally the body was not very hot to the touch, nor pale in its appearance, but reddish, livid, and breaking out into small pustules and ulcers. But internally it burned so that the patient could not bear to have on him clothing or linen even of the very lightest description, or indeed to be otherwise than stark naked. What they would have liked best would have been to throw themselves into cold water, as indeed was done by some of the neglected sick, who plunged into the rain-tanks in their agonies of unquenchable thirst, though it made no difference whether they drank little or much. Besides this, the miserable feeling of not being able to rest or sleep never ceased to torment them. The body meanwhile did not waste away so long as the distemper was at its height, but held out to a marvel against its ravages; thus when they succumbed, as in most cases, on the seventh or eighth day to the internal inflammation, they still had some strength in them. But if they passed this stage, and the disease descended further into the bowels, inducing a violent ulceration there accompanied by severe diarrhea, this brought on a weakness which was generally fatal. For the disorder first settled in the head, ran its course from thence through the whole of the body, and even where it did not prove mortal, it still left its mark on the extremities; for it settled in the privy parts, the fingers and the toes, and many escaped with the loss of these, some too with that of their eyes. Others again were seized with an entire loss of memory on their first recovery, and did not know either themselves or their friends.

(115–16)

Like all other epidemics and pandemics, migration and movement led to contagion, virulence and death.

Edgar Allen Poe's story "The Masque of Red Death" that talks of the pestilence ravaging also reminds one that social hierarchies and wealth determine how people might try to protect themselves and also that pandemics and epidemics are great levellers. Narratives that deal with epidemics and pandemics provide a sociological and historical lens through which to view the present pandemic in that they reveal the disparities inherent in society. They reveal that it is those in a less privileged position that are the most vulnerable and suffer the most – something that has been seen in the current times.

The initial human response to such outbreaks of pestilence, pandemics and epidemics is one of denial. There is also false information, particularly by authorities, a tendency to misrepresent facts and data, to not acknowledge the prevalence of the pandemic as was seen in the case of COVID-19 as well. Daniel Defoe in *A Journal of the Plague Year* (1722) writes of the bubonic plague of 1665, the Great Plague of London that wreaked havoc on the city. In it he notes that the authorities in many London neighbourhoods hid the actual mortality figures. Defoe's account narrates how people in London had to deal with restrictive measures with those infected forced to remain locked in their homes. The inconvenience of a lockdown, of asymptomatic people spreading the contagion – Defoe's account is startling in its resonances with the COVID 19 pandemic.

Epidemics and pandemics are periods of crises that affect humanity and that is the reason why they are studied and are of importance not just to virologists, doctors, biologists and scientists but to the humanities and social sciences as well. Paula Treichler in *How To Have Theory in an Epidemic* observes that an

> epidemic is cultural and linguistic as well as biological and biomedical . . . [we need] a careful examination of language and culture to think carefully about ideas in the midst of a crisis, to use our intelligence and critical faculties to consider theoretical problems, develop policy and develop long-term social goals.[6]
>
> *(Nayar)*

Albert Camus' *The Plague*, possibly the most well known and most read text in the times that we are in, apart from so much more speaks of the need to live in the moment as uncertainty becomes the norm. Camus' novel speaks of the cholera epidemic that struck Oran in 1899, though the novel is set in the 1940s. This looking back, which was referred to earlier, is a feature of many narratives that deal with pandemics and epidemics. *Station Eleven* by Emily St. John Mandel reveals the effect of the swine flu pandemic that wipes away most of the world's population. The novel brings in characters from various parts of the world and spans several decades to show how humanity bears the brunt of it all and somehow manages to hold on. *One Hundred Years of Solitude* speaks of the plague of insomnia that troubles the Buendia family in the town of Macondo. Garcia Marquez brings in the idea of storytelling and of collective memories that are so very important for humanity.

T.S. Eliot's *The Waste Land* (1922) reflects the pessimism following the devastation caused by two important events in the first quarter of the twentieth century, the First World War and the Spanish Flu. Both Eliot and his wife suffered from the Spanish Flu in December 1918, as did Edgar Allen Poe and his wife and Katherine Anne Porter and the man she loved. There are lines in *The Wasteland* that speak of times when the epidemic raged, the ravages and the destruction, "heap of broken images" with "no shelter", "no relief", of just "stony rubbish" everywhere and "fear in a handful of dust".[7]

This volume had its origin in a special issue of an online magazine *Café Dissensus*.[8] A few of the contributors of that issue are part of this volume. However, their chapters in this volume have expanded from what was there in that issue. More scholars joined this project and are now part of this volume that consists of chapters on many of the texts referred to earlier and many other texts that discuss the way pandemics/epidemics have been represented in literary texts – the way they feature in the narrative and/or influence it. Literature, to use a cliché, holds up a mirror to us. That is true of epidemics as well. Literature takes us beyond figures and statistics to reveal how the crises affect the lives of individuals. It also shows the similarity in human response over the centuries and across geographical spaces – in the way fear, anxiety, panic and hysteria, along with suspicion and doubts in a difficult time, become the norm.

As we live through the times of COVID-19, belief systems, superstitions, science and scientific inquiry become key aspects for framing the pandemic, of trying to understand about virulence, about how to cope with issues that arise. They also become part of the collective knowledge and rationality of people and nations. Information, the misuse of it, fake information, mistrust, and questions of reliability, doubt and suspicion become important aspects of the framing as well. As Frank Snowden in *Epidemics and Society* notes that disease, medicine, health and epidemics are part of historical change and development of any society – "infectious diseases . . . are as important to understanding societal development as economic crises, wars, revolutions, and demographic change". He goes on to say that

> every society produces its own specific vulnerabilities. To study them is to understand that society's structure, its standard of living, and its political priorities. Epidemic diseases . . . have always been signifiers, and the challenge of medical history is to decipher the meanings embedded in them.[9]

In her 1978 essay on *Disease as Political Metaphor*, Susan Sontag demonstrated that the trope of the infectious malady has been used through human history as a metaphor to represent, describe and critique failures of the polis by critics of culture and politics and we see it in the real world.

In the first chapter in the volume, Sipra Mukherjee examines two narratives from eastern India – Fakir Mohan Senapati's short story "Rebati" and Suryakant Tripathi Nirala's memoir *Kulli Bhaat* to explore the difference in the way pandemics are portrayed in Indian literature. Unlike novels written in the West where epidemics/pandemics dominate the narrative, novels written in regional languages in India present the disease as one just afflicting the physical body. Many of these texts do not work in the conventional binaries of tradition and modernity, masculinity and femininity. This prompts her to question whether a different kind of literary historiography is required to engage with these texts critically. Using the idea of cultural amnesia as propounded by G.N. Devy Mukherjee goes on to analyse the two texts that share a cultural tradition – they are by authors who belonged to the East of India though they wrote in different languages, Odia and Hindi – enabling an examination of them together.

Tania Chakravertty in her chapter "The Trauma and the Triumph: Katherine Anne Porter's 'Pale Horse, Pale Rider'" uses the perspectives of gender studies and trauma studies to examine the short story that addresses the challenges and demands placed on a young woman as she tries to find autonomy in her life. Set against the background of the First World War and the Spanish influenza pandemic that added to all the misery and spread faster due to movement of soldiers the story fictionalizes some of Porter's own experiences. Using a feminist critical perspective to analyse the story, Chakravertty places the protagonist in the context of first-wave feminism. Notions of trauma and collective memory figure in her reading as Miranda's life is also altered by the epidemic. The epidemic brings in the idea of collective trauma. Miranda's individual trauma is set against the historical background and the collective trauma it generates. "Pale Horse, Pale Rider", Chakravertty argues, is a literary text as traumatic memory and reveals an interaction between memory and death.

In "Pandemic and Man-less Society: Problematizing Gender, Sex and Sexuality in Christina Sweeney-Baird's *The End of Men*" Goutam Karmakar discusses Sweeney-Baird's 2021 novel that refers to a "male pandemic" that gradually spreads all over the world. This pandemic affects a social–cultural upheaval due to its gendered nature – it only affects men. This results in a change in the patriarchal power structures. The chapter evaluates the gendered relationships that ensue as a result of the male body being a diseased one. It probes into the idea of whether gender constructs could be questioned in a world where the virus does make a physiological distinction. Karmakar also examines the way the pandemic brings out the vulnerabilities in a disease-ravaged society in the novel.

Riti Agarwala's "*The Decameron*: Re-reading the Uncanny Riddle of Plague" discusses how disease and "dis-ease" that is an important part of *The Decameron* is, at the same time, unsettling and helpful in trying to make sense of such troubled times and works towards an interpretation of it. The chapter reads and analyses this iconic plague text examining the way the epidemic works as it functions as the background to the narrative that Boccaccio presents. Voicing a collective imagination that is connected by the plague, the text brings in the idea of storytelling as important to our social consciousness. Giving space to individual voices, Agarwala notes that the text has a therapeutic role. Mourning, melancholy and laughter are all worked in as the world depicted is poised on the brink of change.

Published in 1826, Mary Shelley's *The Last Man* presents human reactions to moments of crises, to disease and death that spares no one, that reveals the flaws in human society and human behaviour. Sarottama Majumdar in "*The Last Man*: Pandemics and the Existential Dilemma" discusses the paradoxes in the novel in the light of Mary Shelley's conclusion to the novel which she holds as an assertion of hope and resilience of the human spirit. The pandemic brings out the fissures that make a biological tragedy a possibility. Majumdar examines the moral and ethical dilemmas faced by a young band of men and women in the novel whose efforts, though in vain, nevertheless bode well for humanity and speak of the continuity of the human race while bringing important existential conundrums to the fore. The existential questions raised in the novel, Majumdar argues, are even more pressing and relevant in the times we live in.

In "Epidemic Anxiety and Narrative Aesthetics in Sarat Chandra's *Palli Samaj* and *Pandit Mashay*", Subham Dutta explores the way the epidemics of cholera and malaria influence the novels of Sarat Chandra Chattopadhyay with reference to two novels – *Pandit Mashay* and *Palli Samaj*. This chapter argues that Sarat Chandra's use of epidemics in his novels unravels tensions that involve hierarchies, caste, orthodoxies and the liberal, individualistic worldview. Using Lefebvre's ideas of spatiality, Dutta examines the way epidemics create a disproportionateness in the social and cultural fabric of society represented in the novels that renders a reorientation of the dynamics of the rural setting of the two novels under consideration. This chapter also analyses the impact of epidemics on the social realist narrative mode of the novels and tries to ascertain how the use of anxiety caused by epidemics works to bring about a fluidity in Sarat Chandra's narratives.

In "Albert Camus' Rejoinder to the Absent God and the Absurdity of Existence in *The Plague*", Sacaria Joseph argues that the ideas of the absurdity of existence that the Existentialists grappled with emanate from the attempts made by human beings to reconcile the silence of God against the cries and prayers of humanity for deliverance from the troubles and suffering that the plague unleashes. This chapter analyses the responses of Paneloux and Rieux in *The Plague* with a view to understand Camus's answer to the question of the silence of God when humanity is suffering and the larger question of the nature and character of human existence which is similar to the response of Rieux in the novel. This, Joseph argues, is Camus' response to the absurdity of human existence. This chapter also argues that the spirit and mission of Rieux in the novel resonates in the present times, in a world grappling with a pandemic.

Amit R. Baishya in "'It Mattered Not From Whence It Came; But All Agreed It Was Come . . .': Plague Narratives as Narratives of Media and Foreignness" brings in zombie narratives to argue that such narratives draw on tropes and narrative frameworks that one encounters in plague texts. This chapter focuses on two aspects of zombie/plague narratives – as narratives of media and as expressions of fear and panic about foreignness. This arises from the fact that plagues are often associated with the figure of an outsider, a foreigner. Analyzing the opening of Daniel Defoe's *A Journal of the Plague Year* and the Hollywood film *World War Z*, this chapter examines the way in which these aspects reveal the connections between contagion and how media works to represent them. Baishya considers how panic created through various ways plays an important role in these times of crisis and catastrophe.

In "Forgetting Difference: The Plague in Hindi and Urdu Literature", Ishan Mehandru focuses on two works written in India, in Hindi-Urdu, Rajinder Singh Bedi's short story "Quarantine", and Suryakant Tripathi Nirala's memoir *Kulli Bhat* (translated into English as *A Life Misspent*). These two works published in the same year speak of the lived experiences of epidemics that ravaged India in the twentieth century. This chapter analyses the way in which the experiences of the epidemics, disease and contagion are marked by gender, sexuality, caste and religion even in times when death and uncertainty ignore privilege and difference.

A text that has been re-read in the current times has been Defoe's *The Journal of the Plague Year*. Sanghita Sanyal, in her chapter, examines a puppet animation film production of the text, *The Periwig Maker*. Defoe's text has been recontextualized several times, and this modern one done in 1999 has Gothic elements worked in. The film resonates wonderfully, particularly in the light of the times we are in. Working in moral and philosophical questions about responsibility, about how the plague changes the way people behave, the film presents an emotional response to such moments of crisis, when death is a regular feature. This chapter analyses the adaptation as an important way to understand human response to epidemics and pestilence.

Subarna Bhattacharya's "Pestilence, Death, Fear and a Testimony of Female Outrage: The 1897 Bombay Plague in the Writing of Pandita Ramabai" speaks of the importance of medical catastrophes in the historiography of colonial India. This chapter analyses Pandita Ramabai's, a firebrand women's rights activist and social worker of contemporary Maharashtra, letter to *The Bombay Guardian*, in 1897, that vehemently spoke against the actions of the colonial government in regard to the plague control measures taken. This chapter also brings into focus George Lambert, an American Mennonite missionary's *India: The Horror-stricken Empire* (1898) to reveal that it worked to serve an imperialist agenda. While being a critique of colonial policies, Pandita Ramabai's "Letter" also added to the national-ist narrative of the period. Bhattacharya, in her chapter, reveals how this difficult time of sickness, disease and death was also, simultaneously, a political period of pressurizing and resistance.

In "Pandemic as a Disaster: Narratives of Suffering and 'Risk' in *Twilight in Delhi*", Sumantra Baral questions whether pandemic literature comes under the domain of disaster studies and whether we could read the narratives of suffering and 'risk' in a text or narrative when the world has moved towards "second moder-nity". Through a reading of Ahmed Ali's *Twilight in Delhi* from a neo-historical as well as from an eco-critical perspective, this chapter grapples with these questions. The 1918 influenza flu or Bombay Fever provides a definite backdrop to this novel, and this opens up the possibility to discuss the way this pandemic figures and mostly is absent from the nationalist historical discourses. Focusing on important issues of the time – nationalism, progressive writing, protest against orthodoxy and funda-mentalism, love, marriage, pain, death and the influenza flu, Ahmed Ali's novel reveals the life of a community on the threshold of change. This chapter examines the various challenges that the novel brings to the fore and to a new writing style – the progressive, realist mode – which works wonderfully to encapsulate it all.

Paramita Dutta in "Pandemic Fear: Death and the Ruin of Civilization in Jack London's *The Scarlet Plague*" discusses the pandemic fear of death, self-preservation and the ruin of civilization in Jack London's novel. Reading the novel in the light of the times that we are in allows for a reflection of the way in which belief systems and behavioural patterns that are seen in the society, in the world we live in portrayed in this novel. Such a reading Dutta argues works to provide a framework with which to contextualize some of the events that have been so much a part of the COVID-19 pandemic.

Sayan Aich Bhowmik's "Is this the '*way the world ends*'? Dystopic space and utopian dream in Atwood's *Oryx and Crake*" analyses Margaret Atwood's *Oryx and Crake* from the perspective of dystopic spaces. Arguing that there is a very fine dividing line between an idealized and utopian space and that space degenerating into a claustrophobic dystopia this chapter examines Atwood's novel which presents a post-apocalyptic world after a pandemic has wiped out the entire civilization. The virus that has caused the plague was actually meant to create a more intelligent species constituting the best in human beings. Aich brings in references to the US foreign policy in Afghanistan and its repercussion that culminated in 9/11 in order to explore how, in order to create a dominant capitalist world order of free trade and thought, the monster created turns its back on its creator to wreak havoc.

In "Power and the Pandemic Through Two Gothic Tropes", academic and author Tabish Khair looks at the pandemic of the present times through the lens of two gothic figures – the vampire and the zombie. This chapter argues that there has been a shift in popular, cinematic perceptions of the vampire and the zombie over the past few decades, which is in keeping with a change in the nature of capitalism and then goes on to explore the trope of the zombie to analyse some reactions to the COVID-19 pandemic.

In the last chapter of this volume, "Follow the Dead: Digital Obituaries as Rituals of Selective Remembrance During the COVID-19 Pandemic", Yash Gupta examines American obituaries that were published online during the pandemic. Considering them as journalistic rituals that create a remembrance in the public domain, this chapter takes into analysis many such pandemic-specific obituary pages such as *Time's The Lives Lost to Coronavirus* and *NBC's The Loss*, while focusing on the *We Remember*, a compilation of online obituaries hosted by CNN. Gupta argues that obituaries highlight cultural preferences while working to establish social norms. The obituary is a form that highlights an individual's contribution to society and is ritualistic in nature while bringing in the anxieties about death. This chapter focuses on obituaries published in the pandemic with the purpose of recontextualizing studies of digital obituaries within the setting of the pandemic that is so much a part of our lives.

The Polish author Olga Tokarczuk speaks about how the COVID-19 pandemic has dealt a blow to the belief that humans are masters of the world. It has, she says, forced us to accept a slow way of life, a natural rhythm and has also increased distrust and worsened inequality.[10] The chapters in this volume discuss various aspects of narratives from the West and from India that belong to a much larger time period in order to forge a critical debate about contagion, pestilence, epidemic, fear, trauma, memory and storytelling. The fact that these chapters have been written during the time when the world is in the throes of a pandemic lends an immediacy and perspective that is based on lived experiences. It is no longer out there, in the texts under consideration and analysis, it is happening in our lives as we try to forge new meanings in media, literature and popular culture – an attempt to make some sense amidst all the confusion.

Notes

1 Intizar Husain 10.
2 Tumbe.
3 https://thenewcriterion1926.files.wordpress.com/2014/12/woolf-on-being-ill.pdf.
4 Khair, "Inside the Tortoise".
5 Referred to in Davis, "The Forgotten Apocalypse".
6 Quoted in https://thebastion.co.in/ideas/what-the-humanities-can-teach-us-during-a-pandemic/.
7 www.poetryfoundation.org/poems/47311/the-waste-land.
8 *Café Dissensus*.
9 Quoted in Nayar.
10 www.dw.com/en/literature-that-makes-you-think/av-55223061.

Works Cited

Assman, Jan. "Collective Memory and Cultural Identity." Translated John Czaplicka. *New German Critique*, vol. 65, Spring 1995, pp. 125–33.

Camus, Albert. *The Plague*. Penguin, 1980.

Caruth, Cathy. *Unclaimed Experience: Trauma, Narrative and History*. John Hopkins UP, 1996.

Davis, David A. "The Forgotten Apocalypse: Katherine Anne Porter's 'Pale Horse, Pale Rider', Traumatic Memory and the Influenza Pandemic of 1918." *The Southern Literary Journal*, vol. 43, no. 2, Spring 2011, pp. 55–74.

Defoe, Daniel. *A Journal of the Plague Year*. Edited by Paula R. Backscheider. W.W. Norton and Co., 1992.

Eliot, T.S. *The Wasteland*. www.poetryfoundation.org/poems/47311/the-waste-land.

Garcia Marquez, Gabriel. *One Hundred Years of Solitude*. Penguin, 2007.

Husain, Intizar. *Basti*. Translated by Frances W. Pritchett. New York Review Books, 2007.

Khair, Tabish. "Inside the Tortoise: On the Literary Responses to the Ongoing Pandemic." *The Hindu*, 19 Dec. 2020. www.thehindu.com/books/inside-the-tortoise-on-the-literary-responses-to-the-ongoing-pandemic/article33361774.ece.

La Capra, Dominik. *Writing History, Writing Trauma*. John Hopkins UP, 2001.

Mandel, Emily St. John. *Station Eleven*. Vintage, 2015.

Nayar, Pramod K. *What the Humanities Can Teach Us During a Pandemic*, 2020. https://thebastion.co.in/ideas/what-the-humanities-can-teach-us-during-a-pandemic/.

Pulugurtha, Nishi, editor. "Pandemics/Epidemics and Literature." *Café Dissensus*, no. 57, Feb. 2021. https://cafedissensus.com/2021/02/14/contents-pandemics-epidemics-and-literature-issue-57/.

Saramago, Jose. *Blindness*. Translated by Giovanni Ponteiro. Houghton Mifflin Harcourt, 1995.

Snowden, Frank M. *Epidemics and Society: From the Black Death to the Present*. Yale UP, 2019.

Sontag, Susan. *Illness as Metaphor*. Farrar, Straus and Giroux, 1977.

———. *Disease as Political Metaphor.* www.nybooks.com/articles/1978/02/23/disease-as-political-metaphor/.

Thucydides. *The Peloponnesian War, Book II: "Crawley".* Translated and rev. edited by T.E. Wick. Modern Library, 1982.

Tokarczuk, Olga. *Literature That Makes You Think.* www.dw.com/en/literature-that-makes-you-think/av-55223061.

Treichler, Paula. *How To Have Theory in an Epidemic.* Duke UP, 1999.

Tumbe, Chinmay. *The Age of Pandemics 1817–1920: How They Shaped India and the World.* Harper Collins, 2020.

Woolf, Virginia. *On Being Ill.* https://thenewcriterion1926.files.wordpress.com/2014/12/woolf-on-being-ill.pdf.

I
Memory and Contagion

1

"VERNACULAR REALITIES" IN EPIDEMIC LITERATURE

Reading Fakir Mohan Senapati's "Rebati" and Suryakant Tripathi Nirala's *Kulli Bhaat*

Sipra Mukherjee

Literatures from India have frequently carried portrayals of disease and epidemics on their pages. Difficult as it is to gain a sufficiently deep knowledge of the many bhāsā literatures of India, these representations are frequent enough to be visible even at a cursory glance across the few vernaculars that one does know. Outbreaks of cholera have been a frequent occurrence on the Indian subcontinent and have found faithful portrayals in innumerable novels, so have the other diseases that have swept across the subcontinent: malaria, kala-azar or the Black Fever, plague, influenza, smallpox – all deadly diseases that left thousands dead every time they struck. In these innumerable representations of disease in the Indian literatures, however, the portrayals of the epidemics do not dominate the narrative in the way that the plague does in Mary Shelley's 1821 novel, *The Last Man*, or in Camus' novel *The Plague* (1947). Constituting a part of the novel, diseases and epidemics, or even the Spanish flu pandemic, are not presented as the singular significant event that controls the entire plot. Even *Azar*, the recent 2017 Assamiya novel by Dhrubajyoti Borah on the kala-azar that devastated colonial Assam, centres its narrative on the criminal negligence of the colonial administration towards the lives of the general people. Michael Heffernan's essay "Fin de Siècle, Fin du Monde?" (2000) explains the recurrent subject of disaster and a consequent post-apocalyptic world as the *fin de siecle* syndrome of the European world that assumed an end of the world with the end of the century. But as one goes through the continued publication of these novels into the twenty-first century, the *fin de siecle* explanation grows shaky, and at least one apocalyptic novel published every year has as its subject a deadly pandemic.[1] Perceived and portrayed as disasters that reveal humanity as a species that has remained threatened and vulnerable despite (or because of) its advances in science, most of these European and American novels see the pandemics as metaphors denoting points of crises that lead us to question the path that human civilization has taken.

DOI: 10.4324/9781003294436-3

In the Indian bhāsā literatures that feature epidemics, one finds the questions raised are different. The issues here are of, what may perhaps be termed, "smaller" magnitude. They relate not to the advances of science or the trajectory taken by civilization, which are the queries raised in so many of the world's English literatures, but to the corporeality of the disease and the suffering it causes. In most of these books, the epidemics remain just that, a disease of the physical human body, and do not function as metaphors of evil or wrong-headed "progress". It is within this frame of the very visceral misery and terror that the writers explore the expected questions of human destiny, the arbitrariness of human misery, the futility of human endeavour as they re-view, as do the English novels, the values of compassion, brotherhood and responsibility.

A Different Literary Approach

This striking difference with the Indian narratives encourages one to ask whether a different literary approach is required to explore these texts meaningfully. Many literary texts of India do appear placed awkwardly when situated within the frameworks that see the physical and the spiritual, the traditional and the modern, the masculine and the feminine, in binary opposition to each other. The lines do not coincide, and the parameters do not agree with these paradigms that are frequently used in literary analysis and criticism. The texts I will attempt to explore are puzzling because they resist such categorization and consequently are difficult to "understand". This difficulty may in part be due to the "disfiguring colonial epistemology" that G. N. Devy talks of that has created "false frameworks of cultural values" (2–3) and induced what he terms "cultural amnesia" (1992). Mudimbe in *The Invention of Africa* talks in a similar vein of the colonizing structure and its resultant epistemology:

> Because of the colonizing structure, a dichotomizing system has emerged, and with it a great number of current paradigmatic oppositions have developed: traditional versus modern; oral versus written and printed; agrarian and customary communities versus urban and industrialized civilization; subsistence economies versus highly productive economies. In Africa a great deal of attention is generally given to the evolution implied and promised by the passage from the former paradigms to the latter.
>
> *(17)*

A similar "passage" from "the former to the latter" that occurred on the Indian subcontinent could not have left literature entirely untouched. We are all, as Talal Asad wrote in 1992, the same year as Devy's *After Amnesia*, willingly or unwillingly "conscripts of western civilization" (1992). It can be equally argued, however, that the modern Western criticism could not have entirely displaced the earlier traditions and ways of thought. To quote Devy again, "did or did not the earlier current leave behind it any silt which modified the new current?" (1). This juxtaposition of the earlier and the new currents may be the reason for the critic's unease with the effeminacy of many of Sarat Chandra Chattopadhyay's heroes, who may be looked at askance if placed within the masculine–feminine binary, could be one example. Another could be the complex portrayals of tradition and modernity that we find in so many of the vernacular texts dealing with epidemics. Characters cling to traditional practices and ignore modern medical scientific ways to fight disease. The texts may present these characters as traditional, conservative, courageous, gracious as they face mortality, and/or ignorant. All these features come together without any apparent contradiction, just as the portrayal of modern hospitals may be portrayed as the glorious advance of science, marked by indifference and heartlessness.

It being quite impossible, and academically unsound, to make sweeping statements about the corpus of Indian bhāsā literatures, given both its immensity of size and diversity of range, I will limit my exploration to two texts authored in 1898 and 1938. Given the innumerability of the Indian bhāsā literatures, one is always more ignorant than knowledgeable of its entirety. Following Devy's suspicion of the term "India" as a "product of colonial historiography", with its "disfiguring colonial epistemology", this chapter will approach the prose writings more as sharing linguistic traditions of the eastern region or "*kshetra*" of the Indian subcontinent, than of being writers of any "imaginary cultural unit or unity" (2) called India. The two texts are authored by writers who hailed from the eastern provinces of India, though they wrote in different languages.[2] Fakir Mohan Senapati was from Balasore, Odisha, and Suryakant Tripathi Nirala, who began learning Hindi only after his marriage took him to Dalmau, North India, was from Mahishadal, Bengal. The ravages of cholera are depicted in Fakir Mohan's short story "Rebati" (1898), and the horrors of the influenza epidemic that swept through India in 1918 are portrayed in one chapter of Suryakant Tripathi Nirala's *Kulli Bhat* (1939). Despite the literature authored by these writers being part of the established classical canon, their works reflect the complex dialectics of the little traditions and the great, of the mārga and the deši, that seem to have been integral to what may be termed the "vernacular reality", following Upton Dell's coinage of the term "vernacular architecture" to refer to regional architecture (Dell), before the "cultural amnesia" set in.

Is There a Causal Logic in Fakir Mohan Senapati's "Rebati"?

"Rebati" is a story of a girl's desire for learning and life cut short unceremoniously by an outbreak of cholera that claims the lives of her family, and ultimately her own. The story begins in a rural setting portraying a simple, honest family who can more or less comfortably make ends meet and so have no complaints. The girl Rebati sits next to her father Shyambandhu in the evenings as he, having lit an oil lamp, recites from the *Bhagvat*. Rebati had picked up some of the hymns and would sing them to her father's great delight. The inclusion of a hymn, an aspect that we find in Nirala's text too, adds to the reader's appreciation of the "space", or "*kshetra*", which forms the context of the story:

> "Whither shall I take my prayers, Lord
> If Thou turnest a blind eye?"
> *(Senapati 69)*

Education is in the air, as is evident in the opening of the village school consequent to the villagers requesting a visiting Inspector of Schools, and news arrives of a girls' school nearby. When her father decides to educate her, Rebati is happy and excited at the prospect. And then cholera happens, killing all the family one after the other, including the gentle young man Rebati, was to marry. There is no evident causality to explain this trajectory of the plot. There is no complication and subsequent denouement, no weighty decision or momentous step is taken by any character, and no hubris is displayed by the protagonists as in Fakir Mohan's novels, *Chha Mana Atha Guntha* (*Six Acres and a Third*) and *Prayaschitta* (*The Penance*). The only connecting thread running through the plot seems to be that of chronos or time, as events follow one another chronologically.

Yet the story has frequently been read with a causal trajectory in mind. Rebati's grandmother's angry reaction to the girl's education has been read by some as indicating that causality. The deadly epidemic that kills the family is read as punishment for the girl's aspiration for literacy, though any other reaction from the grandmother would have been unreal considering the age and rural setting of the character. With her wild hair and agonized eyes, the grandmother does approximate the archetypal image of the woman prophesying doom. Yet this reading of the epidemic as Rebati's karma is weakened by the author's careful mention that the cholera struck more than 4 years after Rebati's education had begun. Fakir Mohan also makes it a point to depict Rebati as an obedient, gentle, religious-minded young woman, entirely in accordance with the diktats of tradition. Rebati's education is suggested by the young man Rebati was to marry, and the decision is taken by Rebati's father. That both these decisions were taken by the males in Rebati's life should be sufficient for the girl's desire for education to pass muster in traditional society, and pacify whatever angry gods there be. That Shyambandhu believes his daughter's education will make it possible for her to "read the Bhagawat and the Vaidehisha Vilas" also makes education non-threatening to tradition, custom and religion.

Despite these aspects of the narrative, reading the grandmother's cry of anger that rings through the latter part of the story, "Rebati! Rebi! You fire, you ashes!" as the vengeance wreaked by the gods of tradition has been a frequent reading. The story as "an allegory for women's education and identity politics, its contestation of the patriarchal discourse" (Mohanty, "Rebati's Sisters" 42) has been another. The second is a more secular reading of the story, which draws validation from Fakir Mohan's own interest in the spread of education as Dewan in the many princely states of Orissa, when he "assisted in the spread of education in Nilgiri, Keonjhar, Anandpur and Dompara" (Mohanty, "Rebati's Sisters" 44). This interpretation of the story may find the missing "causality" in what Sudipta Kaviraj has termed the nineteenth-century intellectual's "unhappy consciousness" in the context of colonial modernity. When he authored "Rebati", Fakir Mohan was serializing his novel *Chha Mana Atha Guntha* in the literary monthly *Utkal Sahitya* (1897 to 1899) a novel that critiques the imposition of colonial structures upon the rural order. The author's desire for modernity via education in "Rebati" could have sat uneasily on his mind as Kaviraj argues it did for some colonial writers: "If he chose modernity, he had to choose subjection as its condition, or so it appeared to him", writes Kaviraj of the Bengali novelist, Bankim Chandra Chattopadhyay (167). But this explanation of the unhappy consciousness fails to fully satisfy. The satirical tone used by Senapati in the novel *Chha Mana*, a tone that includes a critique of the colonizer as well as self-mockery of the educated colonized, is missing in the story "Rebati". Fakir Mohan's characteristic irony is limited to a few brief references to the zamindars and shopkeepers who remain outside the story in "Rebati". The description of the father Shyambandhu Mohanty, Basudev the young teacher and Rebati are not laced with irony or sarcasm. On the contrary, Fakir Mohan appears to have gone uncharacteristically far in portraying these human beings as good and merciful ("*bhitara-bahara sundara*") and who use the little power their social positions afford them with kindness and generosity. Shyambandhu, the zamindar's accountant responsible for collecting rent

> was a straight forward person, and the tenants respected, even liked him. He never demanded a paisa extra from anyone . . ... He never let the zamindar's muscle man cast his shadow in the village; he'd pump the fellow's palm, . . . tucked two paise into the waist-fold of his clothes for buying himself tobacco and saw him off.
>
> *(68)*

Even Bana the village washerman, a veteran of 50 or 60 cremations, who turns up to cremate Shyambandhu is described in a "straight", rather than "arched", manner:

> He turned up with a towel around his waist; an axe hung from his shoulder. As Bana saw it, if your time was up you'd have to go today or tomorrow, but why miss a pair of new clothes when there was a chance now?
>
> *(72)*

Bana's way of thinking may be seen as "typically Indian" in its fatalistic inclinations, and may be considered as indicating another "way" to read the story. Yet Senapati's story "Rebati" does not otherwise appear to portray a fatalistic universe or an absence of agency in the characters. As in his novels like *Chha Mana Atha Guntha*, Fakir Mohan's characters in "Rebati" demonstrate sufficient power. Shyambandhu as the zamindar's accountant and Basudev, as the school teacher, are both characters who command a degree of agency in their world. In fact, the power of the characters, including Rebati's, in the larger world where life and death are decided is confirmed by Rebati's grandmother mourning the death of young Basudev: "*Jaha apona kia tohiko elajo kia* (What can be the remedy when one has brought it on himself)". It is, in fact, this understanding that stokes her fury, "Rebati, Rebi! You fire! You ashes!" as the line reads in the 1996 literal translation made by Leelavati Mohapatra and Kamalakanta Mohapatra. The later 2019 translation in *The Greatest Oriya Stories Ever Told* by the translators Leelavati Mohapatra, Paul St. Pierre and Kamalakanta Mohapatra reads, "Rebi! You fire that turns all to ashes!" The changed translation articulates unequivocally Rebati's role in bringing about ruin.

Such a reading sees the characters as "protagonists", a word that etymologically means "the first actor", or the main character in the struggle/contest (agón). Reading the characters as playing a pivotal role in determining their own lives and bringing on disease and death gives the story a rational causality in accordance with the conventions of literary realism. Ulka Anjaria describes the novel *Chha Mana* as a highly self-critical text that also concerns itself with "the experience of the 'soft' power of literary conventions on the subjects of colonial modernity". The powers of these conventions were, and are, normative rather than coercive, and Anjaria traces "the mode of critique in Fakir Mohan's satire to the nature of its object, which we might define as colonialist logic" (4795). In the story "Rebati", however, "colonialist logic" has no direct presence. Though the village school happens through the visiting Inspector, and the unseen zamindar is associated with the colonial machinery, much of the village continues in the pre-modern, feudal world. Shyambandhu's family is described as a family that is cash-poor, yet "quite comfortable" in reality:

> His salary was two rupees a month. He could raise a little more . . . four rupees a month. With this he could somehow make both ends meet. Well, not just; no, to speak the truth, he was quite comfortable. His family never complained of lacking this or that. They had everything they needed: two drumstick trees in the backyard, besides a patch of spinach and vegetables; two cows, which never went dry simultaneously, so that a little curd and milk could always be found in the pails. Mohanty's old mother made fuel-cakes from cow-dungs and husks, so they hardly had to buy any firewood. The zamindar had given him three and half acres of rent free land for cultivation; and the produce was just about enough.
>
> (68)

Interpreting this description of the agrarian economic order as different from the capitalist colonial order marked by the acquisitive and exploitative spirit would, however, be simplistic, and Fakir Mohan's minor characters give ample proof of the continuity of human greed through the changing economies. Rebati and her family, though, remain outside both the greed and colonial logic. Cholera strikes suddenly, without any *reason*: "One fine Phalguna day, like a bolt out of the blue, struck the epidemic of cholera" (71).

A Different Way of Thinking?

"Is there an Indian way of thinking?" Ramanujan asked in his 1989 essay, and went on to write about the answers that may be made to this question. "The problem was posed to [him] personally", he writes, "at the age of 20 in the image of [his] father" (42) who moved with ease between astrology and astronomy, turbans and collar studs, muslin dhotis and serge jackets, and made short shrift of Ramanujan's discomfort with such "inconsistency" (44): "don't you know the brain has two lobes?" (43). Ramanujan goes on to discuss context-sensitive way of thinking that characterized Indians to the more context-free way of thought that dominated Western philosophy and, possibly, modern Indian thought. Reading Fakir Mohan's story "Rebati" with Ramanujan's essay in mind, one finds a near-echo of Ramanujan's father's "don't you know the brain has two lobes?" in Shyambandhu's equanimous response to his mother's anxious query on Rebati's education: "Never mind, Ma", said Shyambandhu, "let her study if she wants to. Haven't you heard that Jhankar Pattanaik's daughters can read the Bhagawat and the Vaidehisha Vilas?" (Senapati 70). Unlike the urban intellectual from the metropole, agonized by "the unhappy consciousness", Shyambandhu appears fairly confident in using education as a *tool*. He does not see his choice of modernity as a choice that implies subjection to the colonizer's ideology. Rebati's grandmother's opposition too is not based on fear of Rebati being inspired to modernity and individualism but based on her fear of breaking a taboo. Based on the political geography, this could signify a rural–urban divide that remained true at least till the end of the nineteenth century. In capturing this rural context, filtered as it is through both the physical senses and the minds of the characters conditioned by diverse ideologies, the story's telling is dominated by precision. This precision, which may be said to be in keeping with literary realism, privileges the real over the fantastic but does not unequivocally privilege the secular over the metaphysical. A chain of events are narrated, connected by their sequentiality. Responses, gestures and emotions are reported, and through these, a story is told. The voice of the narrator does not intrude with opinions, conjectures or suggestions. There is neither insinuation of doom or acquittal nor any implication of reward or punishment that may be read into the plot. The story uses the discourse of the realism novel but goes beyond the verisimilitude of realist representation in its quest for reality. There is a sense of the space, the *kshetra*, the characters inhabit. One way of entering into this *kshetra* could be through the idioms and the references included in the language. No word or idiom is ever free of its context. It is always mediated through the culture and history of the world that remains outside the frame of the text. The language of "Rebati" incorporates a diversity of idioms that speak of colonial modernity and traditional piety, humanity's aspiration and the terror of facing an uncontrollable universe.

In 1854 London, when cholera broke out in Soho, the British physician John Snow traced the epidemic to a water pump, in a step-by-step diagnosis much like a detective tracking down a criminal:

> On proceeding to the spot, I found that nearly all the deaths had taken place within a short distance of the [Broad Street] pump . . . With regard to

the deaths occurring in the locality belonging to the pump, there were 61 instances in which I was informed that the deceased persons used to drink the pump water from Broad Street, either constantly or occasionally . . . the handle of the pump was removed on the following day.

(Snow 1854)

Attempting such a strategic, methodical tracking down of a cholera outbreak may have been possible in the cities of London or even Calcutta and Puri. But in Pata-pur, the rural hinterland of Cuttack, where the rain gods needed to be propitiated as much as the zamindar's musclemen, into whose palms Shyambandhu tucked the two paise so that their shadow did not fall on anyone from his village, reality was different and more difficult in its multi-layered nature. Within this multi-layered reality, the concept of human agency is more amorphous than crystallized. Rita Kothari writes of one particular Gujarati ghazal by Ramesh Parekh that she found difficult to translate into English. It included the words "*Na thaya*", which means "It did not happen" as a refrain:

So what did not happen? The poem goes on to describe an ironic and poignant predicament when "we" . . . were tantalisingly close to fulfilment, but "it did not happen". Festivals at our home did not becomes ours, we dipped our hands in flowers but they did not become fragrant. And the last line: "Don't say Ramesh it did not rain today, say, it must have, we did not get drenched". The passive construction, the collective we, the arrangement of opening and closing lines, and the philosophical view that we may try, but it may not be in our hands – all of this that came together in Gujarati was difficult to achieve in English.

(Bhargava)

This is neither an absence nor a denial of agency. It would possibly be nearer to an understanding of the limits of human agency as included in the very concept of agency. Straitjacketing the tragedy of a lively young girl as being explicable through hubris[3] or hamartia or some other reason, within a trajectory of cause and effect, could seem as naive, or worse, as evidence of human arrogance aspiring to explanations beyond their ken. Satya Mohanty's description of Fakir Mohan's realism as "complex and sophisticated, not simply mimetic" ("Introduction" 2) may guide us towards an understanding of this short story not as one that is ruled by causality, secular or religious, but as a story replete with the randomness that is part of the world. In keeping with this world perhaps, the telling of the story lays itself open to more than one interpretation, masterfully evading any clear, and simplistic, trajectory of causality.

Nursing of Fellow Humanity

This different understanding of agency runs through Nirala's *Kulli Bhaat* as well. This book, *Kulli Bhaat*, is Nirala's attempt to pen the biography of a dear friend and has been translated into English by Satti Khanna as *A Life Misspent*. The chapter that deals with the epidemic begins with the young Nirala receiving a telegram that informs him of his wife having fallen "gravely ill":

> I travelled to the riverbank in Dalmau and waited. The Ganga was swollen with dead bodies. At my in-laws' house, I learned that my wife had passed away. My cousin had come over . . . but he had taken ill himself and returned home. I left for our ancestral village . . . As I was walking towards my house, I saw my cousin's corpse being carried to the cremation site. My head grew dizzy; I sat down on the ground to get a hold on myself. At home I found my cousin's wife lying ill on a pallet. "How far has the funeral procession travelled?' she asked. I had nothing to say. They had . . . a baby girl who was still nursing . . . Words cannot describe how pitiful the scene was, how help-less, how tender".
>
> *(Nirala,* A Life Misspent: *Chapter 9, n.p.[4])*

His sister-in-law passed away on the third day. The nursing child was also sick.

> I slept that night holding her. She, too, passed away in the morning. I bur-ied her in the riverbank. Then Uncle died. One more corpse to cart to the Ganga . . . My family disappeared in the blink of an eye . . ... In whichever direction I turned, I saw darkness.
>
> *(Nirala, A Life Misspent 9)*

Nirala describes this as his "first opportunity to serve those who were ill", noting also "since then there has been no dearth in my life of calls for such service". The original Hindi in Nirala's text reads, "*Tab se ab tak kisi-na-kisi rup se phursat nahi mili*" (Since then, in some form or the other, I have had no respite (from seva)) (Nirala, *Kulli Bhaat* 44). "Phursat" is a word very difficult to translate into English, which perhaps explains why the excellent translation leaves this word out, trans-lating instead an approximate sense of the sentence. The Hindi word for "serve" that Nirala uses is "seva", and he confirms the continuity of "seva" in his life in a sentence that also, wordlessly, affirms the continuity of human suffering. The epi-demic is not a singular, apocalyptic event, but one in an unending chain of events that brings sorrow to people. That he was not a silent witness to this continued suffering of humanity has been told and retold in stories of Nirala's legendary generosity, an aspect of his personality that contributed to his persistent poverty. It is also reflected in his poems like "Bhikshuka" and "Woh Todti Patthar"[5]. His editorship of the Ramakrishna Mission publication *Samanvaya* was "of importance in directing him to a study of Vedanta, reflections of which are found throughout his work" (Rubin 117). In his poem "Panchvati-prasang", Nirala speaks of devoted service through the character of Lakshmana, who does not feel the need to "know liberation" because his devotion to his brother Rama "suffices" (Nirala, "In the Forest of Panchvati" 51). Seva as an ethic is represented in almost every portrayal of the epidemics. It is not medical science, the hospitals or the doctors who are placed centre stage in these depictions, but the person who nurses.

Sarat Chandra Chattopadhyay's novels house an array of such characters who nurse friends, strangers, acquaintances and adversaries to health through epidemics: Kamal, Rajen, Abhaya, Srikanta, Rajlakshmi. *Pather Dabi* shows Bharati, a young Bengali Christian girl nursing the near-unknown Tewari, when the latter falls ill with smallpox in Burma. Tewari used to be an extremely caste-conscious Hindu, who had been harsh in his discriminatory behaviour and the observance of the purity-pollution rules with this particular young woman. Helpless and alone when he catches the deadly virus, he is nursed back to health by Bharati who decides against taking the terrified Tewari to the city hospital because very few returned alive from there. Allusions to the colonial public medical system on the subcontinent are usually marked by their absence in these narratives; and when they are present, the governmental facilities are seen as more dangerous than beneficial to patients.

"Bhavbhay Darunam" ("The Terror of Being")

The savagery of the influenza epidemic that swept through India in 1918 is described briefly in *Kulli Bhaat*. This was a pandemic that

> killed more people all over the world than any epidemic before or since; it ranks with the Black Death in Europe and Asian outbreaks of plague as the most destructive in history. In India roughly 12,500,000 persons, or 4 per cent of the total population, are said to have been killed by influenza in the autumn of 1918.
>
> *(Chaudhuri xxxvi)*

Nirala's account of this pandemic takes up only one chapter in his book of 16 chapters. Though briefly stated, the depiction is one of colossal destruction. "This was the strangest time in my life", writes Nirala. "My family disappeared in the blink of an eye" (9). In the original Hindi, Nirala uses the words, "*Dekhte dekhte ghar saaf ho gaya*", a sentence that underscores the sudden and absolute emptiness of his home. The word "saaf" (clean) with its ironic and self-flagellating undertone may have been felt with greater intensity by the writer who, writing the memoir in 1939, had recently lost his young daughter Saroj. Satti Khanna has described this work as one that makes us consider "*bhavbhay darunam* (the terror of being)". Epidemics were dreaded events in India, and contemporary narratives describe deserted villages and fleeing villagers.[6] The scale of the tragedies was such that comprehending them in terms of the rational or the clinical was difficult. Humans drew upon the realm ruled by the irrational and the supernatural to make sense of such gigantic realities. The phrase "*bhavbhay darunam*" is taken from the devotional song that Nirala's young wife sings, "*Shri Ram Chandra kripalu bhaju man/haran bhavbhay darunam*" ("Sing praise of Ram, who banishes the terror of being"). As in

Fakir Mohan's "Rebati", the words bear powerful emotions for the characters. The use of these words by Khanna is significant in their bridging of the alleged gulf between a realist novel and a devotional lyric. Through the words *bhavbhay darunam*, an echo of the song that Nirala's young wife had enchanted her audience with, the reader is led into a reality apprehended through mythology, folklore and other narratives where the paradigm of the realist novel is also included, but as one possibility.

Drawing from many cultural texts, Nirala's wife Manohara had sung three songs one after the other in the chapter preceding this which speaks of the epidemic. The first is the bhajan, "*Shri Ram Chandra kripalu bhaju man*". The second is a ghazal: "*Agar hai chaah milne ki to hardam lau lagaataa jaa*" ("If you desire to meet, let your mind dwell on me"). Nirala notes how the audience was "ready to renounce the world for the love this stirred in them. People cast questioning glances at one another. Whom was this song dedicated to?" (Nirala, *A Life Misspent* 8), while the husband Nirala preened himself silently as being the only one to whom the song could be addressed. The next song is a fast-paced dadra:

> *Sasuji ka chhokda, meri thadi pe rakh diya haath*
> ("My mother-in-law's son laid his hand on my chin
> I could have slapped him straight, but I held my pain in").
> *(Nirala,* A Life Misspent *8)*

What is left unspecified in this song is whether the "Sasuji ka chhokda" is the husband or a brother-in-law, a silence that adds an ambiguity to the lyrics. There is no transition, explanation or excuse given as the singer moves from one song to the next, speaking of different possible renunciations, fusing the gods and the lovers into one richly coloured canvas.

Nirala's own desolation and despair at the loss of his family, though left un-worded, are not un-communicated. One comprehends them through the references and idioms used:

> I would go sit on a mound by the Ganga and watch the file of corpses brought to the river. It is impossible to describe my feelings. The mound of sadhus in Dalmau is famous for its height. The Ganga made a sharp turn below it. The corpses were laid together.
> *(Nirala,* A Life Misspent *9)*

Kulli Bhaat meets him there and asks if he would like to go with him to visit Ramgiri Maharaj's ashram. This chapter ends with the words, "We set out for the ashram".

This mound that Nirala chose to seat himself on was the "avadhut-tila", translated by Khanna as "the mound of the sadhus". "Sadhus" is a generic term for sanyasis or ascetics. Not every sadhu, however, would be recognized as avadhut. Avadhuts frequently belonged to the Shaiva Nath sampradaya.[7] They were marked by their fierce independence from any institutionalized religion and by their indifference to social and religious norms, a characteristic that has earned them the reputation of being mad or eccentric. The young Nirala would go here every day to see the Ganga. The avadhut-tila is a high mound, writes Nirala. The word "ooncha" (high) is mentioned twice within a space of three lines, perhaps suggesting the philosophical detachment which the young man was trying to impose upon his mind as he grappled with grief. He would sit and observe the corpses being brought in as he thought "sometimes . . . of the ascetic sadhus, sometimes of the ephemerality of the world" (Nirala, *A Life Misspent* 9). The passage brings together vedantic Hinduism symbolized by the Ganga which intersects with the smaller, often breakaway traditions of faiths symbolized by the avadhut-tila and the ashram. Dalmau, the town itself, situated in the Lalganj *tahsil* in the district of Rae Bareilli is a very old town that is known for its associations with Vedantic Hinduism, being situated on the banks of the Ganges. But it is also famous for its connection with Sufi culture, being the town where Mulla Daud composed his "Romance of Laur and Chanda", the first surviving Indian Sufi romance and a work that draws heavily on local folklore. Through his friendship with Kulli, the ostracised Dalit who is also gay, Nirala learns of the richness of Dalmau's history, with its fort, gardens, ashrams, bathing ghats, monastery and poetic tradition.

Both Indian English novelists and those who wrote in the vernaculars engaged with the modern form of the novel. "Some of the invisible binaries the early novelist had to negotiate in order to forge a new form", writes Meenakshi Mukherjee, were those of "the oral and the written, poetry and prose, evocative and rational" (*Early Novels in India* xiii). It is significant that both Fakir Mohan and Nirala are hailed for the distinctive modernity they introduced through their innovation in form and language. Senapati, writing the first short story in his vernacular Odia and Nirala, writing possibly the first biography of a common man, are both unquestionably modern in their inclinations. But they chose to focus on the "vernacular" rather than the "Anglicised" spaces in their works, thwarting easy connections between the modern and the Western. They also draw from widely different discourses to present rural and suburban India, as they attempt to perceive, what Satya Mohanty describes as "the vantage point of the downtrodden poor" (Mohanty, "Introduction" 66). This use of an eclectic mix of discourses was shared by quite a few vernacular writers. Umasankar Patra writes of Natabar Samantaray who, like Ramanujan and Ramanujan's father, "fits the figure of the juggler, 'happy anomaly'", and is one who "resists labels, as his work amalgamates 'mathematical precision' with deep investment in contextual and historical grid of texts" (64).

When describing an evening of songs, Nirala writes of "our" inclination to imitate the English in the field of literature, culture and even politics while ignoring "the splendour of our own culture":

> The singing began with ghazals. The audience was hard on singers who did not know courtly ghazals but sang devotional songs instead. The singers of devotional songs were mostly older women. They were drawn to what the

fashionable younger women sang, but did not know the new style. It is no different today in the field of literature. I wonder why we have been quick to accept English ways, but are far slower with the ghazal. Why is it that English food and clothing and sitting arrangements have become our own, but the Persian language and the poetry of Hafiz remain unfamiliar? . . . What we should have passed on to our daughters was the splendour of our own culture. What had been passed on instead led to stifled thought and cultural indigestion.

(Nirala, A Life Misspent 8)

In its dependence on oral narratives and community traditions, the world in these texts is different from the civilizations of the Book that Derrida writes of. "The idea of the book", Derrida writes, "is a totality, finite or infinite, of the signifier; this totality of the signifier cannot be a totality unless a totality constituted by the signified preexists it, supervises its inscriptions and its signs, and is independent of it in reality" (18). Within the civilizations of the Book, beginnings and ends may be stated, and closures may be possible. But such well-defined and pre-determined totalities may be difficult to arrive at in the spaces indicated by Nirala's and Fakir Mohan's texts. This difficulty is due not only to the diminished control of "civilization" over spaces distant from the better-regulated centres. Nor is the difficulty to be located squarely within the greater vulnerability that poverty imposes upon human life. The difficulty is possibly also due to the plurality that forms the climate of ideas in such spaces. Even the official documented histories of these places, Dalmau, Mahishadal and Cuttack, reveal them to be spaces that possess a diverse heritage brought in by people of different creeds and races. The cultures here draw from a multiplicity of quotidian cultural texts, both oral and written, a living tradition of the *marga* (classical) and the *desi* (popular) that the writers, being "provincial" men (Nirala, *A Life Misspent* 8), had been acquainted with.

That the tragedy of "Rebati" and Nirala's memoir cannot be encompassed by either a secular causal logic or an "Indian" karma discourse[8] indicates the limitations of these within the given *kshetra*. Much as the "Da. Da. Da." that the thunder uttered in *Brihadaranyaka Upanishads'* sounded differently to the communities of gods, demons and humans, each interpreting the sound in accordance with its own *kshetra*, damyatā, datta, dayadhvam: self-restraint, self-sacrifice and compassion, the texts of the untimely and unnecessary deaths will need to be understood through the Indian *kshetra*.

The ideal of the realist prose narrative possibly faces a greater challenge within the pages of the pandemic novel, when called upon to represent the staggering number of deaths humanity is confronted with. The rational and the secular are both domains that claim explicability. But the realist narrative, defined as it is by the rational and the secular, fails to provide any satisfactory explanation when faced with the randomness and enormity of the tragedy in these texts. Meenakshi Mukherjee writes about the English literatures from India in which "there may be a greater pull towards a homogenization of reality, an essentializing of India, a certain flattening out of the complicated and conflicting contours, the ambiguous and shifting relations that exist between individuals and groups in a plural community" ("The Anxiety of Indianness" 2608). In the vernacular texts of "Rebati" and *Kulli Bhaat*, however, the reality reflected gives us a canvas which portrays a polyphony that interweaves the empirical with the conjectural, the physical with the metaphysical, and confounds the boundaries of "reality".

Notes

1 To name only a few published in the twenty-first century: Laurie Halse Anderson, *Fever 1793* (2000); Kim Stanley Robinson, *The Years of Rice and Salt* (2002); Margaret Atwood, *Oryx and Crake* (2003); Chris Adrian, *The Children's Hospital* (2006); Max Brooks, *World War Z: An Oral History of the Zombie War* (2006); Jeff Carlson, *Plague Year* (2007); Kathy Reichs, *Virals* (2010); Mira Grant, *Feed* (2010); Colson Whitehead, *Zone One* (2011); Peter Heller, *The Dog Stars* (2012); Megan Crewe, *The Wy We Fall* (2012); Yuri Herrera, *The Transmigration of Bodies* (2013); Emily St John Mandel, *Station Eleven* (2014); Laura van den Berg, *Find Me* (2015); Alexandra Oliva, *The Last One* (2016); Deon Meyer, *Fever* (2016); Ling Ma, *Severance* (2018); Peng Shepherd, *The Book of M* (2018) DiAnn Mills, *Airborne* (2020).

2 In the eastern literatures from India, the terrors of the plague, small pox, cholera and the Spanish Flu have been depicted in many Bangla novels by Sarat Chandra Chattopadhyay, an author whom I had included at first, but the depth and complexity of these novels would require a separate chapter devoted to it.

3 The English word "hubris" too, now circumcised within a secular, rational sphere of meaning, originates from the Greek word meaning transgressions against the gods.

4 All quotations from *A Life Misspent* are referred to with the chapter numbers, since I have used the Kindle e-version which has no page numbers.

5 I am indebted to my friend and colleague Arun Hota for hours of help with Nirala's works.

6 There is also a reference to the plague in *Kulli Bhaat*, but that is inconsequential in comparison to the Flu.

7 This is the popular understanding of the term *avadhoot* in North India. However, though mostly worshippers of Shiva, *avadhoots* may also be followers of two other traditions, including the Buddhist tradition.

8 Ramanujan's essay, though, gives us enough reason to question whether karma can really be termed Indian.

Works cited

Anjaria, Ulka. "Satire, Literary Realism and the Indian State Six Acres and a Third and Raag Darbari." *Economic and Political Weekly*, vol. 41, no. 46, 18 Nov. 2006, pp. 4795–800.

Asad, Talal. "Conscripts of Western Civilization." *Dialectical Anthropology: Essays in Honour of Stanley Diamond, vol. 1; Civilization in Crisis: Anthropological Perspectives*, edited by Christine Ward Gailey. U of Florida P, 1992, pp. 333–51.

Bhargava, Shashank. "What Is Untranslatable? Ten Translators from Indian Languages List Their Candidates." *Scroll.in*, 28 Oct. 2017. https://scroll.in/article/855625/what-is-untranslatable-ten-translators-from-indian-languages-list-their-candidates. Accessed 30 Jan. 2022.

Chaudhuri, Supriya. "Introduction." *The Final Question*, edited by Saratchandra Chattopadhyay, translated by Arup Rudra and Sukanta Chaudhuri. Ravi Dayal, Penguin, 2001, 2010.

Dell, Upton. "Vernacular Domestic Architecture in Eighteenth-Century Virginia." *Winterthur Portfolio*, vol. 17, no. 2/3, 1982, pp. 95–119. *JSTOR*, http://www.jstor.org/stable/1180893. Accessed 28 Aug. 2022.

Devy, Ganesh N. *After Amnesia*. Orient Longman, 1992.

Heffernan, Michael. "Fin de Siècle, Fin du Monde? On the Origins of European Geopolitics, 1890–1920." *Geopolitical Traditions: A Century of Geopolitical Thought*, edited by Klaus Dodds and David Atkinson. Routledge, 2000, pp. 27–51.

Kaviraj, Sudipta. *The Unhappy Consciousness: Bankimchandra Chattopadhyay and the Formation of Nationalist Discourse in India*. Oxford UP, 1995.

Mohanty, Sachidananda. "Rebati's Sisters: Search for Identity Through Education." *India International Centre Quarterly*, vol. 21, no. 4, Winter 1994, pp. 41–52.

Mohanty, Satya P. "Introduction." *Six Acres and a Third*. Penguin, 2006, pp. 1–31.

———. "The Epistemic Work of Literary Realism: Two Novels from Colonial India." *History of the Indian Novel in English*, edited by Ulka Anjaria. Cambridge UP, 2015.

Mudimbe, V.Y. *The Invention of Africa: Gnosis, Philosophy, and the Order of Knowledge*. Indiana UP, 1988.

Mukherjee, Meenakshi. "The Anxiety of Indianness: Our Novels in English." *Economic and Political Weekly*, vol. 28, no. 48, 27 Nov. 1993, pp. 2607–11.

———. *Early Novels in India*. Sahitya Akademi, 2002.

Nirala Tripathi, Suryakant. "In the Forest of Panchvati." *A Season on the Earth: Selected Poems of Nirala*, translated by David Rubin. Oxford UP, 2003.

———. *A Life Misspent*. Translated by Satti Khanna. Harper Perennial, 2016.

———. *Kulli Bhaat*. Prabhakar Prakashan, 2022.

Patra, Umasankar. "Translating an Indian Way of Thinking." *Indian Literature*, vol. 61, no. 3(299), May–June 2017, pp. 62–70.

Ramanujan, A.K. "Is There an Indian Way of Thinking? An Informal Essay." *Contributions to Indian Sociology*, vol. 23, no. 1, 1989, pp. 41–58.

Rubin, Daivid. "Nirala and the Renaissance of Hindi Poetry." *The Journal of Asian Studies*, vol. 31, no. 1, Nov. 1971, pp. 111–26.

Senapati, Fakir Mohan, Kamalakanta Mohapatra, and Leelavati Mohapatra, translators. "Rebati." *Indian Literature (Accent on Oriya Short Story)*, vol. 39, no. 2(172), Mar.–Apr. 1996, pp. 68–77.

Senapati, Fakir Mohan, Leelavati Mohapatra, Paul St. Pierre, and Kamalakanta Mohapatra, translators. "Rebati." *The Greatest Oriya Stories Ever Told*. Aleph, 2019.

Snow, John. "The Cholera Near Golden Square, and at Deptford." *Medical Times and Gazette*, vol. 9, 23 Sept. 1854, pp. 321–22. www.ph.ucla.edu/epi/snow/choleragolden square.html. Accessed 29 Jan. 2022.

2

THE TRAUMA AND THE TRIUMPH

Katherine Anne Porter's "Pale Horse, Pale Rider"

Tania Chakravertty

In 1915, Katharine Anne Porter, diagnosed with tuberculosis, was sent to a sanatorium. Before the discovery of antibiotics, long-term isolation was often the option for tuberculosis patients. During the two years of confinement prescribed for her, she decided to become a writer. The diagnosis changed soon, however; she came to know that she had bronchitis, not tuberculosis. After writing criticism of plays and society gossip for the *Critic*, Fort Worth, Texas for about a year; in 1918, she joined the *Rocky Mountain News* in Denver, Colorado. It was in the same year that Porter had a near-fatal attack of the Spanish influenza. She was discharged from the hospital after months of confinement. This traumatic experience is depicted in her trilogy of short novels, *Pale Horse, Pale Rider* published in 1939. The eponymous story of Porter's collection, "Pale Horse, Pale Rider" (1939) is set against the backdrop of the First World War and the Spanish influenza pandemic. Two other long stories appear in the same volume – "Old Mortality" and "Noon Wine" – and in the first and the third, appears the female protagonist Miranda, vivacious and independent, a woman with semi-autobiographical overtones. Before the emergence of the COVID-19 pandemic, the 1918 Influenza pandemic had largely disappeared from cultural memory. Few references to the 1918 pandemic exist in literature, popular culture and history books, and this makes Porter's story a significant record of the outbreak.

Feminism and a Young Woman's Quest for Autonomy

The period in which the story is set is also very significant in history in relation to the women's movement in the West. "Pale Horse, Pale Rider" is set in a time when the word feminism had just come into use in the United States. Feminism appeared in the 1910s and, as historian Nancy Cott says, "signaled a new phase in the debate and agitation about women's rights and freedoms that had flared for hundreds of

DOI: 10.4324/9781003294436-4

years" (3). Though people spoke about woman's advancement, woman's cause, woman's rights, and of course, woman's suffrage, in the nineteenth century they did not call it feminism. Cott further adds:

> [m]ost inclusively, they spoke of the woman movement, to denote the many ways women moved out of their homes to initiate measures of charitable benevolence, temperance, and social welfare and to instigate struggles for civic rights, social freedoms, higher education, remunerative occupations, and the ballot.
>
> *(3)*

From the 1910s to the 1930s, girls began graduating with majors in subjects which had hitherto been confined only to the male sphere – educating themselves to build up their potential for paid jobs outside the home. Katherine Anne Porter's young and educated protagonist, Miranda Gay, longs for freedom, best understood if one takes into account the full trilogy of the collection *Pale Horse, Pale Rider* especially "Old Mortality". We see Miranda Gay, longing for independence and autonomy as a journalist amidst the war. The story addresses the challenges and demands placed on a young woman in her quest for autonomy.

Porter chooses Denver, Colorado for Miranda to begin a new life, away from the South and away from her past. She escapes the South and its feudalistic and oppressive hold on women but has to combat sexism in the mythical West. As this tide of women wanting to educate themselves for jobs and careers became prominent, many educators were uncomfortable about women being educated and trained for work outside the home. The period in which the story is set is also distinct as it was the period of the war emergency, when, by an ironical twist of fate, with millions of men called to the front, more jobs had become open to American women. Trying to cater to the demands made by male soldiers, and to encourage those men directly involved in the war, society demanded support from women. War gave women the opportunity to enter the labour force. Miranda Gay enters the labour force during the First World War and during the Spanish flu pandemic as a reporter.

The Woman Worker: A Threat to Masculinity

Middle-class "civilized" white American men grew up with the conviction from the neo-industrialized nineteenth century that white males ought to possess power because white supremacy and male authority were results of human evolutionary development. White civilized men therefore needed to be firm of character and had to be protectors and guardians of women and children. "Pale Horse, Pale Rider" was penned at a time when this Victorian ideology of viewing masculine and feminine spheres as separate identities was gradually dissolving. Ironically, those who continued to adhere to this Victorian insistence on separate identities between masculine and feminine spheres began to suffer from middle-class male identity crisis. By the 1890s, both masculinity and middle-class identity had begun to suffer. From the 1890s, middle-class men found themselves increasingly employed in corporate offices which meant that they lost their economic independence as they were increasingly forced to become salaried employees of other men. The number of salaried, non-propertied workers grew eightfold between 1870 and 1910. Not only did men lose occupations that had served hitherto as signs of masculinity but there was also the awareness that the office space, a male sphere was also being slowly invaded by women. Though women seldom enjoyed the same advantages or positions as men, the mere presence of females within the male sphere proved unsettling to the concept of middle-class masculinity. Though women usually held posts subordinate to male bosses, yet their very presence seemed to diminish the status of the corporate workplace as a masculine territory. Women began breaching the division between proper spheres of the sexes and also claiming or challenging the traditional male prerogatives. This threat that middle-class men felt in the 1910s and 1920s by women's attempts at self-empowerment is shown so well in contemporary literature, and "Pale Horse, Pale Rider" is no exception. The first part of the story shows Miranda as a journalist, struggling because of the raging war and struggling against sex discrimination at work. In "Pale Horse, Pale Rider", Miranda Gay says how:

> all sorts of persons sat upon her desk at the newspaper office. Every day she found someone there, sitting upon her desk instead of the chair provided, dangling his legs, eyes roving, full of his important affairs, waiting to pounce about something or other.
>
> *(316)*

The woman journalist is made painfully aware that she has entered a male sphere. Somewhat threatened by such overtures, let alone protesting verbally, Miranda decides not even to frown at the intruders. Men keep on keeping her under threat, sometimes singly, sometimes in pairs or groups. On one occasion, she reports "two pairs of legs dangling, on either side of her typewriter" (316). The pair manifest, as she says, "a stale air of borrowed importance" (316) and they try to control her finances, constantly trying to coerce her to buy Liberty Bonds, so much so that Miranda thinks, "They are in fact going to throw me out if I don't buy a Liberty Bond" (316). Gilbert and Gubar in *No Man's Land: The Place of the Woman Writer* trace the origins of modernism; they do mention Freud and the First World War, and they also insist on the importance of the new woman, who ushered in significant social changes. The uncertainties of war, coupled with the entry of women as serious competitors in the economic zone (and the literary), made it, for men, a time of enfeebling anxiety. Arguing along the same lines, Barbara Melosh says, this entry and invasion into the economic and corporate zone, so long considered a masculine sphere of work, forced men to acquire "feminine" sensibilities. She asserts, "Paid work, a predominantly masculine realm in the nineteenth century, became increasingly 'feminized', both as more women entered the labor force and as new managerial and sales jobs required men to practice traditionally feminine strategies of persuasion" (Melosh 7). One man, in his persuasion tactic, becomes "all Patriot, working for the Government" (317), insultingly speaking to the obstinate Miranda; Porter writes, "Look here", he asked her, "do you know there's a war, or don't you?" (317). The other man, the younger one, adds, "We're having a war, and some people are buying Liberty Bonds and others just don't seem to get around to it" (317). Finally after repeated attempts, the older of the two men asks her in a voice "persuasive and ominous" (318) why she has not still bought a Liberty Bond. Along with such coercions, in the newspaper job dominated by men, Miranda is also coerced to appropriate a discourse which is not natural to her. The editor old man Gibbons keeps on instructing her: "Never say *people* when you mean *persons* . . . and never say *practically*, say *virtually*, and don't for God's sake ever so long as I am at this desk use the barbarism *inasmuch* under any circumstances whatsoever. Now you're educated, you may go". (319).

Feminists of the 1910s had associated the independence of women with independent income; obviously, they were outraged at the exploitation of women wage earners by employers. Nancy Cott asserts, "Their Feminism insisted on women's economic independence in principle and defence of wage-earning women in fact" (119). American society, a section at least, continued to view career women as usurpers, and reporters were also discriminated against in many ways like all others. Even as full-time reporters for important newspaper houses, women were often referred to as "researchers" whereas men were the real "writers", hierarchically superior. In "Pale Horse, Pale Rider", Porter in fact refers to an anecdote at a better time, when Miranda and Towney as "real reporters" (319) had been sent to cover a scandalous elopement and they botched the opportunity by showing compassion. Compassion being traditionally considered a "feminine" virtue, Porter writes, how they "had been degraded publicly to routine female jobs, one to the theaters, the other to society . . .. they knew they were considered fools by the rest of the staff – nice girls, but fools" (320). None of these prejudices showed in the surveys conducted, however. In fact, the responses to queries were more tilted towards the positive. One editorial personnel for the *Boston Record* replied to the query whether newspapermen discriminated against their female colleagues, "certainly not. Newspaper men are usually over the average of intelligence. Nowadays that sort of question is absurd" (Cott 226). For some inexplicable reason, newspaperwomen queried by the bureau during 1918 were not much willing to perceive or admit to discrimination on the grounds of sex. Cott writes, "The more insistently the bureau's questionnaire thrust the issue of sex discrimination – especially impalpable sex discrimination – before the newspaperwomen's eyes, the more they shied away from answering the questions" (226). The semi-autobiographical story based on Porter's experiences in 1918 was published two decades later, at a time when many well-liked writers like Olga Knoff were arguing that men were "natural heirs" to work opportunity and women, if and when they took jobs, lacked skill, experience and the proper attitude. Porter's story examines the ideology of the 1930s that love and a home as also paid work were "natural" desires in all women.

Romance and Heterosexual Ties

Whether or not Miranda wants a home is not made clear, but love she clearly desires, as becomes evident in the brief romance that blossoms between her and Adam Barclay, a young Army officer. Porter writes, "Miranda smiled at him gaily because she was always delighted at the sight of him" (323). Adam, "tall and heavily muscled in the shoulders, narrow in the waist and flanks" (324) the same age as Miranda, "twenty-four years old and a Second Lieutenant in an Engineers Corps" (324) shows an immense liking for Miranda. Miranda does not just reciprocate Adam's feelings, at heart she longs for more. "Miranda wished to stop hearing, and talking, she wished to think for just five minutes of her own about Adam, really to think about him, but there was no time" (330). It should be noted that feminists ascribed value to heterosexual ties; feminists wanted to achieve financial independence through a career primarily, and each felt that she could attach a husband and children to her life. In fact, they assigned meaning and value to passionate heterosexual attachment than did any other women's rights advocates before them. In the story, Miranda enjoys a few dates, and a bit of romance with Adam Barclay, the young Army officer, but only for a few days. In "Pale Horse, Pale Rider", romance also eventually gets associated with trauma. During her journalism years with *Rocky Mountain News*, Katherine Anne Porter had contracted influenza. Her landlady, fearing contagion, decided to evict her from her place, and the newspaper's editor finagled her admission to a hospital which was overcrowded. Porter ran a temperature of 105 degrees and had to lie on a wheeled stretcher, because of the unavailability of beds, in a hallway for nine days. Doctors thought she would die, newspapers kept her obituary typed and ready, her family made arrangements for her burial, but then an experimental injection of strychnine made her miraculously recover from the virus. Recover she did but by the time she was discharged from the hospital, she was crippled, frail and bald. The hair that eventually grew back and framed her oval face, however, was white and remained white as long as she lived. Before she fell ill, Porter had been indeed seeing a young soldier named Alexander Barclay. As she lay hospitalized, her young boyfriend contracted influenza and died.

The Great War and the Spanish Influenza Pandemic

In the second decade of the twentieth century, the Great War and the pandemic together precipitated an international crisis unprecedented in human history. Jewel Spears Brooker provides us with the statistics related to the war: "Between August 1914 and November 1918, some nine million soldiers were slaughtered, countless civilians killed, and several times as many people forever scarred, both physically and psychologically" (214). Porter happened to witness both the horrors. She was busy as a reporter during the final phase of the Great War, which also included the Spanish influenza epidemic. John Barry provides the statistics related to the Spanish influenza pandemic in *The Great Influenza*. He mentions,

> the influenza epidemic not only caused the deaths of some six hundred thousand people, but it also left a trail of lowered vitality . . . nervous breakdown,

and other sequella [sic] which now threaten thousands of people. . . . This havoc is wide spread, reaching all parts of the United States and all classes of people.

(392)

In the months immediately before the war ended, estimates Barry, between fifty and one hundred million more were claimed by the Spanish influenza. To Porter, the newspaper woman, this international turmoil was not remote but immediate, at the centre of her waking life. Brooker analyses how modernist classics document the association:

> between the flittering consciousness of the individual and the nightmare of contemporary history and, at the same time, put both into a larger context that at once de-personalizes and de-temporalizes, thus giving the personal and the temporal a shape and significance they otherwise would not have.

(213)

Porter does not just remain faithful to her time and contemporary history, she also remains faithful to art. Within the domains of history and art, Porter shows the continuous reaction of individual consciousness towards external traumatic events. One ought to remember that the incident that caused immense trauma in 1918 was reshaped as art years later in 1932. By that time, Porter had tried to bring her post-traumatic stress under control and managed to instil in herself the objectivity required to create works of art. In 1932, based in Basel Switzerland, immersed in Reformation Art – including the remarkable works of Albrecht Dürer, referred to as the Leonardo of the North – Porter used *The Four Horsemen of the Apocalypse* (1498) and *The Knight, Death, and the Devil* (1513) as the structural and thematic references for her apocalyptic work. In fact, Basel's cultural resources honed Porter's interests in religion and history, art and literature. It is a known fact that contemporary disasters often seem to conform to descriptions in the scriptures with the end of history. One could name the Black Death (1346–1353) of the Middle Ages, also referred to as the Pestilence, the Great Mortality or simply the Plague, the Spanish Flu (1918–1919) and the Great War (1914–1919). Porter in "Pale Horse, Pale Rider", like Yeats, associates contemporary events with an apocalyptic vision. Steeped in the rich culture of Basel, as Porter wrote to Pressly, in Geneva, in November 1932, and she dated her letter "1932 – or is it 1400? Who cares?" (Quoted in Brooker 220).

The story "Pale Horse, Pale Rider" opens with the narrator "[in] sleep [where] she knew she was in her bed, . . . Her heart was a stone lying upon her breast outside of her" (314). This dream within a dream was a technique of narration used by Dante and many other medieval writers. Dante's *Divine Comedy* and *The Knight, Death and the Devil* by Dürer manifest the individual's journey through life. And as Miranda wakes up, she finds herself in the sweep of contemporary history – the war. The second work of Dürer, *The Four Horsemen of the Apocalypse*, manifests the large sweep of history. In the Book of Revelations, Chapter 6, the four horsemen symbolize Conquest, War, Famine and Death. As the story opens, in her first dream, Miranda confronts Death, the pale rider, seated on a grey horse with the Devil as his companion. She mounts her own (pale) horse, Graylie, and attempts to outrun them and leave them behind, "Come now, Graylie, she said, taking his bridle, we must out-run Death and the Devil" (315). Death the stranger continues to ride

> beside her, easily, lightly . . . his pale face smiled in an evil trance, he did not glance at her. Ah, I have seen this fellow before, I know this man if I could place him. He is no stranger to me.
>
> *(315)*

Death continues to loom large over the young lovers in the incipient stage of their relationship. As they go out together, on a fine fall day, at "the first corner they waited for a funeral to pass" (324). Somewhat distressed, Adam and Miranda refer to the Spanish Flu as a plague:

> "They just gave it", said Adam, "for no reason. The men are dying like flies out there, anyway. This funny new disease. Simply knocks you into a cocked hat".
>
> "It seems to be a plague", said Miranda, "something out of the Middle Ages. Did you ever see so many funerals, ever?"
>
> "Never did . . ."
>
> *(326)*

In fact, Miranda's landlady Miss Hobbe also calls it a plague; as she finds Miranda with influenza, she shrieks:

> "I tell you, they must come for her *now*, or I'll put her on the sidewalk . . . I tell you, this is a plague, a plague, my God, and I've got a houseful of people to think about!"
>
> *(345)*

John Barry says that though influenza usually selects the weakest in a society to kill, the very young and the very old, the Spanish Influenza in 1918 killed the young and the strong.

> Studies worldwide all found the same thing. Young adults, the healthiest and strongest part of the population, were the most likely to die. Those with the most to live for – the robust, the fit, the hearty, the ones raising young sons and daughters – those were the ones who died.
>
> *(238–39)*

In the United States, not only did it kill men in the military, it killed fifteen times as many civilians. Barry notes that this influenza, for it was after all only influenza, left almost no internal organ untouched:

> the brain showed "marked hyperemia" – blood flooding the brain . . . The virus inflamed or affected the pericardium – the sac of tissue and fluid that protects the heart – and the heart muscle itself, . . . The amount of damage to the kidneys varied . . . The liver was sometimes damaged. The adrenal glands suffered "necrotic areas, frank hemorrhage, and occasionally abscesses. . . . Muscles along the rib cage were torn apart both by internal toxic processes and by the external stress of coughing. . . . And, finally, came the lungs. . . . Only one known disease – a particularly virulent form of bubonic plague called pneumonic plague, which kills approximately 90 percent of its victims – ripped the lungs apart in the way this disease did. So did weapons in war.
>
> *(240–41)*

Edwin Kilbourne, a scientist who has specialized knowledge on influenza, confirmed seven decades after the Spanish Influenza pandemic that the condition of the lungs was "unusual in other viral respiratory infections and is reminiscent of lesions seen following inhalation of poison gas" (Quoted in Barry 241). Ironically, the cause was neither poison gas nor the pneumonic plague; it was unthinkable that it was only the influenza. Exactly a century later humanity has been struck by another pandemic, the COVID-19 pandemic, an infectious disease caused by the SARS-CoV-2 virus.

The Trauma and the Triumph

As soon as Miranda says that she may have contracted influenza, Miss Hobbe, her landlady, exclaims, "*Horrors*" (343) and instructs her to go to bed. Adam comes over, nurses her, feeds her, gets her medicines and also tries to arrange for an ambulance to take Miranda to the hospital. It is in one of those moments that she begins to confide in him about her nightmares, and her fear about him:

> "I'm glad you're here, I've been having a nightmare. Give me a cigarette, will you, and light one for yourself and open all the windows and sit near one of them. You're running a risk", she told him, "don't you know that? Why do you do it?"
>
> *(345)*

And also it is in one of those moments that Miranda asks him to sing with her:

> "Let's sing", said Miranda. "I know an old spiritual, I can remember some of the words". She spoke in a natural voice. "I'm fine now". She began in a

hoarse whisper, "'Pale horse, pale rider, done taken my lover away . . .' Do you know that song?"

"Yes", said Adam, "I heard Negroes in Texas sing it, in an oil field. . . ."

"There's a lot more to it than that", said Adam, "about forty verses, the rider done taken away mammy, pappy, brother, sister, the whole family besides the lover –"

"But not the singer, not yet", said Miranda. "Death always leaves, one singer to mourn. 'Death'", she sang, 'oh, leave one singer to mourn –"

(349)

The Spanish Influenza attacks both Miranda and Adam dies, leaving her, the sole singer to mourn. Darlene Harbour Unrue remarks that "the world-weariness of Miranda in 'Pale Horse, Pale Rider' [was] Porter's own state of mind at the time" (Quoted in Davis 57). Indeed, keeping in mind that the fictionalized narrative was written years after the actual incident, David A. Davis feels that her silence regarding the pandemic till 1932 suggests that she tried, either consciously or unconsciously, to repress her memory. The memory obviously was repressed but could not be obliterated. In a 1963 interview, Porter said how the pandemic had affected her:

> It simply divided my life, cut across it like that. So that everything before that was just getting ready, and after that I was in some strange way altered, really. It took me a long time to go out and live in the world again. I was really "alienated," in the pure sense. It was, I think, the fact that I really had participated in death, that I knew what death was, and had almost experienced it. I had what Christians call the "beatific vision," and the Greeks called the "happy day," the happy vision just before death. Now if you have had that, and survived it, come back from it, you are no longer like other people, and there's no use deceiving yourself that you are
>
> *(Quoted in Davis 57–58)*

"Pale Horse, Pale Rider" becomes a piece of literature as traumatic memory showing a constant interplay between memory and death. Trauma becomes more complex when it occurs on a mass scale. In fact, Porter's story portrays not just individual trauma but also collective trauma, and the presence of the influenza pandemic complicates the distinction between the two. Basing her study on Freud's *Beyond the Pleasure Principle*, Cathy Caruth says the term *trauma* is understood as a wound inflicted not upon the body but upon the mind. But what is alarming is that:

> the wound of the mind – the breach in the mind's experience of time, self, and the world – is not, like the wound of the body, a simple and healable event, but rather an event that, like Tancred's first infliction of a mortal

wound on the disguised Clorinda in the duel, is experienced too soon, too unexpectedly, to be fully known and is therefore not available to conscious- ness until it imposes itself again, repeatedly, in the nightmares and repetitive actions of the survivor.

(3–4)

To Caruth, trauma occurs as a reaction to an overwhelming experience of sud- den or catastrophic events, and the response to the event is often delayed, and manifests itself in "uncontrolled repetitive appearance of hallucinations and other intrusive phenomena" (11). Porter uses the flashback technique and also weaves memories into her plot. Most of the action in "Pale Horse, Pale Rider" takes place roughly a day before Miranda is taken ill, but Miranda's internal monologue takes the reader to even far beyond the immediate past. Caruth argues that, in cases of trauma, "a rethinking of reference is aimed not at elimi- nating history but at resituating it in our understanding, that is, at precisely permitting *history* to arise where *immediate understanding* may not" (11). As Porter fictionalized her traumatic past experience, she simultaneously blended indi- vidual trauma with collective trauma, by linking her personal experience to the experience of millions – the survivors of the war and survivors of the Spanish influenza pandemic.

When Miranda regains consciousness, she finds everything changed. By the time she recovers, the Armistice has been signed and the war is over; and there is a total absence of pestilence and death. Under normal circumstances, Miranda would have tried to forget everything, the war and the pandemic and gone on living, "but she encounters a complication that challenges her will to forget" (Davis 68). Miranda also learns that Adam has died from the virus, obviously having contracted the flu from her. Though she keeps up a stoical demeanour during her discharge from the hospital, she says to herself:

> Adam, she said, now you need not die again, but still I wish you were here; I wish you had come back, what do you think I came back for, Adam, to be deceived like this? . . . She said, "I love you" and stood up trembling, trying by the mere act of her will to bring him to sight before her.

(363)

Miranda fails to repress her memory of Adam, it is a memory which she holds dear, but this memory gets juxtaposed with her memory of the Spanish Influenza pandemic, a memory she detests. Davis rightly says, "Miranda's personal memory of the pandemic is a confusing tangle of love, horror and guilt. Yet it remains her only connection to Adam, so she cannot allow herself to forget the memory with- out abdicating her love for him" (69). In "Pale Horse, Pale Rider" as in *A Farewell to Arms* (1929), trauma is aestheticized and bound by fictionalization. LaCapra, in *Writing History, Writing Trauma* speaks of the symptomatic returns of trauma. He asserts that this immersion in trauma or the state of being haunted by trauma can be countered by narrative. In a similar vein, Peter Brooks says that narrative can first provoke and then bind emotional energies, just as the repetition compulsion does: "Analysis works toward the more precise and orderly recollection of the past, no longer compulsively repeated, insistently reproduced in the present, but ordered as a retrospective narrative" (227). This model of narrative has its basis in psychoanalysis. Moreover, as Porter fictionalizes personal experience, the reader also partially shares the traumatic experience. Miranda, the sole singer left to mourn, does mourn but in silence and in dignity.

Works Cited

Primary Text

Porter, Katherine Anne. *Pale Horse, Pale Rider: The Selected Short Stories*. Penguin Books, 2011.

Secondary Texts

Barry, John M. *The Great Influenza: The Story of the Deadliest Pandemic in History*. Penguin, 2004.

Brooker, Jewel Spears. "Nightmare and Apocalypse in Katherine Anne Porter's 'Pale Horse, Pale Rider'." *The Mississippi Quarterly*, vol. 62, no. 2, 2009, pp. 213–34. Mississippi State UP. www.jstor.org/stable/26476735. Accessed 20 Oct. 2021.

Brooks, Peter. *Reading for the Plot: Design and Intension in Narrative*. Knopf, 1984.

Caruth, Cathy. *Unclaimed Experience: Trauma, Narrative, and History*. The Johns Hopkins University Press, 1996.

Cott, Nancy F. *The Grounding of Modern Feminism*. Yale University Press, 1987.

Davis, David A. "The Forgotten Apocalypse: Katherine Anne Porter's 'Pale Horse, Pale Rider', Traumatic Memory, and the Influenza Pandemic of 1918." *The Southern Literary Journal*, vol. 43, no. 2, 2011, pp. 55–74. U of North Carolina P. www.jstor.org/stable/23208856. Accessed 20 Oct. 2021.

Melosh, Barbara. *Gender and American History Since 1890*. Routledge, 1993.

3

PANDEMIC AND MAN-LESS SOCIETY

Problematizing Gender, Sex and Sexuality in Christina Sweeney-Baird's *The End of Men*

Goutam Karmakar

The current crisis of the COVID-19 pandemic is immense and brings a dystopic world alive in the twenty-first century. The alarming spread of the contagious virus around the world, the unprecedented loss of life, the lack of adequate medical support, the closure of public spaces and the prolonged isolation have all contributed to the chaos, which is likely one of the greatest socio-pathological crises humanity has faced in a century. The sprouting of the contagious virus SARS-CoV-2 in Wuhan, China, and its eventual spread across international borders suggests the locomotive ability of the febrile virus. The vulnerability of human lives owing to the viral infection triggers the fear of human beings' supposed end and turns the ominous literary dystopic worlds into a reality. The oeuvre of pandemic fiction, bearing its seed in the history of pandemics and plagues over the years, creates worlds (sometimes speculative) fraught with disease and despair. Mary Shelley's *The Last Man* is the earliest speculative pandemic fiction that speculates on Europe in the late twenty-first century being distorted by a mysterious plague which eventually spreads across the globe and threatens the very existence of human beings. The threatened condition of human beings owing to the outbreak of contagious disease is not a new phenomenon, but a medically advanced world in the twenty-first century ravaged by a mysterious virus, outpowering human agency, may be unprecedented. This unprecedented phenomenon of viral outbreaks necessitates the "thinking (of) the pandemic" (Horton 1), which is expected to alter the socio-economic transactions between human beings. The thinking of a pandemic suggests the topsy-turvy social order and intensifies the class divisions. Žižek predicts "new forms of class struggles will erupt" (qtd. in Horton 1) and also thinks the lockdowns have curtailed democracy as the "shared space of communication and interaction are under private control" (qtd. in Horton 1). In *Pandemic! COVID 19 shakes the world*, Žižek writes that "limitations and constraints are definitely not only internal: new strict rules of behaviour are being enforced", ensuing the "struggle

DOI: 10.4324/9781003294436-5

against oneself" (21). The internal and external restraints of the pandemic-ravaged world trigger the thinking of altered human relations. The thinking of pandemics also induces the literature on pandemics, keeping in view the class struggles, gendered relations and crisis of the twenty-first century.

The topos of recent pandemic literature derives its inspiration from the current pandemic situation and extends the temporal line to accommodate future years. Pandemic fiction speculates years beyond the present while holding the memory of the past catastrophic outbreaks of disease, suggesting the continuation of disease-inflicted humanity. The speculative quality of pandemic literature, on the one hand, serves as ominous reflections of the future and as cautionary tales for humanity, on the other hand. The speculative nature of pandemic narratives furthers the imagination of writers, who invent peculiar diseases and viruses that send chills down the spines of the readers. The very thought of a pandemic instrumenting the geo-social and socio-pathological relations and interactions sets "illness as metaphor" (Sontag v) of fear, anxiety, alteration of socio-economic dynamics and unpredictability.

Christina Sweeney-Baird's *The End of Men* (2021) contributes significantly to the oeuvre of pandemic literature, more so due to its timely publication during the pandemic-ridden times. The novel speculates on a future (between 2025 and 2031) when a virus infects only men, while women survive without being affected by the virus. The high mortality factor of the virus kills thousands of men in Scotland and in other parts of Europe. The "male pandemic" gradually spreads worldwide and infects the male population, in turn affecting socio-cultural and gendered relationships around the globe. The global male population is exposed to the virus, and they stand on the verge of their supposed end. The fragility of men reverses the patriarchal power structure, with the world's future resting in the hands of women only. The cover page of the novel inscribes: "Only men carry the virus. Only women can save us" (Sweeny-Baird 2021), suggestive of the pandemic as a means of altering gender relations and gendered space. When considering the male diseased body, gender politics takes an unexpected turn. The impact of the pandemic is far-fetched and rings the knell for men, thereby triggering the thought of a world devoid of males. The imagination of a man-less society arouses several kinds of dread, and the fear of the mysterious contagious disease proves to be morally contagious as well. The panic and trauma spread across the globe faster than the virus, which subjected the disease and the diseased bodies to political scrutiny, surpassing the bio-medical premises. The "fear of contagion increase(s) vices such as avarice, greed, and corruption", which lead to "moral and physical death" (Riva et al. 1753). The disease affecting men alone further complicates the positions of sexually minor groups and exposes their vulnerabilities to a point of non-recovery. This chapter seeks to examine the male pandemic as a socio-political instrument for altering gender relations vis-à-vis male diseased bodies, medically treated as "ontologically distinct entities" (Cantor 347) and also seeks to re-evaluate how the biological sex-specific viral infection intensifies the anatomical distinction between male and female. This will further problematize the idea of sex and gender fluidity vis-à-vis the reconstructed pandemic-affected society.

Diseased Body, Gendered Relations and Pandemic

The outbreak of contagious diseases and their transmission across distant places is not a new phenomenon. The uncontrollable transmission of the disease adds to its geo-social significance, which changes transportation, migratory patterns and socialization of human beings. The transmission and transportation of the viral disease have led to "a shifting perception in time and space" (Huber 455). The variability in the perception of time and space induces the formation of a localized space, curtailing global relationships and inter-spacious transactions. The situation is complicated further if the disease is anatomy or biological constitution specific, as it will inevitably categorize human beings and will create unwanted rifts between the two categories of people. As such, a situation of disease-induced crisis is depicted in *The End of Men*, as the peculiar virus solely attacks and infects male bodies, while sparing female bodies. The first case of the virus attack was received at a hospital in Glasgow, United Kingdom, by Doctor Amanda Mclean. The man was detected with common flu-like symptoms and was treated with paracetamol, and he seemed to be stable. But within a while,

> the patient is dying. His breathing is laboured with shallow pant of a body not coping with the basic requirements of taking in air. His skin has the grey pallor of someone whose bodily systems are shutting down and his temperature is climbing higher and higher.
>
> *(Sweeny-Baird 17)*

The infection can hardly be detected by Amanda, who, along with other medical personnel, labours behind the patient whose health deteriorates rapidly and unbelievably. The dark-haired, handsome lad seems to lose the fight against the unknown and undetected disease as his organs gradually fail and the patient dies at "12.34 pm, 3 November 2025" (Sweeny-Baird 19). The young patient's sudden death leaves the health staff distraught as the deterioration has been rapid and unprecedented. Moreover, the death of a young patient suggests "something has gone seriously wrong" and the doctors "have been unable to fix it" (Sweeny-Baird 19) relates to Amanda Mclean after losing her patient to "just a flu" (Sweeny-Baird 19). The arbitrariness and fatality of the disease ensue waves of panic across the medical team at A&E hospital, demanding a close analysis of the disease. Amanda Maclean notices that the disease only affects men, killing six men with similar symptoms in a single day. She writes an e-mail to Leah Spicer, an official in the health protection department in Scotland, "They're all men. Too small a sample size so far obviously but I've never seen that before. May be men are more vulnerable to it?" (Sweeney-Baird 26). In connection to this e-mail, Leah Spicer writes an e-mail to Raymond McNab, a senior in the health protection department, suggesting his disbelief in the case of the flu and also making a remark about Amanda's psychological fragility, which perhaps sanctions his ignorance of Amanda's cautionary message. Raymond supports Leah and refers to Amanda as a "stark raving lunatic who's trying to waste the limited resources and time of this institution" (Sweeney-Baird 27). This is a common practice when anything unusual happens, and the outbreak of an epidemic is initially often met with ignorance and a refusal to accept the severity of it. As Tory Gates writes about his experience of a pandemic in the essay "Change and Embracing It" (2020) that "we are good at ignoring things" (10) and "we are terrified of anything we do not understand or refuse to understand" (11). The fatal virus threatens human beings on the one hand, while on the other hand, the denial of its existence compounds the threat further. Here, Giorgio Agamben's critical position on the COVID-19 pandemic can be recalled. He presents the COVID-19 symptoms as a "sort of influenza" (Agamben 11), which, in his opinion, is media hyped to create a "climate of panic" and to establish "a state of exception", restricting mobilization and suspending the normal pattern of living (Agamben 11). The initial response to the early reports of men dying of flu was to dismiss them as bits of rumour and hyped concern about the normal flu, which can be treated with simple infection-controlling medical techniques. The ignorant approach is criticized, as is Agamben's view of seeing the symptoms of the COVID-19 virus-affected bodies as mere influenza. The first reporting of the flu was done by the *New York Times*, while the media in the United Kingdom largely remained silent about the flu. The flu, only affecting men, highlights its bizarreness, which appals Lisa Michael, Professor of the Department of Virology, at the University of Toronto. Dr. Amanda speaks to *The Times of London* about the "new" plague which has escaped Scotland, primarily due to the negligence of the authorities, who have been reluctant to acknowledge the severity of the virus and to contain the infection. Journalist Maria Ferreira writes an article "The Plague is Here and Someone Should Have Warned You" (Sweeney-Baird 63) which highlights the delay in responding to the plague, thereby increasing the risk factor and exposing infected people to the world. To this the people of the United Kingdom react to the article by stating,

> The fucking *Washington Post* article – that a reporter in the United States of fucking America has managed to simultaneously make us look incompetent and corrupt, as though we knew there was a problem that we refused to fix and couldn't have fixed it even if we tried?
>
> *(Sweeney-Baird 69)*

The US newspaper reporting the spread of the flu due to the negligence of UK authorities is received with criticism by UK citizens, breeding a politics of representing a nation in negative light. The scepticism bred by the reporting of the foreign media creates a political divide. Thus, politics initiates a division by pandemic between states.

Moreover, the fact that the virus infects only men increases the danger level for them. This alters gender relations, creating a situation where women are at the helm of power. The virus immune female biological composition puts women at the centre of health protection, treatment, political power and research, while the male population around them dwindles away. This presents a situation of power subversion, subjecting men to the protection of women. The women, assuming the charge, endeavour to safeguard their male counterparts. They thus take the charge of mediating the news of the tremendous spread of the viral infection. The likes of Dr. Amanda Mclean and journalist Maria Ferreira break the male-controlled media space and male-regulated information. As Maria Ferreira writes in her *Washington Post* article,

> I think my editor, and lots of other men who are gatekeepers to information around the world, are terrified. They are so frozen with panic that they can't bear to look reality in the face. So, I'm here to do their job for them.
>
> *(Sweeney-Baird 65)*

The trans-mediation of information about the rapid transmission of a fatal disease is required to adopt precautionary measures across the world to contain the disease geo-socially. Also, the allusion to men as "gatekeepers of information around the world" suggests the dominance of men in the premises of the media and their power over women in particular spheres. Maria oversteps the male-dominated medical premises to circulate the information and news about the plague across the continents. This is an indication of the subversion of the patriarchal power structure as the "male plague" has horrified men, consequently instigating their states of denial. The women taking charge of mediating the news and treating the viral disease echo the words written on the cover page of the novel – "only women can save us".

The overpowering of the virus on men reduced their identities to vulnerable diseased bodies, eventually bringing men under the radar of vigilance and subjecting them to isolation. Men with the disease are perceived as being unable to mobilize in public, limiting their public interactions and connections. They are looked at with pity or fear by those who are subjected to dying. Men's bodily disorders have a socio-political impact, robbing them of their power. The assumption of men's identity as carriers of the contagious viral disease renders the virus/disease as a "distinct entity, quite distinct from their manifestation in the individual patient" and the treatment is therefore "directed towards the disease rather than the person" (Cantor 349). The patient, rather than being viewed as an individual, is perceived as a disease-carrying medium which requires treatment. This is evident through an incident of a man stepping into an isolated cottage of Catherine with her son, Theodore. After losing her husband to the plague, Catherine is left with her only son, vulnerable to the virus. On seeing a man trespassing in her presumably safe and cocooned space, Catherine is initially frightened of being raped or killed by the man. She responds to the sight of a stranger in a conventional way in a male-dominated society, taking advantage of a lonely woman. But soon she is reminded of the disease, and she at once perceives the man as a weak and vulnerable object, defeated by the virus. Catherine firmly says, "I came here with my son. I'm a host and my son is infected, he's just upstairs. I came here to die with him"

(Sweeney-Baird 133). While saying this, she steps towards the man, enough to frighten him and to reduce him to look like "a cow being led to slaughter with bulging eyes and a mouth dry and twisting with terror" (Sweeney-Baird 133). Another instance of male vulnerability is exposed when Dr. Amaya Sharvani, a pre-eminent paediatric geneticist, says to Dr. George, a male doctor: "I have to say, it's a pleasant surprise with a male doctor, discussing all of this (about the plague). There's not many of you left" (Sweeney-Baird 166). This indicates the astonishment of women at the bare survival of men and the dwindling condition of men in the pandemic-affected neo-world. Men around the world are exposed to "bare life", as Agamben opines:

> Bare life, and the fear of losing it, is not something that unites people: rather, it blinds and separates them. Fellow human beings, as in the plague . . ., are now seen only as potential anointers whom we must avoid at all cost, and from whom we should maintain a distance of at least one meter.
>
> *(15)*

The exposure to "bare life" presents men with biological constitutions vulnerable to the virus, rather than social beings.

Male Plague and Sex/Gender Identity

The advent of the "male plague", identifying the male chromosome, intensifies the gender divide. Common perception holds sex as biologically given and gender as a social construct, which is deconstructed by presenting the assumption of "a sex with the question of identification" as a folly (*Bodies That Matter* 3). "No longer construed as natural, fixed, ahistorical or given, the body is now often viewed as a pre-eminently socio-cultural artifact (or construct)" (Vertinsky 148), body is seen as a result, rather than a pre-given object. But the identification of sex by the chromosomes XX and XY becomes mandatory in detecting the reason behind the virus's affecting only men. The doctors discuss,

> The Plague virus requires the absence of a specific gene sequence. The body's resistance to the Plague – through its ability to fight the high white blood cell count it generates with speed – is present in the X chromosome. In around 9 per cent of men their X chromosome has the necessary genetic protection. Thanks to their XX chromosomes, all women are safe. The others, the billions of other men, are vulnerable to the virus.
>
> *(Sweeney-Baird 165)*

The chromosome biologically determining human sex becomes the regulating factor for providing immunity to the virus. The virus being biologically sex specific perhaps subverts the idea that the body is not "pre-determined". This very phenomenon of viruses affecting male bodies perhaps intensifies the notion of sexed bodies, but without privileging male bodies over those of females. Within the medico-social paradigm, the (re)intensification of sexed bodies complicates the concept of body, particularly the diseased body. The proliferation of male diseased bodies subverts the notion that women are eternally wounded, medically not privileging the female body over that of the male. Rather, the male-affecting virus challenges the notion of the female as the "weak" and vulnerable sex, while the male is the physically stronger and disease immune one. This notion naturalizes the consideration of women being inferior to men, which bears connection with the sexed body since "deployments of power are directly connected to the body – to bodies, functions [and] physiological processes" (Foucault 152). Male diseased bodies become the subject of social gaze and pity in the novel, (re)identifying male-ness with vulnerability. The (re)identification of the male as the vulnerable segment of a pandemic-affected society realigns gender–sex identity. Here, in the pandemic-affected society, men being outnumbered by women, and men being subjected to women's gazes of astonishment and pity, reverse the gender norms. The male plague overturns the stereotypical gender roles of men protecting women to women protecting men, as "only women can save us" (Sweeney-Baird).

However, the concept of gender–sex identity becomes more complicated when it crosses the traditional sex-gender binarization to include transgender people. In the novel, the author makes an interesting reference to trans men and women and to the LGBQIA+ community at large. The novel tries to highlight the most vulnerable and marginalized sections of society and attempts to assess the impact of the male pandemic on them. Due to the virus, trans men and trans women face a peculiar problem. Trans men, due to their XX chromosome, are immune to the virus, while trans women, due to their XY chromosome, are vulnerable to the virus. Tanya, a trans woman, explains to Amanda Mclean about the psychological anxieties and convolutions in the trans and LGBTQIA+ community:

> the Plague distinguished on the basis of sex and there was no fucking with it. None at all. It was the first time I had experienced a huge divide in the trans community. There wasn't anger or discord, just stunned desolation. Trans women on this side – you're all probably going to die. Trans men on that side – you're all going to be fine.
>
> *(Sweeney-Baird 355–56)*

Tanya further expresses the helplessness and fragility of trans women and gay men – "Trans women were rendered helpless in the face of their XY chromosomes, and gay men became a super-minority" (Sweeney-Baird 356) which she calls a "nightmare". The Plague's sex distinction, as well as the notion that "body (or sex) is also discursively gendered" (Motschenbacher 2), may then complicate gender–sex identity. With the notion "gender is a social construct" and that "sex/gender need not be aligned" are challenged with a sex-specific disease. The basic constitution of the XY chromosomes of trans women, despite their assumed identity as women within the socio-cultural paradigm, does not render them immune to the virus, whereas trans men who are socially identified as men are immune to the virus because of their XX chromosomes. The sex-specific disease in a way reminds the trans community of their assigned sexed identities at birth, which they have struggled to get rid of. The Plague, therefore, underlines their sex assigned at birth as their basic identity, which now has become a glaring reality. As Tanya says to Amanda:

> It was really hard being trans in 2025, and being gay often wasn't a picnic. But the plague made everything so much worse. The process of supporting trans individuals, campaigning for expanded rights and making the world a better place for trans people became irrelevant to a lot of people.
>
> *(Sweeney-Baird 356)*

This weakens marginalized groups and harms the mental health of those in the LGBTQIA community. The murderous plague's devastating effects on trans women who are vulnerable to the disease and gay men who are reduced to a bare minimum highlight the murderous plague's devastating effects. The very problem of sex/gender identity, posing an identity crisis for the trans community, perhaps questions the notion of fluidity of sex and gender (both being discursive in nature). Gender fluidity arises from the notion that "one's own gender, which may or may not correspond to the sex assigned at birth" (Tasikowski et al. 1) and that one may align with any gender depending on one's socio-cultural awareness. Furthermore, the discursive generation of sex implies that sexual identity and responses are not explicit but rather implicit in the socio-cultural context. But with the male-specific plague, this notion seems to be disarrayed, as the Plague questions "the very criterion by which we judge a person to be a gendered being" and examines the "criterion that posits coherent gender as a presupposition of humanness" ("Doing Justice to Someone" 184). The enquiry into trans identity questions the very ontology of trans non-binary beings in the face of the pandemic. The awful comments on trans women as they must have died as "the last thing the world needs is a man dressed up as a woman – it needs real men, and [they] should have stayed [so]" (Sweeney-Baird 356), render their trans identities as insignificant, instigating prejudice and hatred towards them. Their "plurality of the self" ("Doing Justice to Someone" 183) is denied, while reinforcing a gender-binarized society.

Conclusion

The narrative that zooms into a pandemic-ridden world, therefore, instigates the imagination of a society that will deal with a disease that not only redefines the social norm but also redefines gendered relations. The Male Plague affects and effaces men in a way that speculates on a woman-dominated world, where men take the back seat, helpless, vulnerable and forced to leave the world's reins at the hands of women. This may sound intriguing, especially given the possibility of power subversion in a patriarchal society, but it is important to recognize that eradicating the male population is a dangerous suggestion that is bound to create an imbalance in society. The imbalance in society in turn will affect women, the trans community and other minorities. The Male Plague convolutes the problems at various levels, as the pandemic does not prove itself to be a great equalizer, but a great discriminator, as it distinguishes between the basic composition of sex. The fixity of the body has been socially refuted, but the basic composition of XX and XY chromosomes remains unchanged, which is the determining factor for providing immunity to the virus. The body, thus, becomes the focus of identity, which again complicates the "body/gender dissonance", increases "social challenges (e.g. discrimination, stigma, estrangement, isolation)" and triggers "mental ill-health experiences" (Jones et al. 2).

Works Cited

Agamben, Giorgio. *Where We Are Now? The Epidemic as Politics.* Eris, 2020.

Butler, Judith. *Bodies That Matter.* Routledge, 1993.

———. "Doing Justice to Someone: Sex Reassignment and Allegories of Transsexuality." *The Transgender Studies Reader*, edited by Susan Strykar and Susan Whittle. Routledge, 2006, pp. 183–93.

Cantor, David. "The Diseased Body." *Medicine in the Twentieth Century*, edited by Roger Cooter and John Pickstone. OPA, 2000, pp. 347–66.

Foucault, Michel. *The History of Sexuality, vol. 1: An Introduction.* Pantheon, 1978.

Gates, Tory. "Change and Embracing It." *After the Pandemic: Visions of Life Post Covid 19*, edited by Lawrence Knorr, et al. Sunbury, 2020, pp. 10–16.

Horton, Richard. "Thinking Pandemic." *Offline*, vol. 397, Feb. 2021, p. 1.

Huber, Valeska. "The Unification of the Globe by Disease? The International Sanitary Conferences on Cholera, 1851–1894." *The Historical Journal*, vol. 49, no. 2, June 2006, pp. 453–76.

Jones, Bethany A., et al. "Exploring the Mental Health Experiences of Young Trans and Gender Diverse People During the Covid-19 Pandemic." *International Journal of Transgender Health*, 2021, pp. 1–14.

Motschenbacher, Heiko. "Speaking the Gendered Body: The Performative Construction of Commercial Femininities and Masculinities via Body-Part Vocabulary." *Language in Society*, vol. 38, 2009, pp. 1–22.

Riva, Michele Augusto, Marta Benedetti, and Giancarlo Cesana. "Pandemic Fear and Literature: Observations from Jack London's *The Scarlet Plague*." *Emerging Infectious Diseases*, vol. 20, no. 10, 2014, pp. 1753–57.

Sontag, Susan. *Illness as Metaphor.* Farrar, Straus and Giroux, 1977.

Sweeney-Baird, Christina. *The End of Men.* The Borough Press, 2021.

Tacikowski, Pawel, et al. "Fluidity of Gender Identity Induced by Illusory Body-Sex Change." *Nature Research*, vol. 10, 2020, pp. 1–14.

Vertinsky, Patricia. "The Social Construction of the Gendered Body: Exercise and the Exercise of Power." *The International Journal of the History of Sport*, vol. 11, no. 2, Mar. 2007, pp. 147–71.

Žižek, Slavoj. *Pandemic: COVID 19 Shakes the World.* OR Books, 2020.

II

Uncanny Dilemmas

4

THE DECAMERON

Re-reading the Uncanny Riddle of Plague

Riti Agarwala

In reconsidering the importance of reading and writing plague narratives, it is inevitable to remember that "past plagues are still present to us, exerting their pressure as shards of cultural memory, traumatic fragments that still have the power to wound even if – especially if – their substance has been 'forgotten'"(Gilman 5).

Situating the Crisis of Plague

Ernest B. Gilman asserts that the *Yersinia pestis* bacterium, first isolated from Chinese strains in 1894 by the Swiss bacteriologist Alexandre Yersin, was identified by epidemiologists to have caused three global pandemics of the bubonic plague:

> the Plague of Justinian, which ravaged the Roman Empire in the sixth century; the Black Death of the fourteenth century; and the outbreak of 1894–1903, which spread from Hong Kong and caused millions of deaths across east and south Asia.
>
> *(Gilman 9)*

This bears witness to how the very phenomenon of virus inflicting humankind is inevitable, repetitive and a part of our "cultural memory" and the "collective consciousness".

The plague bacterium of the fourteenth century is said to have confined itself within the stomachs of rat fleas and the bloodstreams of the black rats on which they fed. The plague bacterium had gradually spread along the trade routes from the East towards the West. *The Decameron*'s description of the Black Death becomes one of the most vivid descriptions of the plague in the Middle Ages. Boccaccio in the Preface to the text very cleverly introduces two principal narratives of disease: the primary narrative of the Black Death and the other of "lovesickness". Where

DOI: 10.4324/9781003294436-7

Boccaccio talks about the Bubonic plague in great detail making us feel the trauma and horror of the plague, lovesickness remains a mystery for the readers which unfolds gradually and intermingles with the plague narrative to create a contrasting narrative of disease that rested on medieval social customs and norms, contributing to the dystopic hell of illness, death and disease. The portrayal of diseases in literature unfurls its intricacies with time, in the way they are read and interpreted. As Ernest B. Gilman cites Sander Gilman, insisting that "the infected individual is never value-neutral", Sander Gilman sees the symptoms of disease as a "complex text" read, and to be read, "within the conventions of an interpretive community" and "in the light of earlier, powerful readings of what are understood to be similar or parallel texts". In Gilman's view, diseases are coded so as to represent our own deepest fears of dissolution and contamination, and to contain these fantasies by projecting them onto the body of the sufferer as a demonized "other" – or by framing them within the boundaries of art (qtd. in Gilman 38).

Reading *The Decameron* in the context of its composition upholds the fact that literature has long been changing our lives in the way it has affected readers. This creates the urge to read and discuss *The Decameron* as a "text" that continues to cast its shadow on the readers; to understand how its context, content and meaning(s) help us to analyse the world around us and how its readership resurrects the importance of the text in the present era of crisis.

In collating narratives of various genres and mood, in the fabric of plague and disease, Boccaccio presents a distinct aesthetics of narrativization where he talks about diseases, the psychological and the physical aspects of it, in a way it had never been done before. The design of the narrative becomes important because the way the narrative reaches the reader decides its impact on the reader and hence one's reception of it. In the author's intention to render both "pleasure and useful counsel" to the readers, one must note that the author balances the role of the reader and the author at the very outset of the narrative; even before the 10 days journey of entertainment begins. The author, who is very much a part of the first day of the journey, not only initiates the course of the journey but also becomes a starting point from where the dynamics of the speaker and listener gradually changes.

The plague is that steep mountain which one needs to climb in order to see the beauty beyond it. However, plague is not the initial impediment only, in some ways it is the mountain that we climb like Sisyphus whenever we confront direct or indirect references to the plague within the text. The Plague, as an event that inhabits the artifice of the text, is tucked in the consciousness of the *brigata*; it peeks in from the nooks and crannies of the tales. The social condition of the characters along with their psychological framework draws us back to the plague narrative in some way or the other.

In perceiving *The Decameron* as a "human comedy" we realize how it upholds the time of flux in which it is situated. The "steep" mountain climb at the beginning of the narrative promises the reader a utopic *purgatorio* which is typically Boccaccio's own invention. Boccaccio's narrative is principally guided by the aim to pass time pleasantly. The author does not seem to bother much about what is "virtuous" and what is "corrupt", he is rather "interested in stimulating the curiosity of the reader by presenting unusual events and characters" (Sanctis 224).

Dealing With the "Gap": The Past and the Present

Alongside the socio-economic changes, the plague had also changed the way human emotions worked: cruelty, selfishness, lack of concern for others, fear, mayhem, loneliness and abandonment chiefly guided the human spirit. It is here that we can very closely relate to previous plagues, and hence plague writing becomes an important sphere whose documentation, be it through fictions or non-fictions, lives through generations. The plague becomes a prism through which we make a journey in the time of flux, to decipher the various ways in which the plague affects people from various walks of life. Very akin to our sense of self-journey and the loneliness that comes with illness, "individualism" is an aspect that is embedded in the semantics and stylization of *The Decameron*.

The Author's introduction, a compact text which has too many hints and implications for the reader, is crucial to the understanding of the text. Pampinea, the first fictional character whose fictional existence itself is questionable, jumps out of a real-life scenario narrated by the author, takes charge of the narrative in the first person voice and shifts the locus of the narrative from the author to the characters. Pampinea is an important character who reveals the subtle merging of micro-narratives in the text. The preface does not remain a vivid dictation or explanation of events on the part of the author, and the stepping of the characters through Pampinea brings in the amalgamation of the fictional and the non-fictional in a very precise way.

Pampinea's entry changes the course of the narrative. The questions she asks her fellow female companions are open-ended and are intended for readers across generations – the resonances for us, who are in a similar situation given the pandemic of the present era, are even more. Pampinea ultimately seems to talk to the readers; from the immediate audience her circle of listeners widens. Followed by Pampinea, the dialogues by the women in the very introduction expose the multifarious directions in which *The Decameron* would make us think; we start playing with the questions and arguments raised and discussed among the characters.

The very concept of a character as the narrator of a story brings in the individual in the formation of the "collective" and in the amalgamation of the individual and the collective. *The Decameron* becomes emblematic of "collective imagination", in the way the pandemic-stricken world has always called for a "new normal". Very much like us, who are experiencing the period of flux in the pandemic grieved lives of ours, preoccupied with the dilemma of "fitting in", where "[o]ur minds are still racing back and forth, longing for a return to 'normalcy', trying to stitch our future to our past and refusing to acknowledge the rupture" (Roy 214), *The Decameron* is a reminder that there is still "a chance to rethink the doomsday machine we have built for ourselves. Nothing can be worse than a return to normality . . . [the pandemic] is a portal, a gateway between one world and the next" (Roy 214).

Storytelling: Relieving Ourselves From the Environs of Illness

Storytelling as a therapeutic medium of listening to our fellow companions' experiences and life narratives has been a popular form of literature when it comes to talking about illness or disease. Storytelling was a well-established form of literary expression even in the medieval times. Stories from various sources influenced and found their place in varied forms of art. As opposed to its rival form, the legend, short stories gave space to combine both the old and the new. However, the "tales"

> called by different names, were the common heritage of all the Latin peoples, but *the* tale – and much less a collection of them where the single stories had been brought together in an organic whole by a story teller – did not yet exist.
>
> *(Sanctis 222)*

Boccaccio can hence be counted as a major initiator of a new form which perhaps is in synchrony with the need to tell the stories of changing times. The setting of the narrative, its content and form, all comes together to contribute to the dynamism of fluid entities that the text constitutes. The metaphor of "play" alongside the sense of "permanent displacement" tricks the reader throughout the narrative, engaging us in the mind game of interpretation.

The garden which we conceive of as a pre-lapsarian world, utopic beyond the filth and dirt of the city; that which has the potential to rejuvenate the tired souls from the city has a strong semantics that syncs with the formal logic of the text. As Aldo D. Scaglione notes:

> We must, then, remember that in the Middle Ages the *villa*, the *locus amoenus*, or the garden are, indeed, an occasion for escape from the closed life of the walled city or the fortress-like house, but without quite plunging into the perturbing disorderliness, the "wildness" of open nature. Places of this kind represent a compromise, a fusion of elements of city and wilderness, symbolical of harmony between reason and the forces of the subconscious. [It is] an appropriate introduction for a gentle opening of the mind – without a direct, sudden, and drastic exposure – to those subterranean phenomena of life, those forces of matter and of the unconscious, which, in their bloom, could frighten and repel the medieval mind. Besides, one ought not overlook the medieval fondness of enclosed gardens as allegorical settings wherein to stage the exclusive, aristocratic scene for actions of courtly love.
>
> *(235–36)*

The characters constituting the basic fabric of *The Decameron* are both characters and storytellers; their role keeps changing within the narrative. They tell stories to the listeners within the boundaries of the narrative and also reach out to the readers beyond the visible narrative frame. The other storytellers hence become both listeners and speakers according to the set design of the text. However, the switching position of the speaker and listener portrays the fluidity in roles even within a deliberately crafted form of the text. *The Decameron* rests very much on this shifting dynamics of something that is given and that which is untold, uncertain.

Boccaccio expresses his intention to especially address the women in the preface. The *brigata* too consists of majority of women. The women of the *brigata* laugh, enjoy, communicate and live as free spirits which again is a change from the preceding medieval convention. The women do defy the medieval women's expected "code of conduct", their reactions are much more balanced but that does not imply that the women of the *brigata* are unruly and shameless to the extreme. Where the *brigata* implicates the collective role of women in the narrative, the tales told by the storytellers reveal a plethora of women who emerge in various roles: the mourning woman, the heroic woman, woman as a saviour, woman as a silent sufferer and many more. The multiple shades of the female character are again a debunking of the convention and a plea to the readers to give space to the "individual" in choosing to read an event of history.

Gender binaries operate from the very beginning of the text. At the very inception of the narrative, Boccaccio asserts that the women cannot bear melancholy unlike the men in love. The author also considers that the women being fragile have too long hidden their flaming desire within themselves, and hence the narrative intends to soothe the "melancholy" of the "delicate ladies". In the medieval belief system

> [m]en's and women's passions are not only held to be different in quality, but also derive from the entirely different medical and pathological traditions. Whereas male lovesickness is classified as a form of melancholy – a malady associated with creativity, interiority and intellect – the female version is considered a disorder of the womb.
>
> *(Dawson 4)*

Lovesickness that inflicts the male lover is exaggerated and in doing so the male lover is himself raised to a pedestal and the beloved remains as a "cause" of his illness in the journey of love. This very narrative exposes the gender logic of heroism that worked behind the concept of courtly love. The gendering of insanity and the way the disease of love infects the "male" is at the same time ironic for the present reader of the twenty-first century. It also brings this realization to readers in the present times that beyond the cultural dynamics of lovesickness as a disease in medieval times, lovesickness might have gendered implications but simultaneously it liberates one from gender roles as love can strike anyone, anywhere. Boccaccio through his deliberate hybridization of narrative and concepts relating to them subverts the very system of "universals" that rules the medieval world. As Francesco de Sanctis puts it "The essential quality of the Middle Ages was transcendence: a sort of ultrahuman and ultranatural 'beyond' outside of nature and man. . . . The basis of this philosophical theology was the existence of universals" (217). Universals had hence created an arch of superficiality which rested on traditional concepts of entities that constitute life. *The Decameron* offers a shift from this monolithic perspective and provides a space for individuality and self-reflection. In the multitude of stories that come to us within the 10 days of "enjoyment" and storytelling, we realize the disruption of old forms and traditions. The author himself is very aware of this process of change that he initiates. In the prologue to Day Four, the author talks of his critics and the way contemporary society would "judge" him. The author is assertive of the move he makes in differing from the conventions and tells the readers that as he portrays the women in an unconventional way, critics might advise him to concentrate on his Muses. The author in turn claims that

> the Muses are women, and although women are not as worthy as the Muses, they do, nevertheless look like them at first glance; and so for this reason, if for no other, they please me. What's more, the fact is that women have already been the cause for my composing thousands of verses, while the Muses were in no way the cause of my writing them.
>
> *(Boccaccio 77)*

Making the Emotions Heard

The depiction of various moods and forms in *The Decameron*, including extremes like the comic and the tragic, is done in such a way that one doesn't always feel a heavy turn in emotions in the journey across the narrative. The way Boccaccio uses laughter too is very balanced, and hence it makes us feel "appeased, not excited. Although we do not laugh our faces are serene and happy; laughter is latently present, and we never feel that it is going to break out irresistibly in a contracted and convulsive way" (Sanctis 227).

Mourning and melancholia, emotions related to both "lovesickness" and the plague, become principal in understanding and relating the text to our own present. Catastrophic and traumatic phenomenon like the pandemic in the twenty-first century and its effect on a large group of people calls for the need to reflect on "collective mourning". Day four of *The Decameron* which portrays tragic events in the venture of love particularly invites us to reconsider and rethink the basic concepts like "love" on which society dwells.

Isabetta, the one who dips the head of her dead lover in a pot of basil and weeps over it to finally be self-consumed in her own tears, is like a "perennial mourner" whose mourning never ends. Where melancholia becomes associated with the "dis-ease" of love, it has an added significance in the way it is related to the context of "death" reminding us of the death in the time of plague. Guido Ruggiero talks about the two aspects of mourning:

> In the end, getting ahead or actually getting a head, as Boccaccio and his readers were well aware, required not just love and passion but, crucially, also

action and virtù in an ongoing negotiation of self with the groups that formed a person's consensus realities in the world of Rinascimento, as Lisabetta negatively demonstrated to all with her tragic death that concluded the central tale of the fourth day of tragic tales. Mourning the tragedies of life was not the answer and definitely not the answer to the devastating mortality of the plague.

(*Ruggiero 121*)

On the other side of things, Boccaccio uses laughter as a medicine to combat the sorrows of the plague. Laughter, simultaneously, is a form of liberation for women from the expected culture of coquetry. Here lies the therapeutic intent of Boccaccio in composing *The Decameron*. The tension-relieving motive of the text perhaps does not overtly let us read it as a "life changing" experience. However, it does tell us stories and experiences of varied kinds which act as a hint to the "change" that is imminent when a generation faces a crisis like the pandemic. This might not be "life changing", but it does affect us in the way we think of the pandemic and the role literature plays in such times.

The process in which meaning gets filtered is inevitably complex and infinite. The ambience of the garden, beyond the urban nomenclatures, provides a larger space for the free play of meaning. The text "makes no positive assertions of a 'higher' reality. Nor does it deny that there is a reality or realities. It simply states that the expression, sharing and understanding of experiences are meaningful and worthy of appropriation" (Tangeras 18). The conclusion of the text with the author's words itself makes this clear. The author is himself very aware of the context he builds to use words and create meaning.

The Decameron makes the reader realize and face the "crisis" through its narrative: a crisis which "constitutes a challenge, as the individual must abandon old assumptions and create new meaning" (Tangeras 13). *The Decameron*, thus, like a transtemporal memento for us, connects to the narratives of past plagues in history and gives us a way to step beyond the labyrinth of obstacles that the pandemic in the current century has brought to us.

Works Cited

Boccaccio, Giovanni. "The Author's Preface." *The Decameron*, translated and edited by Mark Musa and Peter E. Bondanella. W.W. Norton & Company, 1977, pp. 1–3.

———. "The Author's Introduction." *The Decameron*, translated and edited by Mark Musa and Peter E. Bondanella. W.W. Norton & Company, 1977, pp. 3–17.

———. "Fourth Day: Prologue." *The Decameron*, translated and edited by Mark Musa and Peter E. Bondanella. W.W. Norton & Company, 1977, pp. 73–79.

Dawson, Lesel. "Introduction: Sweet Poison." *Lovesickness and Gender in Early Modern English Literature*. Oxford UP, 2008, pp. 1–11.

Gilman, Ernest B. "Introduction." *Plague Writing in Early Modern England*. The U of Chicago P, 2009, pp. 1–27.

———. "The Plague and the World." *Plague Writing in Early Modern England*. The U of Chicago P, 2009, pp. 27–71.

Roy, Arundhati. "The Pandemic Is a Portal." *Azadi: Freedom. Fascism. Fiction.* Penguin Hamish Hamilton, 2020, pp. 203–14.

Ruggiero, Guido. "Sorrow." *Love and Sex in the Time of Plague: A Decameron Renaissance,* edited by Nicholas Terpstra. Harvard UP, 2021, pp. 88–121.

Sanctis, Francesco De. "Boccaccio and the Human Comedy." *The Decameron,* translated and edited by Mark Musa and Peter E. Bondanella. W.W. Norton & Company, 1977, pp. 216–30.

Scaglione, Aldo D. "Nature and Love in Boccaccio's Decameron." *The Decameron,* translated and edited by Mark Musa and Peter E. Bondanella. W.W. Norton & Company, 1977, pp. 230–43.

Tangeras, Thor Magnus. "Intimate Reading: A Narrative Method." *Literature and Transformation: A Narrative Study of Life-Changing Reading Experiences.* Anthem Press, 2020, pp. 17–36.

———. "Introduction." *Literature and Transformation: A Narrative Study of Life-Changing Reading Experiences.* Anthem Press, 2020, pp. 1–15.

5

MARY SHELLEY'S *THE LAST MAN*

Dystopian Fiction and Pandemics

Sarottama Majumdar

Mary Shelley knew about contagious diseases. Her daughter Clara died of dysentery and her son William of malaria at the ages of 1 and 3, respectively. Her husband Percy's drowned corpse was interred in quicklime in keeping with contemporary Italian quarantine rules where the family was residing at the time. The corpse was eventually disinterred and cremated. According to apocryphal sources, Mary Shelley snatched the heart from Edward Trelawney, a friend of Shelley's, who had snatched the organ from the burning pyre. Trelawney later confessed that he had suffered from misgivings about breaching quarantine rules while engaging in this gothic gesture. Mary, who did not subscribe to the theory of quarantine safety, apparently had no such qualms (Wheatley).

Two theories about infectious diseases gained traction in the early nineteenth century; that of "contagion" or transmission by touch or ingestion of diseased bodily fluid and "miasmatism" or infection from the inspiration of infected air ("mal aria" or bad air was a name coined for a disease supposedly spread through miasma). Mary Shelley firmly believed in the latter and felt that precautions such as distancing and quarantine were not only superfluous but potentially detrimental to civic activities and commerce. The grim irony of the debate between contagion theory supporters and miasmatists (such as Shelley) had resonances in her times. By prioritizing the need for ventilation but ignoring precautions about distancing, quarantine and hand washing, later critics have suggested that an upsurge in hospital mortality rates in England at the beginning of the nineteenth century may have been exacerbated by choice thus made (Kannadan).

This confusion about efficacy of different preventive measures in times of pandemics is but one among several connections that can be made between Mary Shelley's *The Last Man* and the medical emergency in which the world has been embroiled in recent times. On 13 March 2020, by which date the reality of SARS-COVID-19 as a pandemic and its global effect had begun to be realized, the *New*

DOI: 10.4324/9781003294436-8

York Times published an op-ed discussing the largely forgotten novel written in 1826. In that article, Eileen Botting notes the chilling similarities between the situation in the Western hemisphere as it was unfolding towards the end of the second decade of the millennium and the global apocalypse described in Mary Shelley's *The Last Man*. The similarities are not confined to the nature and characteristics of the disease as imagined by Mary Shelley with the one the world faces during the recent pandemic but more importantly, to the lacuna she envisaged in political and leadership responses to acknowledging and containing death and damage (Botting). Ultimately, however, it may be possible to argue that Shelley's novel on pandemics and human annihilation is less concerned about the cause and effect of this catastrophe and more about human response as individuals and communities to overwhelming crises.

Dystopia and *The Last Man*

The overall structure of the plot, the sense of doom in progression and apocalyptic finality in its closure aligns *The Last Man* generically to later dystopic tradition. Dystopic or apocalyptic fiction has been enjoying increasing popularity in the last few decades. Texts depicting a dysfunctional present and/or future on various media platforms: print, film, television, web, cyber games and versions in which concepts cross from one to the other have abounded in these decades and have colonized a considerable share of our collective mind space. Apocalyptic science fiction was the generic term which would, before the 1980s, have sufficed to describe works as diverse as the film *The Matrix*, the web series *Hunger Games*, the novel *The Handmaid's Tale* and the video game *The Last of Us*, all of which deal variously with a post-disaster world order slowly or speedily moving towards the extinction of human life as we know it.

Dystopic fiction is that form of futuristic fantasy that deals with a dire and endangered future where scientific or technological innovations lead to invasive threats to human survival from within and without. The dangers depicted typically result from application of artificial intelligence, extra-terrestrial invasion or environmental crises. Few among the aforementioned works deal also, with predictive biological Armageddon such as the 2018 film of the *Maze Runner* series titled "*The Death Cure*" about a pandemic named "Flare" (Stevens). Then with Margaret Atwood's acclaimed 1985 novel *The Handmaid's Tale*, there is an introduction of a tangential new discourse in the biological dystopic genre which is that of reproductive female agency as player in a medical emergency.

Mary Shelley's novel written a century and a half before modern dystopic apocalyptic fiction became popular contains unified in it, many of the aforementioned concerns. What the novel is chiefly prescient about is the betrayal of socio-political hypocrisy and mismanagement that a biological crisis of unprecedented scale unleashes on nations as also the deeply problematic nature of decisions balancing welfare, safety and economics that policy-makers are faced with. Mary Shelley, who kept abreast of medical developments and held strong views, nevertheless presented the ethical dilemma as inherently a cultural one.

The concept of "quarantine" or isolation of people and things (including trade goods) was a response to the contagion theory and one which as mentioned earlier, Mary Shelley, a miasmatist strenuously opposed. Quarantine in the nineteenth century like in the present included isolation and/or embargo on imported trade goods and therefore had substantial impact on international trade. *The Last Man* was Shelley's fictional representation of the futility of contemporary contagion theory responses like quarantine and isolation in the case of a pandemic so that the plague in the novel is as Anne McWhir notes, both a "disease and a metaphor" (26). One of the reasons for Shelley's opposition to large-scale quarantine imposition was political pragmatism. Shelley, the daughter of two radical extremists and spouse of another. was herself more of a conservative pessimist (Sterrenburg 146). The protagonist of her novel *The Last Man* Lionel Verney makes a clear case of how belief in contagion containment in a pandemic can hurt the economy.

> We feared the coming summer. Nations, bordering on the already infected countries, began to enter upon serious plans for the better keeping out of the enemy. We, a commercial people, were obliged to bring such schemes under consideration; and the question of contagion became matter of earnest disquisition.

Verney is concerned about the putative commercial losses incurred through quarantining the uselessness of which the novel demonstrates (Wills). Shelley prioritizes the overwhelming response to communicable disease for a trading nation with far-flung colonial and economic interest in a fictional composition grimly prophetic of recent developments. In the novel, England's response to the occurrence of the disease in its colonies segues empirical assumptions and commercial prudence in an ominous combination. For McWhir and Botting, Mary Shelley true to the legacy of Godwin and Wollstoncraft, imagined that such a crisis unleashed on the world would be as much civilizational as medical and this conclusion in keeping with the others before, could well be another prescient observation on the pandemic the world is suffering from at this present time; especially its reception and effect in the socio-political contemporary global scenario.

The discriminatory empiricist stance adopted by the first world protagonists of the novel and the murky standards maintained in an increasingly panic-imbued atmosphere when contagion and rumour spread globally are again prophetically explored in the novel. The initial response of Lionel Verney, his friends Adrian and Raymond, Perdita, Idris, sisters and wives of the different men in the company is one of the disbeliefs that privileged citizenship cannot withstand the disease spreading.

> Can it be true, each asked the other with wonder and dismay, that whole countries are laid waste, whole nations annihilated, by these disorders in nature? The vast cities of America, the fertile plains of *Hindostan*, the crowded abodes of the Chinese, are menaced with utter ruin. . . . The air is

empoisoned, and each human being inhales death even while in youth and health . . . As yet western Europe was uninfected; would it always be so?

O, yes, it would – Countrymen, fear not! . . . If perchance some stricken Asiatic come among us, plague dies with him, uncommunicated and innoxious. Let us weep for our brethren, though we can never experience his.

The novel moves inexorably to a climax depicting failure of preconceived notions such as those previously referred to; of racial exclusivity and superiority ensconced in the discourse of the times rebutted in entirety with the narrator Verney succumbing finally:

I spread the whole earth out as a map before me. On no one spot on its surface could I put my finger and say, here is safety.

As the unnamed plague spreads and becomes a global phenomenon, the dark underside of government inefficiency as well as hypocrisy paralyses the idealistic protagonist and his companions. In an episode which occurs in the third volume of the novel, a charismatic and popular leader in France, with a huge cultic following identified only as "the imposter" is introduced, who leads his believers to extinction from the contagious disease raging across the world first by assuring them that the disease is in fact not as serious as proclaimed everywhere and that he can save his followers from it and later by withholding and falsifying facts about danger and mortality rates. Another leader, this time in Britain, is portrayed as escaping and abandoning his fellow countrymen, and is later discovered dead in a bunker surrounded by stockpiled provisions while around him people died of sickness and starvation. In a separate instance, reverse migration is portrayed in the return of hundreds of Irish immigrants who go back to Ireland from North America and the intense suffering of the returning migrants, leading to an insurrection and revolution. Such portrayals, though tempting enough since they can be compared with contemporary instances of betrayal or failure of global leadership in the current crisis, or of the suffering of immigrants during pandemics, should not distract the reader from exploring the existentialist and civilizational dilemma at the heart of Shelley's fictionalized depiction of humanity and human continuance brought to the brink of slow disappearance through factors (in this case an unnamed plague) which cannot be overcome.

This dystopic vision of the end of times climaxes in the last chapter of the three-volume novel. As the world is decimated of all but the last man, Lionel Verney and his only living companion, a dog in the concluding tableau is depicted looking down from a height to the morning sun gilding the basilica of St. Peter in Rome as they straddle a world empty of hope. The symbolic significance in the novel *The Last Man*, of the epidemic which first surfaced in Constantinople and whose devastation would finally conclude with the death of the eponymous last man in Rome, is not lost on readers. The sense of pervasive doom and decay that the story about incurable disease and inexorable genocide evoked was considered so disturbing at the time of publication that early copies were suppressed and Mary Shelley herself had to defend her creation against charges ranging from "diseased" to accusations of witchcraft and black magic.

The novel published in England in 1826 found its way into print on the other side of the Atlantic in 1833 in a pirated version. No reprint in the United States was available until the 1960s. However, the response to *The Last Man* was not only negative but also lukewarm. The latter was caused by the fact that the early nineteenth century was witness to unprecedented natural and man-made catastrophes provoking a spate of apocalyptic fiction ranging across the scale from horrific to bathetic. The revolutionary and Napoleonic wars between the last decade of the eighteenth century and the first two of the nineteenth century and rapid global cooling due to the eruption of Mount Tambora in 1815 caused massive environmental disruption and human loss. In 1811, palaeontologists excavated and identified fossils of dinosaurs for the first time and the intellectual possibility that a ubiquitous and powerful species can become extinct began to be processed within academia (Eylott). Around these phenomena and imaginative possibilities, fiction which could collectively be termed "apocalyptic" began to be produced in great numbers. *The Last Man* when first published was received by a sated and disillusioned reading public who had begun to consider prophetic depiction of cataclysm or human extinction in fiction a clichéd idea. Shelley's portrayal of stark desolation shot through with existential quest was thus published in a "hostile critical atmosphere"(Murphy).

1815 was called the "year without summer". The eruption of Mount Tambora in Indonesia caused a dust cloud in Europe blocking the sun, causing constant rain, plummeting temperatures, harvest failure and famine. Starving crowds moved from city to city and many died by the roadside. Though the suffering was not primarily caused by disease, terrible sights must have been witnessed by the Shelley coterie in their northern Italian refuge (Switzerland bordering on this region suffered from the worst food shortages and riots). An estimated two hundred thousand people died in Europe because of the environmental catastrophe. Mary Shelley returned again and again to the depiction of ragged desperate humanoid creature/s lurching on the street: in *Frankenstein* and in *The Last Man*. These scenes remain for the author objective co-relatives of hopelessness and human achievement in one complex whole (Starr).

Apocalypse and Existentialism

As evidence of the civilizational project, in the chaotic concluding scenes there surface, amidst the squalor and panic in the diminishing group of doomed survivors an obstinate desire to continue searching for aesthetic as well sensual fulfilment, a romantic reworking of the often invoked medieval epidemic image: "the masque of death". They live in hedonistic hope that the carnage will clear the stage for the rise of an idealistic, equitable, cultured society, a civilizational rebirth. Verney, the last survivor of the doomed company of dreamers, thus inscribes this vision in his narrative, already shattered but one whose validity through the very act of the surviving inscription cannot be denied. Betty T. Bennett finds in the deliberate biographical incursion in a narrative serving as cultural blueprint, an instance of attempted "romantic dislocation". The complex provenance riddle at commencement when a narrative apparently retrieved by the author from the cave of the Cumean Sybil purportedly penned by one of Apollo's priestesses and projected as self-fulfilling prophecy for the year 2073, an example of fiction as "romantic dislocation" since the prophecy immediately problematizes the identity and location of the first person narrator (Bennett). A deliberate dislocation of authority and obfuscation of narrative frame is thus created.

Mary Shelley's work therefore must be assessed as a positive and humane document in spite of the brooding morbidity of its central thesis. This statement, startling as it may sound, is rooted in the invocation of the writer's Romantic vision coupled with her deep investment in the ethical mores governing human development, scientific advancement and political commitment to universal welfare. This vision of a deeply problematic society spiralling hopelessly into ruin with the symbolic disease acting as a catalyst must be offset by her final epiphanic image of the individual human survivor. Lionel, the protagonist and the last man, is acutely aware of his own imminent death and with it, the conclusion of human existence. As a symbol, however, he represents the human individual who confronts mortality and transcends fears of biological extinction choosing to regale his vision instead with evidences of human achievement and manifestations of immortality of the spirit rather than that of flesh. In that one symbolic gesture of defiance against fear of mortality and concern for mere biological survival as opposed to glorying in the deathless spirit of human endeavour, Shelley's Lionel becomes the medieval "Everyman" and Leonardo da Vinci's "Renaissance Man" whose individual genius is humanity's greatest triumph and its strongest defense against annihilation.

Of the many apocalyptic works written in the 1820s, at least two others are named *The Last Man*. For Thomas Campbell in his poem *The Last Man* (1823),[1] the sole surviving human against certain extinction reaffirms the traditional Christian belief that a "darkening Universe" cannot or should not:

> quench his Immortality
> Or shake his trust in God.

Set against this conventional Anglican dogmatic position is a dark parody like Thomas Hood's *The Last Man* (1826), which adopts grim humour as means to similar ends. This eponymous poem makes a point about survival in a situation reminiscent of the biblical "end of days". Hood's last man is an executioner who regrets the loss of his profession and of companionship after he has executed the only other survivor in the world:

> For there is not another man alive,
> In the world, to pull my legs!

These (dissimilar) mood pieces are texts which, however, tangentially reflect Shelley's concern: that holding fast to existential and communal certainties even in the face of extinction is our only guarantee against absolute annihilation of human identity, history, achievement and aspiration. Shelley's novel is different by every conceivable standard from the two similarly named works by her contemporaries. *The Last Man* is generally considered a roman à clef. Lionel Verne is modelled on Mary herself. He is portrayed as a former radical thinker reformed to moderation by the influence of Adrian, an aristocrat, scholar and idealist modelled on her husband Percy Shelley, while their friend Raymond the Lord Protector and leader of the Greeks is Byron thinly disguised. In a letter addressed to Teresa Guiccioli in 1827, Shelley admitted that inducting these deliberate biographical studies were literary strategies, however, adding "but this is a secret" (Bennett). These characters, their sisters, wives, lovers and children, Lionel, Raymond, Adrian, the women Perdita, Idris and Evadne are intricately related by webs of romantic interest and easily recognizable fictional representations of the Shelley-Byron family circle in Italy in the decades before publication. By the time the novel was written, the only survivor of that brilliant company was Mary. It is easy to see her despair transmuted to the depiction of a desolate decimated world. In the concluding chapter, the protagonist surviving a final shipwreck which drowns the last of the bedraggled survivors realizes he is the last man. This last scene of the three-volume novel is a set piece that is a textbook summation of gothic romantic tragedy – Lionel Verney swims ashore in a desolate world depleted of all human beings. He vows to roam the earth alone except for his canine companion and write the journal of the last days before human dissolution: the text which becomes the novel. Shelley's advocacy of the "intrusion of the self in a work of art" argues for a belief that works mined from "self analysation and display" are likely to appeal to men of imagination and sensibility, as opposed to those who bring to their literary appreciation, neither faculty (Shelley, "Giovanni Villani" 283). Shelley's dismissal of such readers is final, "their criticism stand for nothing" (Shelley, "Modern Italy" 131). But for those with the required characteristics the text in the author's own estimation offers up instead of nihilistic despair, a life-confirming confidence in continuation of human endeavour beyond the exigency of death.

Fear and Contagion

Pandemic discourse is riddled with ironies of the kind that dystopic fiction routinely explores. Pandemics cause fear which is as contagious as the diseases. Fear feeds on unpredictability, death and breakdown of everyday certainties and regurgitates these symptoms exponentially increased. Commercial transactions triggered by panic, it has been demonstrated in both present and past instances, substantially affect the economy which reacts unfavourably resulting in further quotidian hardship, uncertainty and mistrust. John Green forwards a historical instance, "the cholera riots that broke out in Liverpool in 1832 were caused not so much by fear of the disease as by a breakdown in the public's trust in the medical profession". However, the literature which explores pandemics and those which take the pandemic as a metaphor for universal breakdown of certainties and systems must be considered separately. From ancient to modern; Boccaccio, Defoe, Mather, Franklin and Carey all wrote about pandemics but with detachment and objectivity eschewing the gothic for deliberate pedestrianism presenting documentary evidence of a phenomenon within a space–time framework. It is otherwise with writers such as Brockden Brown, Edward Allen Poe and H.G. Wells. For these writers, the disease is a literary metaphor or fictional strategy. This makes the corralling of all fictional instances using the biological apocalypse framework into the dystopic generic fold problematic.

Mary Shelley's novel is planned as a record of the long, inexorable passage to human annihilation but the characters are not portrayed as reacting to the panic that waiting for such an apocalyptic end must entail. There is a sense of suppressed excitement aimed rather at celebrating human achievement until the end than at succumbing to despair at its conclusion. Moreover, Shelley had conjured a narrative about a pandemic which is peculiarly and particularly a human experience. As humans perish horribly, nature returns to pre-lapsarian plenitude. The glory of the world free from human intervention, returning to a state of ancient wilderness and the splendour of natural phenomena in a world devoid of all eyes but that of the last man is a triumphant Romantic trope rather than a cautionary one. This seems yet another example of the prescience of a novel predicting depopulation through disease at the cusp of environmental disaster demonstrating how the reverse would logically be equally possible. Again and inevitably the present global concern about impending environmental doom gaining prominence concomitant with a human medical emergency parallels a similar point made with subtle persistence in the text. The survival of humanity seems to preclude the continuation of natural balance and the reversal restores it in Shelley's dystopian novel. In contrast, Byron's vision, in his 1816 apocalyptic poem *Darkness*, of the end as "*Seasonless, herbless, treeless, manless, lifeless*" is the more conventional one of wholesale destruction and therefore less evocative of comparative juxtaposition. It is possible that for Mary Shelley the novelist, exploring with labyrinthine complexity the interplay between scientific discovery, societal corruption, human genius and annihilation, the fault lines dividing dystopic caution and the conundrum of civilizational progress, grew progressively obscure.

Note

1   All quotations from Mary W Shelley's novel *The Last Man* in this paper are from the first edition of the work published by Henry Colburn from London in 1826 and digitized by *Project Gutenberg* (24 Apr. 2006).

Works Cited

Bennett, Betty T. "Radical Imaginings: Mary Shelley's 'The Last Man'." *The Wordsworth Circle*, vol. 26, no. 3, Summer 1995, U of Chicago P. doi:10.1086/TWC24044553.

Botting, Eileen. *Mary Shelley Created 'Frankenstein' and Then a Pandemic.* www.nytimes. com/2020/03/13/opinion/mary-shelley-sc-fi-pandemic-novel.html.

Eylott, Marie-Claire. "Mary Anning: The Unsung Hero of Fossil Discovery." *Natural History Museum.* www.nhm.ac.uk.

Green, Jim. *Pandemic Panic: Mary Shelley's "The Last Man".* www.librarycompany. org/2020/05/26/pandemic-panic-mary-shelleys-the-last-man/.

Kannadan, Ajesh. "History of the Miasma Theory of Disease." *Essai*, vol. 16, 2018, Article 18. https://dc.cod.edu/essai/vol16/iss1/18.

McWhir, Anne. "Mary Shelley's Anti-Contagionism: 'The Last Man as' 'Fatal Narrative'." *Mosaic: An Interdisciplinary Critical Journal*, vol. 35, no. 2, 2002, pp. 23–38. U of Manitoba P. www.jstor.org/stable/44029980.

Murphy, Olivia. *The Last Man by Mary Shelley Is a Prophecy of Life in a Global Pandemic.* www.sydney.edu.au/news-opinion/news/2020/05/05/mary-shelley-s-the-last-man-is-a-prophecy-of-life-in-a-global-pa.html.

Shelley, Mary W. "Giovanni Villani." *The Liberal*, no. 4, 1823, pp. 281–97.

———. "Modern Italy." *Westminster Review*, vol. 2, 1829, pp. 127–40.

Starr, Michelle. *A Devastating Geologic Event in Indonesia May Have Helped Defeat Napoleon*, 24 Aug. 2018. www.sciencealert.com.

Sterrenburg, Lee. "Mary Shelley's Monster: Politics and Psyche in *Frankenstein.*" *The Endurance of "Frankenstein": Essays on Mary Shelley's Novel*, edited by George Levine and U.C. Knoepflmacher. U of California P, 1979, pp. 143–71.

Stevens, David. *Understanding Dystopian Fiction in the Age of Political Correctness*, 5. Dec. 2017. www.grimdarkmagazine.com/understanding-dystopian-fiction-in-the-age-of-political-correctness/.

Wheatley, Kim. "'Attracted by the Body': Accounts of Shelley's Cremation." *Keats-Shelley Journal*, vol. 49, 2000, pp. 162–82. Keats-Shelley Association of America, Inc. www.jstor. org/stable/30213051.

Wills, Matthew. *Disease Theory in Mary Shelley's 'The Last Man'*, 3 Apr. 2020. https://daily. jstor.org/category/arts/.

6

EPIDEMIC ANXIETY AND NARRATIVE AESTHETICS IN SARAT CHANDRA'S *PALLI SAMAJ* AND *PANDIT MASHAY*

Subham Dutta

Sarat Chandra's novels emerge from a shifting cultural trajectory intimately linked to the issues of transition, anxiety and existential dilemma, precipitated by a host of social, cultural and ecological problems – the virulence of epidemic being one of them. In the two novels that this chapter studies, *Palli Samaj* and *Pandit Mashay*, malaria and cholera emerge as important cultural vectors. Although tangentially, epidemic diseases remain embedded in these narratives as important co-texts. A triad built around the spatial milieu the novels are set in, the socio-cultural and political ramifications of the diseases, and the structure of the narrative informs their artistic chronotopes. The way in which the co-relation between modernity and predominant cultural and social hierarchies influences this triad is an area of inquiry. By delving deeper into the representation of epidemic in Sarat Chandra, this chapter traces how the representation of epidemic offers certain insights into Sarat Chandra's attitude to the epidemic in general. My objective in this chapter is twofold. First, it seeks to analyse how the representation of the epidemic in Sarat Chandra is socially and historically informed. Second, it seeks to demonstrate the relationship between epidemic and narrative spatiality in relation to these two novels.

Sarat Chandra's fiction deals with spatiality in a discursive manner with the invocation of a social *topos* linked with tradition, transition and the conflict borne out of their intersection. The discursivity of Sarat's representational politics can be seen in three ways, as argued by Dhussa and Dutt: first, it alerts to the cultural geography of a particular region; second, it seeks to reconstruct the geography of a specific space; third, the psychological insights that Sarat Chandra shares into the minds of the characters and thereby make them an integral part of the sentimental context of the "entire" region (52). He brings together the multiple aspects of social life, in which the geography of space depicts the myriad aspects of local psychology. The socio-cultural milieu of the village frames Chatterjee's narratives. For

DOI: 10.4324/9781003294436-9

Chatterjee, the village acts as a site of "social protest" (Dhussa and Dutt 43), as well as rural reconstruction. The milieu of Sarat Chandra remains deeply connected to the invocation of an ambivalent spatial site which is produced by the ecological and social transformations brought about by epidemics. This chapter deals with the historical and representational aspects of epidemics. At the historical level, this chapter charts how the rise of epidemics in colonial Bengal coincides with an overwhelming cultural and sociological anxiety. At the representational level, this chapter argues how the epidemic-ridden narratives depict the cultural and sociological anxieties, provoked by epidemics, following a self-conscious aesthetic pattern. To delve into the psycho-social aspects of spatiality, this chapter uses Henri Lefebvre's idea of the *Social Production of Space* (1991) as a critical tool of inquiry.

Epidemics in Bengal: The Intersection Between Tradition and Modernity

In *Colonizing the Body: State Medicine and Epidemic Disease in Nineteenth-century India*, David Arnold notes how the rise of epidemics in nineteenth-century Bengal develops a tradition-modernity dialectic. There is a form of subversion along with an urge for mapping the shaping of the discursive layers of epidemics in Bengal, generating an air of uncertainty, ambivalence, death and desolation. Sarat Chandra's *Pandit Mashay* and *Palli Samaj*, remaining embedded in a rural chronotope, tellingly depict how the virulence of epidemic precipitates a series of changes – social, cultural and ideological. The ways in which these texts engage with the questions of modernity and social transformation wrought by the epidemics illustrate the formation of a new *samaj* where an ethical idealism coheres with a lurking cultural anxiety about a society going astray.

The cultural influence of epidemics is a wide-ranging one. In Bengal, cholera epidemic has an uncomfortably fraught history. Not only did it provoke uncertainties, fears and suspicions about the position of the human body but it also contributed widely to the dissemination of rumours, apparently putting to rest the truth claims of the epidemiological discourses. A recent critical intervention, *The Anthropology of Epidemics* brings to light the anthropological inquiries pertaining to epidemics and how they inform cultural and sociological discourses. As they argue "epidemics represent the impossibility of securing the body-politic" (1). In the introduction of their book, they show how epidemics largely re-alter social relations and generate new subjectivities, engendering moral and spiritual crises that can turn upside down the collective modes of existence. They also focus on how outbreaks cause social exclusion, blame and panic (3). Historians like David Arnold and Arabinda Samanta demonstrate how the nineteenth-century cholera epidemics in Bengal were disruptive of the social order in many ways. It is also noticeable from the colonial reports how ambiguity prevailed over the transmission of Cholera in Bengal. Sumit Sarkar's *Modern Times* offers a curious case study of Bengal where the exponential rise of epidemic diseases makes the colonial state more focused and energetic about public health, bolstering the role of an interventionist state (58).

Arnold's study on cholera and colonialism in India, quite in line with this duality, states that the "initial attitudes to cholera were necessarily affected by the wide social, religious and political gulf between Indians and the British" (119). Arnold further postulates that cholera's impact was compounded by famine in the rural areas. Arnold's study is particularly significant because it alerts us to the forms of ritualization that sprang in the immediate aftermath of the epidemics. He refers to the rise of goddesses Sitala and Maryamma as forms of ritualization against the disease-ridden village lives in India. Cholera, as Arnold shows, did not have that ritualization mainly because "as it appears not to have been as widespread and as destructive as it became after 1857 (130)".

The way epidemics in Bengal created a cultural cross-pollination has been explored by the historian Arabinda Samanta in his recent work. Samanta's work, going beyond the colonial–national binary, seeks to foreground how the cholera epidemics in Bengal compellingly provoked an epistemic entanglement between the colonial and the national forms of knowledge. This epistemic entanglement created interstitial spaces paving the way for a cultural contact zone despite contagion. Samanta also shows the disruptive impact of the epidemics in Bengal. It generated an atmosphere of uncertainty, fear, street fight, panic, rumour and suspicion (Samanta 129–30). Samanta's work is important because it also dwells on the narrativization of epidemics in Bengal. The process of narrativization was invariably marked by factors like social and cultural decay, the rupture in the social order, and an intrinsic quest for social and cultural cohesion. Samanta refers to the novels of Sarat Chandra, as emblematic of this tension:

> the novels of Sarat Chandra Chattopadhyay fit the bill the best. Sarat Chandra provides us with an altogether different archive of knowledge, not just on cholera, but on the process of how a society functions when a pestilence strikes terror among its inhabitants.
>
> *(70)*

Spatiality and the Location

Sarat Chandra's fictional world focuses on a particular social and cultural geography of location constantly haunted by the spectres of the past and the vectors of the present. The village space emerges here as a site of contestation and negotiation, in which different times and different spaces criss-cross each other. Drawing on Lefebvre's ideas on the "Production of Space", this chapter unravels the role of epidemics in altering the social and cultural trajectories of space. In his *The Production of Space* (1991), Henri Lefebvre dwells on the idea of a spatial triad which challenges and subverts the idea of spatial duality:

> Social space can never escape its basic duality, even though triadic determining factors may sometimes override and incorporate its binary or dual nature,

for the way in which it presents itself and the way in which it is represented are different.

(191)

Linking space with human perceptions and responses, Lefebvre conceptualizes an alternative site of triadic spatiality where the "the perceived space", "the conceived space" and the "lived space" entangle. Lefebvre argues that spatiality is coextensive and a generative process, and its production remains implicated in the socio-cultural and political relations of society. He suggests that there should be a harmony between the domains of "perceived", "conceived" and "lived space" so that the individual can operate without "confusion" (40). In Lefebvre's framework, the individual perception remains intimately tied to the construction of "space". In Sarat Chandra's fiction, the apparently harmonic relationship between these three domains of spatiality is altered. Epidemics rupture this relationship and generate new social spaces of assimilation and difference. Importantly, this spatial problematic constitutes an alternative idiom of social realism of the village in Sarat Chandra. His narratives are interjected by the tropes of indeterminacy, contingency and tension. What runs parallel to this is the vision of not only an alternative social order but also an alternative self-reflexive narrative pattern that lends order to these diffuse, dispersed narratives of the chaotic worlds. The ways in which these crises relating to aesthetic representation are engendered by the epidemic anthropology remain subject to critical scrutiny.

The representation of rural space in South Asian literature has largely been subject to discursive scrutiny. Among the recent scholars, Anupama Mohan and Sourit Bhattacharya argue that some of the twentieth-century representations of the village through literature adumbrate the presence of Gandhi and his search for a rural utopia. Comparing the Gandhian model of rural reconstruction and collectivity with Leonard Woolf, Mohan argues: "Read together, both Gandhi and Woolf were significant in centering attention on the village as strategic to any representation of South Asian collectivity" (59). However, Mohan's argument fails to lay out the distinctive character of rural regionalism that remains significant to the narration of a space. British thinker Keith Snell lays out the characteristics of "regional novels", laying out how they are marked by a strong sense of "local geography, topography or landscape" (1). Apart from this, "a detailed description of a place, setting or region whether urban or rural, which bears approximation to the real space" (1) informs the regional aesthetic of a novel. He argues that regional novels, usually, abound with characters from the working middle class. Their relentless strivings for achievements and social transformations shape the narratives with an attempted hold over social realism.

Sourit Bhattacharya, in a recent article on "Regional Ecologies and Peripheral Aesthetics", argues how the rise of Mahatma Gandhi remains inextricably attached to the rise of the "regional novel" in India. Gandhi's departure from the colonial idea of "progress" aligns with a representational discourse that emphasized the notions of collectivity, cohesion and harmony (3). However, as Bhattacharya argues following Keith Snell and Dominic Head's argument, the rise of the regional novel opens up a beleaguered site of articulation in which the traditional–modern, rural–urban divides are questioned and redefined:

> The regional novel is marked by a conflict between cultural traditions and capitalist modernity, which, to read tangentially, is also a conflict between one socio-cultural order that has encouraged for centuries, albeit complexly, veneration of nature, trees, plants, nonhuman animals, lands, and natural resources and has evolved worldviews and religions out of them, and the other that sees these relations as historically and culturally "backward", an obstacle to economic progress.
>
> *(4)*

From Bhattacharya's argument, it is evident that the rise of regionalism coincides with a crisis between tradition and modernity.

Taking a cue from Bhattacharya's argument, I will show how Sarat Chandra's novels embody and perform a regionalist ideological character with its own set of conditions, sensibilities and structures of feeling. What also seems to be noticeable here is the distinct characteristic of the epidemic cultural context that impacts the sociology of rural life in Bengal. Epidemics, in general, bring to the fore a crisis in terms of aesthetic representation with the invocation of certain tropes like narrative tension and uncertainty. However, the ways in which epidemics lend a distinctive character to the worldview of Sarat Chandra and emerge instrumental to the nuanced depiction of the emotions and uncertainties of the rural life is an area worth looking at.

Palli Samaj and Malaria

Written in 1916, the novel, *Palli Samaj*, demonstrates how the problems of malaria bring about a series of institutional and cultural changes. Whereas the presence of malaria brings in an array of cultural problems, uncertainties and social anxieties, there are also some potent signs where the principal characters of the novel take up the gauntlet to serve a social mission. From Sarat Chandra's account, it is perceptible how the arrival of malaria in Bengal coincides with the end of the monsoon and the subsequent onset of the *Durga Puja*. This combined effect of festivity and death generates an air of atmospheric uncertainty in the Palli village of Bengal. The ineluctable presence of this epidemic has been studied by different researchers in medical humanities. They show how the representation of epidemic diseases creates an epistemic assemblage between the "traditional" and the "modern" form of knowledge, where the author figures emerge as mediators.

In his thesis, *Malarial Subjects Empire, Medicine and Nonhumans in British India, 1820–1909*, Rohan Deb Roy demonstrates how the presence of malaria opens up a site where imperial insights about malaria are "reshaped and consolidated" (288).

Deb Roy shows how the authors as "liminal go-between" (289) produced knowledge about malaria in colonial Bengal. The intrusion of malaria into the social and moral fabric of the society evoked a sense of loss, disintegration, powerlessness and hopelessness. The use of quinine countervailed its disruptive presence. Quinine was considered to be an infallible remedy for malaria. Alongside this, malaria provoked anxieties and uncertainties regarding local knowledge. Transmission of the disease coincides with the spread of rumours, stories and unauthorized beliefs. This is how malaria begets an unverifiable sense of orality. The intermediation of Western medicine and the rural knowledge about the disease paved the way for cultural contact. The rigid social structures of village life came into contact with a liberal aspirational openness. Sarat Chandra's *Palli Samaj* is marked by the co-existence of a society torn apart by Malaria and a desire for social reconstruction. *Palli Samaj*, by Sarat Chandra, compellingly depicts this problem.

The major institutional vectors that dominate Sarat Chandra's narrative are caste and gender. In *Palli Samaj*, malaria is hailed as *Rakshashi* (a female demon). This gendering of malaria appears strikingly political in relation to the other female characters of the novel. The novel begins in a somber atmosphere. Father Tarini Ghoshal's death becomes the cause of the protagonist Ramesh's homecoming. The insider–outsider dialectic, integral to the village life, is curiously placed within the narrative. The casteist segregation of space becomes apparent when Beni Ghoshal hesitates to bring Rama to their households as she is a "Kulin Brahmin". *Palli Samaj* remains steeped in these caste-based discriminations. The spaces of discrimination are augmented further when Ramesh arrives in this Palli (village). Ramesh's liberal attitude, his disregard for the rigid caste hierarchies, becomes the cause of his trouble and harassment. However, Ramesh remains committed to his mission and goal of social reformation.

Being both an outsider and insider of *Palli Samaj*, Ramesh occupies a liminal space in the narrative. Although Palli Samaj is Ramesh's ancestral household, he perpetually remains an outsider to this space. Ideologically, he remains an usher of liberal humanist modernity in the village. During the scare of malaria around the village, he thinks about making people aware of the causes of malaria. Ramesh's scientific attitude towards the cure of malaria is further reflected through his ingestion of quinine. His awareness of the presence of wood and wetland as the probable cause of malaria propels him into a mission to safeguard the entire village from the scourge of this disease. However, Ramesh's attitude at social and moral restructuring of the village life receives a jolt. He falls prey to the village machinations. However, the inescapable tangle of an altered social relationship does not dent Ramesh's confidence in carrying out a mission.

The *rakshasi* emerges as a potential threat to the ordered stability of the village life. The rigid "structure of feeling" that the village life inhabits seems to be further consolidated by the danger of malaria. The liberalism of Ramesh seems to go against this structure of feeling. Its incursion not only begets an asymmetry in the ongoing socio-cultural relations but unravels how the perennial problems of illiteracy, casteism and religious discrimination generate a greater existential chaos Ramesh wants his village to be removed from. While Ramesh perpetually gropes in the want of life, Bisheshwari and Rama propel him with an impetus that drives him forward.

Palli Samaj weaves a strange dichotomy of gender and caste. While society remains immersed in caste discriminations and upbraids malaria as *rakshashi*, there are some strong female characters like Bisheshwari and Rama. The way the novel frames a trialectical relationship between Ramesh, Rama and Bisheshwari is notable. The narrator recurrently hints at Ramesh's severance with the village life and politics. Ramesh's dilemma about village life is further compounded by his lack of belonging to the social and cultural conditions of the village. However, the role that Bisheshwari plays is a symbolic one. As if she appears as the substitute "mother-figure" in the novel, she acts as a catalytic force by re-knitting Ramesh's socio-cultural ties with the land that he had left behind. Malaria thereby provokes the necessity of a new world order based on individual action and liberty, exposing the underlying cracks and fault lines of rural society.

With the arrival of Ramesh, the village finds itself faced with the uncomfortable traits of modernity. Bisheshwari's constant presence throughout the narrative hints at an assemblage between tradition and modernity. Malaria's presence simultaneously impedes and facilitates the fusion between this tradition and modernity. It generates deep existential anxiety about the village and its dominant structures of faith and belief at one level. It also engenders the requirement of a mutually binding social order where the individual can carry out the mission of social transformation. Rama and Bisheshwari stand squarely against the demonic presence of the epidemics – "*rakshashi*". Jethima represents an idealized world order with unwavering faith and commitment to ethical action. On the other hand, Rama and Ramesh embody a new world of certitude and faith.

Sarat adopts a social realist narrative mode in *Palli Samaj*. Epidemics not only beget cultural and social uncertainty but also generate uncertainty within the narrative. The sudden arrival of Ramesh, his protest against feudal exploitation, makes inroads into the apparently stable order of the village life. The narrative also registers these changes. The simultaneous arrival of malaria and Ramesh puts the social organizations of the village life into chaotic disarray. Therefore, a sense of brooding uncertainty prevails throughout the novel. The sense of uncertainty is further reinforced by a latent sense of orality and silence. The presence of orality outside the cognizable narrative realism alerts one to the presence of forces that remain specific to the spatial region of the village. The problems of rural life that Sarat Chandra depicts are augmented by the problems of casteist discrimination. Disturbing images of caste-based discrimination haunt the narrative, generating an unresolvable cultural and narrative crisis. Apart from that, *Palli Samaj* also alerts one to an alternative social desire for an idealized world order epitomized by Rama and Ramesh.

Representation of Cholera and Narrative Crisis in *Pandit Mashay*

The presence of epidemics in *Pandit Mashay* is even more telling, poignant and macabre. It centres around the questions of social and moral disintegration owing to the eruption of cholera epidemics. In *Pandit Mashay* too, there is no exception. The rural sentimentalism is juxtaposed against the violent eruption of cholera in the village. Brindaban, the protagonist of the novel, takes up the mission to grapple with the social rigidities of casteism and illiteracy but fails to be of any avail due to the lack of awareness and social and cultural rigidities of rural life.

References to cholera abound in the narrative of *Pandit Mashay* (1914). While *Palli Samaj* is a novel about Ramesh's homecoming and a rediscovery of the lost cultural and social relations, *Pandit Mashay* demonstrates the presence of Brindaban who runs a free school for the illiterate children of the village. The urge for social reconstruction that Ramesh embodies is reflected here as well. However, Ramesh's urge for social reconstruction suddenly comes to a halt with the onset of epidemics in the village. Arabinda Samanta's account alerts us to the virulence of cholera in *Pandit Mashay*:

> Cholera, better known in Bengal as Bisuchika, figures in *Pandit Mashay* (1914) with such a force that it becomes a character itself, pulling events in and out, and finally forcing the novel's inevitable end. Almost all the characters in the novel come into focus when cholera breaks out in the village in an epidemic form, killing people young and old within a very short span of time. Villages in Bengal, often portrayed in literature as idyllic, eking out a sheltered life in complete isolation, free from greed and devilry, are represented by Sarat Chandra in a different hue. Cholera sharpened caste animosities, raked up inter-personal rivalry, and broke down traditional social relations beyond repair.
>
> *(70)*

A novel reconstruction *Pandit Mashay* narrativizes the journey of an epidemic disease into the village and how it makes inroads into the social and moral substructures that govern the rural society.

Cholera epidemics break out due to the contamination of water. The entire village community goes astray because of the unavailability of drinking water. Like Ramesh of *Palli Samaj*, Brindaban as a responsible citizen of the village community carries out the social responsibilities of making people aware of the consequences of epidemics. The dialogues between English-educated, city-bred Keshab and rustic Brindaban are one of the core areas of the novel, spelling out the key debate of the novel that centres around English education, the vantage point of an outsider and a sense of cultural rootedness. The narrative brings to the foreground how the cultivated nature of Keshav's perception of rural development turns out to be grossly inadequate against the culturally rooted perception of Brindaban.

Brindaban's relationship with the rural setting remains based on a sense of kinship and camaraderie. Unlike Ramesh, Brindaban remains an insider in village life. His anxiety about the disintegration of the rural social fabric due to the presence of cholera stems from an insider's perspective. Ramesh in *Palli Samaj* emerges as a liminal figure of modernity and his return to the *Palli Samaj* seems to be an umbilical return in search of a home that is lost forever. Brindaban, being an insider to the dreadful reality of the village, perceives how the space he remains immersed in gets suddenly stripped of its natural habitation. In his thesis on the daktari traditions, Projit Bihari Mukherji argues how the doctors emerge as liminal figures of modernity in colonial Bengal. Mukherji shows how these doctor figures, despite the heterogeneity of their social identities and space, were given an axiomatic social space and bound within a set-up. He records how these *daktars* demonstrate "clear evidence of sympathy" (22) for their fellow countrymen. As Mukherji argues:

> The affective community would have been constituted through the participation of the daktars in spheres of shared 'beliefs, [and] of marriage and a sense of inhabiting the same moral realm'. It is at the level of this emotional identification that we must turn to locate the difference between *daktari* medicine and that practiced by their European colleagues.
>
> *(23)*

Mukherji's study does not take into account the problems and contradictions inherent like this "affective community". The representation of Gopal Daktar in *Pandit Mashay* goes against the conventional ideas of *Seva* (service) and sympathy. On the contrary, Gopal Daktar's position in the novel remains entrenched in the hierarchical circle of power, determined by casteist discrimination.

Since Brindaban had protested against Tarini Mukhujje's indulgence in washing clothes in the pond and thereby contaminating it, Gopal doctor refused to treat the cholera-afflicted son of Brindaban. Brindaban's pleading to him is rebuffed:

> Didn't you know that Tarini Mukhujje is the maternal uncle of this *daktarbabu*? Being a chotolok man from the lower caste, how did you dare to insult a Brahmin just because of money? Didn't you think then that you would have to bow down to this *daktarbabu*?"
>
> *(Translations mine 111)*

Despite Brindaban's recurrent insistence, Gopal harshly retorts:

> My maternal uncle has committed a grave sin! Do you think that I, being a doctor, do not know that you have come to lecture learning some English from Durgadas? Do you really think washing off some clothes in such a large pond contaminates the water! Am I a little boy? It is nothing but your pride in money! This is what happens when a *chotolok* (man from the lower class) becomes rich. Otherwise, how did you dare to close the bank of a Brahmin? Such audacity! Such pride! Go. I will not tread the path of your house.
>
> *(Translations mine 112)*

Gopal's attitude bespeaks the thriving casteist and classist discriminations that inform the core of this village life. Epidemics not only precipitate a social urgency of transformation but also point towards the invisible hierarchies that ravage the country life from within. Sarat Chandra's *Pandit Mashay* brings these hierarchies into sharper focus through a dystopic projection of the village life. The figure of the *daktar*, apart from his liminality between native tradition and Western modernity, gets also crisscrossed by these apparently latent, but often blatant hierarchies of exclusion and discrimination.

Epidemics and Sarat Chandra

Sarat Chandra's compelling depiction of the village life seems to resonate with Ranajit Guha's idea of "History" and "Historicality". In his *History at the Limits of World History*, while reading Tagore, Guha argues how a different sense of *historicality* informs Tagore's works, going beyond the bounds of "historiography" and thereby invoking the "politics" of a radical "possibility" (79). Guha shows how this sense of historicality emanates from the day-to-day struggle for existence and embodies the rhythms of everyday joys and sorrows. *Palli Samaj* and *Pandit Mashay*, too, narrate that sense of everydayness where different times and spaces come together. They remain associated with fluid performativity that remains relevant to the performance of life marked by epidemics in these two novels.

Epidemic works in two ways in Sarat Chandra's fiction: first, it induces the fear and apprehensions of a collapsing social order, and second, it provokes the cultural awareness about the development of a new social order through the efforts of idealized characters. *Palli Samaj* and *Pandit Mashy* articulate this duality of decay and emergence, offering the vignettes of an entangled site ruptured and redefined by the local hierarchies within a changing historical and cultural context. Epidemic acts as a mediator in enacting this duality, subverting the homogeneity of space–time, the village utopia presupposes. It remains quite strongly attached to Sarat's social realism. It not only ruptures and creates an asymmetry within the social and cultural relations but also causes a void in the narrative aesthetic.

From the historical accounts, it can be deduced that the time Sarat Chandra grew up in was a time that was volatile in many ways due to an enduring and persistent resurgence of epidemics. His magnum opus, *Srikanta*, too includes references to plague. It is interesting to look at how the presence of outbreaks coincides with multiple ruptures in the novels. In *Palli Samaj*, Ramesh's advent to the rural life as an outsider exposes him to the underlying problems of village life. The issues are social, cultural and ecological. As a modern man, he displays exemplary vigour through his attempt at social reconstruction with an awareness of the difficulties of village life. However, Ramesh's "lived" space emerges strikingly discordant with the "conceived" space that was part of his cultural imaginary of the village life.

Conclusion

The presence of epidemics, thus, implicates a rupture leading the social ties to an irreconcilable end. With a scathing outlook towards social ills, Sarat Chandra depicts how epidemics unveil the problems underlying the social structure of village life. Furthermore, *Pandit Mashay* narrativizes this distinction between an optimism of social reconstruction and the disruptive social reality fraught with casteist hierarchies. Malaria and cholera, in these novels, wreak havoc on human will and aspirations, quite like "fate" in Greek tragedies. The ruptures that these novels embody are demonstrated at the ideological, social and individual levels. The urge for social transformations that these narratives depict, evoking a quaint sense of regionalism, nonetheless, embody a narrative journey between two worldviews. While one remains embedded in the orthodox casteist and social hierarchies, the other – represented by Rama, Ramesh and Brindaban – embodies the promise of a liberal utopia, outside the age-old time-warp and its attendant hierarchies. The discursivity of this journey is enacted by the overwhelming presence of epidemics with a strong focus on human life and its regionalist attributes.

Works Cited

Arnold, David. *Colonizing the Body: State Medicine and Epidemic Disease in Nineteenth-Century India*. U of California P, 2002.

Bhattacharya, Sourit. "Regional Ecologies and Peripheral Aesthetics in Indian Literature: Tarashankar Bandyopadhyay's Hansuli Banker Upakatha." *South Asian Review*, vol. 42, no. 4, 2021, pp. 387–402. doi:10.1080/02759527.2021.1905482.

Chatterjee, Sarat Chandra. *Pandit Mashay*. Gurudas Chattapadhyay and Sons, 1911.

———. *Palli Samaj*. Sri Pradip Kumar Sarkar, 1960.

Dutt, A.K., and R. Dhussa. "Novelist Sarat Chandra's Perception of His Bengali Home Region: A Literary Geographic Study." *GeoJournal*, vol. 5, no. 1, Springer 1981, pp. 41–53. www.jstor.org/stable/41142500.

Guha, Ranajit. *History at the Limit of World-History*. Columbia UP, 2002.

Henri, Lefebvre. *The Production of Space*. Blackwell Publishers Ltd., 1991.

Kelly, Ann H., et al. *The Anthropology of Epidemics*. Routledge, 2020.

Mohan, Anupama. *Utopia and the Village in South Asian Literatures*. Palgrave Macmillan, 2012.

Mukharji, Projit Bihari. *Nationalizing the Body: The Medical Market, Print and Daktari Medicine*. Anthem Press, 2011.

Roy, Rohan Deb. *Malarial Subjects Empire, Medicine and Nonhumans in British India, 1820–1909*. Cambridge UP, 2017.

Samanta, Arabinda. *Living with Epidemics in Colonial Bengal: 1818–1945*. Routledge, 2018.

Sarkar, Sumit. *Modern Times: India 1880s–1950s: Environment, Economy, Culture*. Permanent Black, 2015.

Snell, Keith. *The Regional Novel in Britain and Ireland*. Cambridge UP, 1998.

Williams, Raymond, and Tristram Hunt. *The Country and the City*. Vintage, 2016.

7

ALBERT CAMUS' REJOINDER TO THE ABSENT GOD AND THE ABSURDITY OF EXISTENCE IN *THE PLAGUE*

Sacaria Joseph

Introduction: The Omnipotent God and the Question of Evil and Suffering

Perhaps nothing has bewildered the philosophical mind over the ages more than the question of the existence of evil in its manifold manifestations in the world and the concomitant human suffering and mortality against the background of the notion of the existence of an omnipotent and omnibenevolent God. The ancient Greek philosopher, Epicurus, articulates the complexity of the issue through his famous trilemma:

> if God exists and he is unable to prevent evil, it means he is not all powerful; if he is able to prevent evil, it means he is not all-loving, given the existence of evil; and if he is able to prevent evil, and is also all-loving, then evil will not exist, but it does, so he cannot be both all-loving and all-powerful at the same time.
>
> *(Guite 424)*

David Hume, the Scottish Enlightenment philosopher reformulated the Epicurean trilemma in his *Dialogues Concerning Natural Religion* published in 1779. During a discussion among Philo, Cleanthes and Demea on the nature of God's existence, Philo asks his fellow philosophers, "Is he [God] willing to prevent evil, but not able? then he is impotent. Is he able, but not willing? then he is malevolent. Is he both able and willing? whence then is evil?" (Hume 63). In the guise of Philo, Hume postulates the difficulty in reconciling the belief in an all-powerful and benevolent God with our everyday experience of pain, suffering and evil in the world.

The questions that baffle the world smitten by COVID-19 pandemic (the agent of evil, suffering and death) are exactly the questions that baffled Epicurus as well

DOI: 10.4324/9781003294436-10

as David Hume. As COVID-19 pandemic began claiming helpless human lives indiscriminately, people from all walks of life and of all faiths across the globe began offering prayers and conducting various religious rituals as part of their entreaties to God in order to free the world of the deadly coronavirus. Close to two years into the pandemic, the world is still writhing under the ghastly grip of the deadly virus. One begins to wonder if there exists an omniscient, omnipotent and omnibenevolent God. If He does exist, why has he turned a deaf ear to the desperate cries of His children for deliverance? Even if He has not done so outright, one thing is evident – He has not responded to their cry for deliverance by intervening in their lives so far! And the baffling question – "why does God continue to remain indifferent to the suffering and death of His children?" – continues to haunt the theistic world. This is a rather unsettling scenario, a moment of intellectual and spiritual crisis for those who believe in an omniscient, omnipotent and omnibenevolent God. The scenario is nothing short of an existential crisis giving rise to a state of absurdity. "The world itself" appears as Albert Camus says, "a vast irrational" where "men vie with one another in proclaiming that nothing is clear, all is chaos" (Camus, *The Myth of Sisyphus* 31). As Camus goes on to say,

> At this point of his effort man stands face to face with the irrational. He feels within him his longing for happiness and for reason. The absurd is born of this confrontation between the human need and the unreasonable silence of the world.
>
> *(Camus, The Myth of Sisyphus 31–32)*

From the viewpoint of Camus, the rationale behind the deafening silence of God can be described, "either God does not exist and the world is absurd or God exists and it is He, then, who is evil" (Omnibus 45).

Unable to reconcile the notion of the existence of God with the pervasive presence of evil, senseless suffering and death in the world, Camus registers his protest saying, "The objection will be raised of evil, and of the paradox of an all-powerful and malevolent, or benevolent and sterile God" (Camus, *The Rebel* 287). In his novel, *The Plague*, Camus proposes a resolution to the paradoxical scenario through the contrasting responses of two characters – Father Paneloux, a Jesuit priest who is the voice of organized religion, and Dr. Bernard Rieux, a surgeon, humanist and atheist, who is the voice of science and rationality – to the plague that smote the coastal city of Oran in Algeria landing its people into an existential crisis and reducing their life into a state of absurdity.

Camus sees the question of evil, suffering and death as an existential issue. Therefore, in 1946, some months before *The Plague* was published, Camus told a group of Dominican monks in Paris, "I am your Augustine before his conversion. I am debating the problem of evil, and I am not getting past it" (Todd 337). Camus dwells on this complex issue in *The Plague* and posits an answer, which, in fact, is his philosophical response to the absurdity of human existence and not a conventional theodicy. From an existential philosophical perspective, this chapter will analyse the contrasting responses of Paneloux and Rieux to the same existential crisis plaguing the Algerian city of Oran in order to focus on Camus's rejoinder to the question, how human persons can come to terms with and respond to their experience of evil, suffering and the ravages of death in the world in the background of the notion of the existence of an omniscient, omnipotent and omnibenevolent God.

Existentialism and Absurdism

Existentialism became popular in the 1940s on account of the deep sense of despair ensuing from the aftermath of the Great Depression and World War II. The Great Depression, one of the most catastrophic economic disasters of the twentieth century, began with the unprecedented dramatic crash of the American stock market on Thursday (a day that later came to be known as Black Thursday), 24 October 1929, and continued for a longer than expected period. "By the time the crash was completed in 1932, following an unprecedentedly large economic depression, stocks had lost nearly 90 percent of their value" (Bierman). Ripples of the Great Depression soon spread to Europe and the rest of the world resulting in a worldwide economic recession that continued until 1946. World War II was the deadliest global conflict in human history with unparalleled inhumanity unleashed by human beings on their own species resulting in the largest number of deaths in any known human conflict. The use of nuclear weapons in the war announced the possibility of the annihilation of humankind at will. In the aftermath of World War II, ironically, humankind came across themselves as totally devoid of rationality; and the world they inhabited seemed to be governed by no benevolent or rational principle or entity. Among a group of thinkers and writers who would later be called existentialists, the image of a thoroughly confused, disillusioned, alienated and preposterous individual facing a broken, chaotic, uncertain, irrational and absurd world that he or she could neither understand nor accept emerged as the common philosophical metaphor for the existence of human beings in the world.

Existentialism may be seen as a response to the failure of modern humanity to find itself "at home" in the apparently unfriendly and unfamiliar world. As a subjective interpretation of life and existence, Existentialism is concerned with the human existence in its totality. The Spanish existentialist philosopher, Miguel de Unamuno's assertion that one "philosophizes not with the reason only, but with the will, with the feelings, with the flesh and the bones, with the whole soul and with the whole body" (Unamuno 584), sums up the philosophical method of the existentialist philosopher. Existentialism was as much a literary movement as a philosophical one. The major writers and thinkers who used this style of philosophizing differed widely in their approaches and views. However, while each of them dealt with the thoroughly unsettling existential human condition in his own distinctive manner, some of them also proposed ways to handle or approach it.

Absurdism emerged as an offshoot of existentialism in the post–World War II Europe, especially, in war-ravaged France. With the publication of Albert Camus' 1942 philosophical essay, *The Myth of Sisyphus*, absurdism as a movement is said to have been inaugurated. Absurdism holds that the effort of humanity to find meaning or rational explanation in the universe ultimately fails, because no such meaning exists. Talking about meaning, Camus says "I don't know whether this world has a meaning that transcends it. But I know that I do not know that meaning and that it is impossible for me just now to know it" (Camus, *The Myth of Sisyphus* 51). Therein lies the sense of the absurd.

> A world that can be explained even with bad reasons is a familiar world. But, on the other hand, in a universe suddenly divested of illusions and lights, man feels an alien, a stranger. His exile is without remedy since he is deprived of the memory of a lost home or the hope of a promised land. This divorce between man and his life, the actor and his setting, is properly the feeling of absurdity.
>
> *(Camus,* The Myth of Sisyphus *13)*

Addressing Absurdity: Suicide, Leap of Faith and Exercise of Human Responsibility

In his essay on Kafka, Eugene Ionesco says, "Absurd is that which is devoid of purpose . . . Cut off from his religious, metaphysical, and transcendental roots, man is lost; all his actions become senseless, absurd, useless" (quoted from Esslin, *The Theatre of the Absurd* 23). If our sense of the absurd is the result of our futile search for meaning in an essentially contingent and meaningless universe, we can respond to this absurdity of our situation in three possible ways – by taking a leap of faith, by taking refuge in suicide or by facing the absurdity with courageous despair.

According to the Danish philosopher, Soren Kierkegaard known as the father of existentialism, the pursuit of the transcendental or the spiritual by a "leap of faith" is the means to counter absurdity. To pursue the transcendental is to believe in and to quest after the ultimate reality that lies beyond the phenomenal and empirical reality and that is believed to have meaning in itself. A belief in a reality beyond the phenomenal and empirical reality calls for a "leap of faith", that is, the acceptance of a transcendental reality outside the boundaries of reason. In other words, it is the belief in something that cannot be confirmed either empirically or rationally. As Kierkegaard maintains, based on our ordinary human experience, we cannot come to conclude that the ultimate transcendental reality, God, exists. Only our faith makes us believe in the existence of God. This faith is not based on any empirical or rational proof but on acts of leap that we keep undertaking relying on our belief and trust in a transcendental reality, God. To believe in God is to believe in the absurd, that is, to believe in that which is contrary to reason as in the case of the Christian belief in the incarnation of the Son of God.

> The absurd is that the eternal truth has come into existence in time, that God has come into existence, has been born, has grown up. etc., has come into existence exactly as an individual human being, indistinguishable from any

other human being, inasmuch as all immediate recognizability is pre-Socratic paganism and from the Jewish point of view is idolatry.

(Kierkegaard, Concluding Unscientific Postscript
to Philosophical Crumps *177)*

In the book, *Fear and Trembling* that Kierkegaard wrote under the pseudonym, Johannes de Silentio, he argues that it is Abraham's belief in the absurd that makes him agree to sacrifice his son, Isaac, as per the command of God. The absurdity of Abraham's situation lies in the fact that it is God Himself who promised Abraham that He would make the latter the father of a great nation; and now it is God Himself asking Abraham to sacrifice his son, Isaac. How can a nation emerge from Abraham without the survival of his son? The scenario does not make sense; it is absurd. When faced with this absurdity, Abraham decides to take a leap of faith, and hence, prepares to sacrifice his son. "He [Abraham] had faith by virtue of the absurd, for [him] human calculation was out of the question" (Kierkegaard, *Fear and Trembling/Repetition: Kierkegaard's Writings* 35). Kierkegaard goes on to comment on Abraham's leap of faith, "God could give him a new Isaac, could restore to life the one sacrificed. He had faith by virtue of the absurd, for all human calculation ceased long ago" (Kierkegaard, *Fear and Trembling/Repetition: Kierkegaard's Writings* 36). It is his leap of faith that makes Abraham accept the absurd. Chapter 22 of the Book of Genesis in the Bible depicts Abraham's unquestioning faith and obedience to God. When viewed through the kaleidoscope of faith, what is absurd is transformed into the mysterious and ineffable way of God.

> When the believer has faith, the absurd is not the absurd – faith transforms it, but in every weak moment it is again more or less absurd to him. The passion of faith is the only thing which masters the absurd – if not, then faith is not faith in the strictest sense, but a kind of knowledge. The absurd terminates negatively before the sphere of faith, which is a sphere by itself.
>
> *(Hong and Hong 7)*

A "leap of faith" according to Camus is a philosophical suicide because it calls for the sacrifice of human reason and the reality of the human condition – the absurd. "Christianity is the scandal, and what Kierkegaard calls for quite plainly is the third sacrifice required by Ignatius Loyola, the one in which God most rejoices: The sacrifice of the intellect" (Camus, *The Myth of Sisyphus* 40). One's leap of faith implies one's belief in the existence of God, an external source and centre of meaning. However, the existence of God is an assumption with no rational foundation. If God does not exist, the entire exercise of the "leap of faith" itself is rather absurd. By believing in God, one is creating a false meaning; and in doing so, one stifles one's own ability to think. And if God does exist, in the background of all the pain, suffering and evil in the world, God would appear to be nothing short of a psychopath or a sadist. Hence, human existence would look even more absurd.

Recognizing the absurdity that characterizes human existence, the German philosopher, Arthur Schopenhauer, says, "For man's greatest offence/Is that he has been born" (Schopenhauer 254). According to Schopenhauer, human persons are absurd playthings in the hands of the blind and irrational "Will" that divides and objectifies itself into innumerable wills with the highest objectification and manifestation found in human persons. Since the Will keeps striving relentlessly without any rationale in order to preserve itself, the individual wills, especially the ones objectified in human persons, strive with one another. "It is one and the same will, living and appearing in them all, whose phenomena fight with one another and tear one another to pieces. In one individual it appears powerfully, in another more feebly" (Schopenhauer 253). This endless striving and conflict between individual wills objectified in human persons make human existence a veritable theatre of the absurd.

> The unspeakable pain, the wretchedness and misery of mankind, the triumph of wickedness, the scornful mastery of chance, and the irretrievable fall of the just and the innocent . . . It is the antagonism of the will with itself which is here most completely unfolded at the highest grade of its objectivity, and which comes into fearful prominence.
>
> *(Schopenhauer 253)*

The presence of the Will makes life an unquenchable desire. Therefore, the only progress human existence makes is in terms of increasing misery. Such being the tragic predicament of human existence, as a way out of this absurd quandary, Schopenhauer proposes that human persons should deliberately will to free themselves from the control of the Will, and will against the desire and will of the Will to preserve itself. When they do so, they surrender their will to live. This stage of will-lessness is the stage of resignation – a state of peace and tranquillity as well as freedom from suffering. The surrender of the will to live is tantamount to suicide. What suicide results in is a cowardly avoidance of the absurd rather than facing it head-on, and thereby, making the scenario even more absurd. Escaping the reality of existence by means of suicide "is confessing that life is too much for you or that you do not understand it . . . It is merely confessing that that 'is not worth the trouble'" (Camus, *The Myth of Sisyphus* 13). Suicide is a declaration that life is not worth living. Recognizing the absurdity of existence is not the same as regarding life as not worth living. Therefore, Camus rules out the possibility of suicide as a way to counter the absurd.

Camus is of the opinion that only if we accept the absurd, we become free to create our own subjective meaning in the absence of any possible objective meaning. Therefore, he argues that we should accept the absurdity of existence and continue to live in spite of the perceived and experienced absurdity. Since the acceptance of absurdity being the only way to counter absurdity, talking about Sisyphus, Camus says, "The Struggle itself towards the heights is enough to fill a man's heart. One must imagine Sisyphus happy" (Camus, *The Myth of Sisyphus* 111).

Our experience of the absurd makes us realize that the universe is fundamentally devoid of absolutes, and as individuals, we are really free to live without appeal to any superior absolute entity and define absolutes and universals subjectively. If we acknowledge the absence of objective meaning in existence, and continue our engagement with life, we can gradually develop our own subjective meaning from life; and this can make us happy like Sisyphus whom we may consider happy.

Camus says, "Thus I draw from the absurd three consequences, which are my revolt, my freedom, and my passion" (Camus, *The Myth of Sisyphus* 62). While his notion of "revolt" might be understood as his feeling of outrage and rebellion against his absurd and tragic condition, and a defiant refusal to be broken by it, his notion of "freedom" may be understood as the freedom from the confines of the religious and other absolutes and their moral codes. His notion of "passion" may be understood as the passionate experience of life at every moment on account of the fact that since we are devoid of objective meaning, every present moment must be lived fully to arrive at our own subjective meaning. The absurdists adhere to this line of thinking even though Kierkegaard would call it demoniac madness.

Leap of Faith: Paneloux's Panacea to Absurdity

The absurdity of the inhabitants of Oran in Camus' novel, *The Plague*, is the helpless situation they face where their life is mercilessly and relentlessly snatched away by the inscrutable plague. In the novel, as Camus' Paneloux, the spokesperson of Christianity, preaches his first Sunday sermon to the people of Oran, he argues that the plague that struck the people of Oran is a punishment from God for their sinful life. His argument is in line with the Pauline theory of divine retribution. According to St. Paul, "sin entered the world through one man, and death through sin, and in this way, death came to all people, because all sinned" (Romans 5:12). In and through the Fall of the first human parent, Adam, both human life and human nature were adversely and irrevocably affected. Everyone – "even those who did not disobey an explicit commandment of God, as Adam did", become prey to death (Romans 5:14). Sickness, the agent of death, is the consequence of the Fall of humanity in and through the Fall of Adam.

Thus, the plague, according to Paneloux, is a manifestation of divine retribution upon a people who lived an essentially mercenary and profligate life. The narrator of the novel tells us that while the young people in Oran pursued their "violent and short-lived" passions, the older people gave themselves over to "games of bowls", "banquets and 'socials,' or clubs where large sums change hands on the fall of a card" (Camus, *The Plague* 6). In the spirit of the biblical retributive justice – "You will always harvest what you plant" (Galatians 6:7) – Paneloux thunders to the people of Oran, "Calamity has come on you, my brethren, and my brethren, you deserve it" (Camus, *The Plague* 80). He drives the idea home forcefully, saying that God has "visited all the cities that offended against Him, since the dawn of history" (Camus, *The Plague* 82). Now it is the turn of the sinful Oran from which God has turned his face away. "God's light withdrawn, we walk in darkness, in the thick darkness of this plague" (Camus, *The Plague* 81). According to Paneloux, repentance alone will save them from the darkness and death looming large over their city.

However, after witnessing the suffering and eventual death of a plague-stricken child, Jacques Othon, Paneloux realizes that when confronted with an intensely tragic human predicament like the painful death of an innocent child, the theology of divine retribution does not suffice. He realizes that the ways of God are too mysterious and inscrutable for the finite human intelligence to comprehend. Paneloux's example reminds us of the sceptical teacher in the book of Qoheleth (Ecclesiastes) in the Bible. With advancing age, the teacher in Qoheleth comes to realize that God being a mystery far beyond human comprehension, the hallmark of the wise is nothing but trust in Him. Paneloux's example also reminds us of another biblical character, Job, who also learns a similar lesson through immense suffering; Job too submits himself to the inexplicable and ineffable ways of God.

Like the sceptical teacher in Qoheleth and the virtuous sufferer, Job, Paneloux too comes to the conclusion that when faced with the intense suffering inflicted by the plague, one must either make a leap of faith in the Kierkegaardian sense and accept everything as part of the mysterious divine will and plan or give up one's faith in God altogether. Paneloux urges the people of Oran to take a leap of faith. He decides to take the leap himself. As he becomes unwell, he accepts his sickness as part of the will and plan of God; he refuses to consult the doctor and get treated – evidently, a misguided application of the concept of the leap of faith. When he dies, nobody knows if he died of the plague or of other causes, because he had refused to get tested for the plague. According to Camus, the concept of the leap of faith is tantamount to a philosophical suicide, because it implies the naïve acceptance of an intangible and uncertain reality (God), the refusal to face truth (the absurdity of human existence characterized by the absence of any objective meaning and significance in life), and the refusal to take responsibility for one's own life.

Stoic Exercise of Human Responsibility: Bernard Rieux's Antidote to Absurdity

Camus is of the opinion that if we accept the absurdity of existence as the reality of our life, we are free to create our own subjective meanings and resolve our problems ourselves. Human responsibility, therefore, is at the heart of Camus' philosophy; when humans have no absolutes, and no God to turn to, they must learn to rely on themselves. Confronting the absurdity of his existence, Sisyphus has learned to take the absurdity head on and create his own personal meaning and live a happy life. Therefore, the scientific-tempered and practical-minded Dr. Bernard Rieux, Camus's spokesperson in *The Plague*, does not subscribe to the theory of divine retribution; nor does he find consolation in taking a leap of faith. Against all odds, he keeps on working hard to develop a cure for the plague. He is conscious of the fact that his struggle against the plague is symbolic of his struggle against human suffering. The narrator of the novel who, the reader realizes towards the end of the novel, is none other than Rieux himself says:

> None the less he knew that the tale he had to tell could not be one of a final victory. It could be only the record of what had . . . to be done, and what assuredly would have to be done again in the never-ending fight against terror and its relentless onslaughts, despite their personal afflictions, by all who, while unable to be saints but refusing to bow down to pestilences, strive their utmost to be healers.
>
> *(Camus,* The Plague *251–52)*

To his friend Tarrou's question as to whether he believes in God, Rieux answers saying, "No – but what does that mean? I'm fumbling in the darkness, struggling to make something out". To Tarrou's further question, "Why do you yourself show such devotion, considering you don't believe in God", Rieux answers saying, if he believed in an all-powerful God, he would cease curing the sick and leave that to Him. The narrator of the novel goes on to remark, "in this respect Rieux believed himself to be on the right road – in fighting against creation as he found it" (Camus, *The Plague* 106–7). Rieux finds creation unfinished and imperfect; he also realizes that the notion of an omniscient, omnipotent, omnibenevolent and interventionist God is not intelligible to him. Therefore, with stoic courage and commitment, he goes about fulfilling his role (every human being has a similar role) in contributing to the betterment of his flawed and battered world even if his effort yields no result.

Conclusion

In general, people expect God to intervene in human affairs. Their prayers and religious rituals are manifestations of their effort to make God intervene in their lives as per their expectations. Anticipating divine intervention in human affairs, people tend to abdicate their responsibility and place it on the shoulders of their God. After having learned lessons from the Holocaust, Camus seems to highlight the example of Rieux to those who tend to abdicate personal responsibility. It would be the height of human naiveté and irresponsibility to expect God to intervene in human lives in answer to their prayers and religious observances after He remained silent and indifferent to the fate of His "chosen people" during World War II. Except in religious and mythical narratives, God has never been found to intervene in the world – be it in times of natural calamities, man-made catastrophes or pandemics. If God were to handle issues that human beings themselves are capable of handling, unfortunately, little would be left of human knowledge and agency.

The spirit and mission of Rieux in *The Plague* are both an inspiration and an invitation to all in times of pandemics to face all odds with courage and commitment. His example also urges us to take the responsibility for finding the means of deliverance from the COVID-19 pandemic on our own shoulders by relying on the manifold human capacities and working to the best of our ability, instead of expecting God to intervene and provide deliverance. Camus's novel underscores the significance of human not divine agency in delivering humanity from all forms of suffering and evil. *The Plague* – and literature of pestilences, epidemics, and pandemics in general – is, thus, best read as human attempts to come to terms with the widespread fear and despair ensuing from human experiences of pestilence, epidemics and pandemics in particular, and the pain and suffering that characterize human life in general.

The novel seems to tell us that it is time we faced the absurdity of human existence (if we regard existence as essentially absurd as Camus did) with a courageous despair like that of Sisyphus and find our own subjective meaning and happiness. It is time we faced the torments of our lives with a stoic spirit and a commitment like that of Bernard Rieux. It is time we took responsibility for our own lives both during and after the COVID-19 pandemic. It is time we lived before God as though He does not exist.

Works Cited

Bierman, Harold. *The 1929 Stock Market Crash*. Edited by Robert Whaples, 26 Mar. 2008. http://eh.net/encyclopedia/the-1929-stock-market-crash/. Accessed 28 Aug. 2021.

Camus, Albert. *The Rebel*. Translated by Anthony Bower. Vintage, 1956.

———. *The Plague*. Penguin, 1980.

———. *The Myth of Sisyphus*. Penguin, 1981.

Esslin, Martin. *The Theatre of the Absurd*. Penguin, 1968.

Guite, Haulian. *Confessions of a Dying Mind: The Blind Faith of Atheism*. Bloomsbury, 2017.

Hong, Howard V., and Edna H. Hong. *Soren Kierkegaard's Journal and Papers*. Translated by Howard V. Hong and Edna H. Hong, vol. 1A–E. Indiana UP, 1967.

Hume, David. *Dialogues Containing Natural Religion*. Edited by Richard H. Popkin, 2nd ed. Hackett, 1998.

Kierkegaard, Soren. *The Journals of Soren Kierkegaard*. Edited by Alexander Dru. Oxford UP, 1938.

———. *Fear and Trembling/Repetition: Kierkegaard's Writings*. Edited and translated by Howard V. Hong and Edna H. Hong, vol. 6. Princeton UP, 1983.

———. *Concluding Unscientific Postscript to Philosophical Crumps*. Edited and translated by Alastair Hannay. Cambridge UP, 2009.

Onimus, Jean. *Albert Camus and Christianity*. Translated by Emmet Parker. Gill and Macmillan, 1970.

Schopenhauer, Arthur. *The World as Will and Representation*. Translated by E.F.J. Payne, vol. 1. Dover Publications, 1969.

Todd, Oliver. *Albert Camus: A Life*. Translated by Benjamin Irvy. Knopf, 1998.

Unamuno, Miguel de. "The Tragic Sense of Life." *Images of the Human: The Philosophy of the Human Person in a Religious Context*, edited by Hunter Brown, et al. Lola Press, 1995, pp. 583–87.

III

Moving Between Language and Media

8

"IT MATTERED NOT FROM WHENCE IT CAME; BUT ALL AGREED IT WAS COME . . ."

Plague Narratives as Narratives of Media and of Foreignness

Amit R. Baishya

This chapter emerges from pedagogical strategies deployed in classes on zombies that I teach at the undergraduate level. While one genealogy of zombies can be traced back to Caribbean folklore surrounding the figure of the *zombie*, the other major trajectory emerges from narratives of the plague. Inspired by Boluk and Lenz's "transhistorical" approach to plague narratives, this chapter adopts a minimalist approach to compare the opening sequences of Daniel Defoe's *A Journal of the Plague Year* and the big-budget Hollywood film *World War Z*. I juxtapose these sequences together in my classes to illustrate how the "communicability of texts becomes inseparable from the communicability of plague" (Boluk and Lenz 128). I adopt a minimalist reading strategy here focusing only on the opening sequences to compare transhistorical continuities inhering in these Euroamerican representations of pandemics from the eras of early and late capitalism. Besides the affinities between the communicability of plagues and the communicability of texts/media, I consider how plagues are imagined as emerging from elsewhere. Furthermore, plagues are associated with the figure of the foreigner, the outsider or the other (figures increasingly racialized in the modern era). I begin with an analysis of the opening passage from *A Journal* and move to an "Intermezzo" that functions as a threshold looking ahead from Defoe's text to later plague/apocalyptic narratives. The "Intermezzo" broaches the representation of media and infection in zombie films predating *World War Z*. I then turn to an analysis of the opening scenes of *World War Z* to consider how it distills the themes of otherness, the connections between media and actual contagions, and how the media forms through which information spreads impact the velocities of affects like panic.

DOI: 10.4324/9781003294436-12

A Journal of the Plague Year: **Biological and Media Contagions**

Here is the opening scene of Defoe's retrospective fictional portrayal of the London plague of 1665:

> It was about the beginning of September, 1664, that I, among the rest of my neighbours, heard in ordinary discourse that the plague was returned again in Holland; for it had been very violent there, and particularly at Amsterdam and Rotterdam, in the year 1663, whither, they say, it was brought, some said from Italy, others from the Levant, among some goods which were brought home by their Turkey fleet; others said it was brought from Candia; others from Cyprus. It mattered not from whence it came; but all agreed it was come into Holland again.
>
> We had no such thing as printed newspapers in those days to spread rumours and reports of things, and to improve them by the invention of men, as I have lived to see practised since. But such things as these were gathered from the letters of merchants and others who corresponded abroad, and from them was handed about by word of mouth only; so that things did not spread instantly over the whole nation, as they do now. Hence it was that this rumour died off again, and people began to forget it as a thing we were very little concerned in, and that we hoped was not true; till the latter end of November or the beginning of December 1664 when two men, said to be Frenchmen, died of the plague in Long Acre, or rather at the upper end of Drury Lane.
>
> *(5)*

I tease out three major threads from these passages that reverberate in future texts. First, as Sontag writes: "there is a link between imagining disease and imagining foreignness" (136). Sontag goes on to say that:

> Part of the centuries-old conception of Europe as a privileged cultural entity is that it is a place which is colonized by lethal diseases coming from else-where. Europe is assumed by rights to be free of disease. (And Europeans have been astoundingly callous about the far more devastating extent to which they – as invaders, as colonists – have introduced their diseases to the exotic "primitive" world . . .)
>
> *(138)*

H.F.'s (Defoe's narrator) speculations about the "origins" of the plague conflate the pandemic with foreignness – the source seems to be from the "hot" zones either in the Mediterranean or in Asia.[1] (The racialization of places like "Turkey" and the "Levant" and the Eurocentrism that Sontag notes emerges in later years). H.F.'s speculations also gesture towards the connections between the mobility of the plague and the mobility of goods and people in the period of early capitalism. As Sontag writes, trading ports like Amsterdam and Rotterdam were the transit points of the plague, "brought by seamen, then transported by soldiers and merchants" (138). Waterways function as openings that introduce the illness into the closed economy that is the nation's imagined "geo-body" (Winichakul) via the circulation of capital. Ships are the carriers of the virus and remained so at up to the predominance of automobiles and air travel.

The second paragraph from Defoe's passage introduces three related but distinct trajectories that circumnavigate later narrativization of plagues. The first is about the connection between media and contagion, the second is about the speed of transmission, and the third an almost fleeting connection instituted between rumour and panic. Discussing the homology between actual and media plagues (now encapsulated by the term "virality"), Sean Cubitt delves into etymology and writes:

> There is a disturbing etymological puzzle underlying [contagion] . . . "Contagion" appears to be a late fourteenth-century coinage, appearing in the wake of the Black Death in mediaeval French and Middle English, from the Latin roots "con", meaning "with", and "tangere", the active verb "to touch". The puzzle comes from another word we associate at least equally closely with electronic media, "contact". Here the root words are the same, with the only exception that "contact" comes from the passive form "tactum", "to be touched". Oddly, most people probably feel positive connotations about "contact", but negative connotations from "contagion".
>
> *(ix)*

The paradox here lies in the fact that what is agential is viewed negatively and what is passive is viewed positively. Underlying this difference in connotation though is a homology about the speed of transfer through the metaphor of tactile contact. Whether "to touch" or "to be touched", both plagues and electronic media are characterized by the rapidity of transfer and the speed with which they move from one bodily interface to another.

Defoe was writing during the consolidation of the era of print capitalism and not of electronic media. But he anticipates later theses about speed – whether it is Karl Marx's thesis in *Capital* about capital "annihilating space with time" (539), or Benedict Anderson's musings about "simultaneity", or Paul Virilio's connections between speed and politics. Note the connection that H.F. draws between newspapers and rumour and the instant spread of information across the "whole nation" in the era of print capitalism, and compares it with this passage from *Imagined Communities* on newspapers as "one-day best-sellers":

> The obsolescence of the newspaper on the morrow of its printing . . . creates this extraordinary mass ceremony: the almost precisely simultaneous consumption ("imagining") of the newspaper-as-fiction. We know that

particular morning and evening editions will overwhelmingly be consumed between this hour and that . . . The significance of this mass ceremony – Hegel observed that newspapers serve modern man as a substitute for morning prayers – is paradoxical. It is performed in silent privacy . . . Yet each communicant is well aware that the ceremony he performs is being replicated *simultaneously* by thousands (or millions) of others of whose existence he is confident, yet of whose identity he has not the slightest notion. Furthermore, this ceremony is incessantly repeated at daily or half-daily intervals throughout the calendar. What more vivid figure for the secular, historically clocked, imagined community can be envisioned? *At the same time*, the newspaper reader, observing exact replicas of his own paper being consumed by his subway, barbershop, or residential neighbors, is continually reassured that the imagined world is visibly rooted in everyday life.

(35–36, italics mine)

I italicized the temporal markers in the passage because implicit in them are theses about the speed of transfer – via simultaneity, newspapers make information "viral" at a velocity which is virtually unimaginable in forms of face-to-face contact. In doing so, they also precipitate the velocity with which rumours and one of its associated affects, panic, spreads across the nation's geo-body.

H.F.'s distinction between the "before" of the era of newspapers and the print capitalism saturated "now" is, however, misread by Boluk and Lenz: "Instead, H.F. explains, prior to the rise of newspapers, 'such things' were 'handed about by word of mouth only,' a process that allowed such rumors to gradually die off" (133). This misreading occurs because they stop at the segment which says "the rumour died off again" in Defoe's paragraph and do not consider what rumour connotes as a speech act and how it facilitates not only the spread of panic, *but the rate and velocity with which it spreads like a contagion.* Note what Gyanendra Pandey, says about rumour, speech acts ostensibly without signature:

Rumor moves in a direction almost contrary to that of testimony: generalizing, exalting to extraordinary (even miraculous) status, and employing the sweeping terms of deluge and just desserts (actual or impending). In rumor, language is transformed from a mode of (possible) communication to a particular kind of imperative condition, communicable, infectious, possible (and almost necessary) to pass on.

(165–66)

Pandey draws upon the registers of what Anjuli Kolb calls "disease poetics" to describe the modality of rumour as a speech act. Rumour naturalizes the political dimensions of speech ("deluge") and is also figured via the lexicon of contagion ("infectious").

One of the affects associated with the spread of rumours is panic. A detour via etymology will prove useful. In her meditations on the physics of terror,

Adriana Cavarero says that panic derives from the Greek *"panikos"* which leads us back to the "tellurian power" connected to the god Pan. Cavarero writes:

> Panic fear, or panic terror, was what the ancients called the feeling of total fear, sudden and unexplainable, caused by the presence of the god. Although for the ancients as well as for the modern psychological lexicon, panic is primarily an individual experience, it is easy to see why the term lends itself to designating those collective experiences in which terrorized masses flee . . . The contiguity of bodies makes masses especially susceptible to the contagion of terror, transmitting and heightening its effects.
>
> *(5)*

H.F. is not saying that the rumours die off. Instead, through a comparison with the "before" of face-to-face communication and the "now" of print capitalism, he is emphasizing the speed of transfer. Rumours lie dormant like a virus and can be reactivated like zombies. However, the spread of the contagion of rumour in conditions of face-to-face communication occurs slowly and *successively*. It spreads from two infectious apertures in the body – the mouth to the ear. Defoe depicts this slow spread of panic in the first part of the novel by the gradual rise in the number of deaths as the infection spreads parish by parish. Print capitalism accelerates the spread of rumour and panic through space–time compression. For the public that participates in the ritual of daily newspaper reading, the experience is not successive, but simultaneous. As a witness to both the "before" and the "now", H.F.'s specter of comparison is a meditation on speed, which as Aldous Huxley said later is the "only new pleasure invented by modernity" (Duffy 2). While Huxley is talking about the pleasures of the automobile, I refer to the other aspect of the polyvalent connotations of speed in the accelerating ages of mechanical reproduction: its capacity to spread panic and anxiety. Defoe is putting his finger on that experience which has increasingly become so familiar for us.

Intermezzo

As a spatial figure, a border is different from a threshold. Borders demarcate insides and outsides. A threshold encompasses the inside in the outside and vice versa. I use this "Intermezzo" as a threshold as I look forward to a lineage of literatures on the plague that follow *A Journal* and backwards from *World War Z* to trace a small history of media as captured in the zombie film.

Let's first consider the trope of the plague as phenomenon that is brought by the "foreigner". Donald Trump's notoriously racist characterization of COVID-19 as "kung flu" follows a long history of the racialization of Asian Americans in the United States. However, other locations like the Islamicate East, South Asia and Latin America are also substitutable in the disease poetics in the Euroamerican ecumene. Consider Mary Shelley's *The Last Man* which with its deployment of the "last man" trope anticipates the figuration of the lone witness of the zombie apocalypse in texts like *28 Days Later*. In *The Last Man*, the world-destroying plague originates in Constantinople ("Stamboul") as a "curse from Allah" (152). In this period of high Orientalism that shapes Romantics like Byron and Mary Shelley, the novel makes a "bid for infectiousness and contagion originating in the Muslim East as primary motors of a universal history" (Kolb 91–92).

Kolb's magisterial *Epidemic Empire* institutes strong connections between the discourses on terrorism (centring in our conjuncture on "radical Islam") and discourses on contagion and its associated disease poetics that are the enduring legacies of colonialism. One text she considers is Albert Camus' *The Plague*, which despite being a novel set in Algeria isn't always read as a novel "about Algeria" (133). *The Plague* departs from the usual script about plagues as arising from elsewhere; here, the plague emerges from within Oran. However, in crucial ways it also follows the disease poetics evidenced in *A Journal* that triangulates otherness, media and speed. Here's a representative passage from the beginning:

> It was about this time that our townsfolk began to show signs of uneasiness. For, from April 18 onwards, quantities of dead or dying rats were found in factories and warehouses . . . From the outer suburbs to the center of the town, in all the byways where the doctor's duties took him, in every thoroughfare, rats were piled up in garbage cans or lying in long lines in the gutters. The evening papers that day took up the matter and inquired whether or not the city fathers were going to take steps, and what emergency measures were contemplated, to abate this particularly disgusting nuisance. Actually the municipality had not contemplated doing anything at all, but now a meeting was convened to discuss the situation . . .
>
> But the situation worsened in the following days . . . Things went so far that the Ransdoc Information Bureau . . . which ran a free-information talk on the radio, by way of publicity, began its talk by announcing that no less than 6,231 rats had been collected and burned in a single day, April 25. Giving as it did an ampler and more precise view of the scene daily enacted before our eyes, this amazing figure administered a jolt to the public nerves. Hitherto people had merely grumbled at a stupid, rather obnoxious visitation; they now realized that this strange phenomenon, whose scope could not be measured and whose origins escaped detection, had something vaguely menacing about it. Only the old Spaniard whom Dr. Rieux was treating for asthma went on rubbing his hands and chuckling: "They're coming out, they're coming out", with senile glee.
>
> On April 28, when the Ransdoc Bureau announced that 8,000 rats had been collected, a wave of something like panic swept the town.
>
> *(15–17)*

Kolb conducts a "depth" reading to compare the rats as an allegorical epitomization of "disappeared life" that aligns with the "absent natives" in the novel (157–60). I bypass the allegorical depths to conduct a "surface" reading of the continuities with Defoe. Defoe's relative vagueness about temporal markers ("about the beginning of September") contrasts with Camus' precision about the progression of *chronos* ("April 24", "April 25") and the numbers of rats collected. The steady anchoring in *chronos* has the talismanic power to propel plot. The mass ritual of reading the evening newspaper becomes a civic exercise to put pressure on the public authorities. Space–time compression and the spread of panic are accentuated by another mass mediatic form: the radio. Radio broadcasts "jolt . . . the public nerves", and later impel a "wave of something like panic". Otherness, too, irrupts suddenly – in a town populated largely by Frenchmen (seemingly bereft of autochthonous Algerians), the "Spaniard" seems to gesture inscrutably towards a mystical form of knowledge unavailable to the denizens of Oran. Finally, the nervous condition of the town ebbs and flows – anxiety rises with the numbers revealed by the radio broadcast, while it ebbs at the end with another broadcast about numbers. Compare this to H.F.'s statement about the beginning of the plague that the rumours die off in September, only to be resuscitated in late November to early December. In an era of heightened mediatic simultaneity, the ebb and flow of panic and anxiety occurs on a day-to-day basis, compressing temporal experience.

World War Z is one of my least favourite zombie films. It simplifies the complex "quasi-epistolary" (Bishop 49) narrative technique of Max Brooks' novel, focusing primarily on the travails of a white male protagonist saviour played by Hollywood superstar Brad Pitt. I agree that the film "reeks of racial demonization" (Arab zombie hordes overrun walled Jerusalem) and is a classist phobic fantasy about "the danger of proximity with the diseased poor" (Luckhurst 186). However, the opening credit sequence, running for approximately 2.08 minutes with an interesting combination of montage and diegetic and extradiegetic sound, is a distillation of several themes discussed earlier about narratives of the plague and of how zombie films represent media.

Like plague narratives, zombie films are narratives of media contagion. This connection between media and zombie contagions occurs in two ways. First, we can read zombie films as a progressive genealogy of media forms – consider, for instance, the role of the television and radio in George Romero's *Night of the Living Dead*, video game simulation in the *Resident Evil*, the surveillance camera in *28 Days Later*, and the use of cell phone imagery in the Native American zom-com, *The Dead Can't Dance*. In such films, new media forms both become a medium for spreading panic while it also shows how their embeddedness in the quotidian presupposes particular forms of spectator positions from their audiences. Second, Boluk and Lenz discuss the infectious living dead category of media like writing – how forms like the book can both transmit viruses and exist like zombies that can be resuscitated by later readers. The dead letter becomes, reinfused with life. This point can be extended to later media products like the photograph and the moving image. Consider the terms that Andre Bazin uses to describe photographs and moving images – "time embalmed" and "change mummified", respectively (8). In both cases, Bazin describes these plastic arts with terms that represent forms of life-in-death. The opening sequence of *World War Z* distills these different threads in a short space. Without further ado, I step over the threshold to describe and analyse this sequence in the concluding segment.

World War Z: Networked Infection

I agree with Bishop that the film is a shift from a

> localised siege narrative to an international kind of "road trip" movie, a shift largely tied to the popularity of zombie-themed videogames and the expectations and demands of viewers accustomed to such narratives, but also realizing . . . that a globalised Gothic includes "increased mobility".
>
> *(51)*

This view is correct if we consider former UN representative Gerry's (Brad Pitt) movements that track the planetary spread of the virus. However, while the plot unfolds on a planetary scale, the opening sequence begins by resituating Euroamerica as a privileged cultural entity. The film first zooms in on the local/national space before it spreads out to the rest of the planet. In this moment of zooming in, it seems far more akin to the opening narrative gambit of *A Journal*.

The opening sequence operates on a conceit – what happens over a significant amount of time seems to be compressed within a single day. The first two wide shots of the sequence show the waves rolling in and the day dawning. The extradiegetic music is sombre and slow-paced. The third shot shows the rising sun peeking through the skyscrapers in an American city (probably Philadelphia, as the reference to JTL radio in one of the first spliced voiceovers reveals). The succeeding montage then alternates between three sets of images: the quotidian early morning rhythms of American life, images of everyday life from South and East Asia, and a steadily accelerating series of animal imagery. Simultaneously, as the musical tempo begins slowly accelerating, the soundtrack is overlaid with extradiegetic snatches of media broadcasts – the JTL early morning radio show and bits of information from TV shows and news. The voiceovers from television suture mundane bits from early morning talk shows and ominous snatches about an infectious outbreak from news reports. Shots of airport information boards and departing aircraft alternate with automobiles lined up near a clogged US border post. If the aircraft replaces the ship as the iconic mode of international travel in late modernity, the automobile facilitates the conquest of national and transcontinental land space. But like the waterways in Defoe, they also become conduits for the plague's entry into the nation's geo-body.

There is an increasing reliance on television footage in the latter half, as images of a talk show, a lifestyle show, beached dolphins, a talking head warning of the dangers of carbon emission, skeptics who warn about the U.N.'s reluctance to restrict international travel, bureaucrats who say that everything will be fine, a horrifying grainy clip of a scene of violence caught by a surveillance camera, and a doomsday skeptic succeed each other. Meanwhile, images of predominantly empty spaces in the "West" are often juxtaposed with crowded spaces in Asia. While there are three shots of crowds in Western spaces (the first of people alighting from a train, the second of a rock concert and the third of a crowded urban street), the only shot from the "East" that is relatively empty is that of a "Matha" ice cream seller on a bicycle in India. The ice cream seller is in the foreground, and a hazy sheen of dust is in the background. Animal imagery begins with wide shots of avian flocks taking to the sky, then shifts towards grainy shots of insect swarms and as the music reaches a fever pitch to align with the accelerated montage towards and focuses on predatory animals like wolves and scavengers like vultures. In this accelerated montage, images of people in masks alternate also recur, signifying that the plague has reached its crescendo.

Through an astute juxtaposition of images of varying length, sound and extradiegetic music, this segment draws on existing tropes of what Priscilla Wald terms "outbreak narratives". In such narratives, disease is exported "as a commodity in the dangerously promiscuous spaces of a global economy conceived as an ecology" (7). While this aspect is nascent in *A Journal*, it is heightened manifold in *World War Z*. Crowds, a dusty haze and dirt – a standard visual trope about South Asia in Hollywood productions – are omnipresent in the Indian sequences evidenced by the dusty filter and the shots of cramped public spaces. People are also wearing masks in the East Asian locales. Given that the plague slowly approaches the Western spaces as the segment progresses, the insinuation that the disease originates elsewhere is clear. The global economy conceived as ecology is evident from three shots of flocks of birds flying paralleled with the display board of an airport and an aircraft leaving. If planes are the primary mode of mobility in a networked globe, flocks of birds, too, cross national borders. If airports have replaced naval ports as the primary entry points that introduce pathogens into the geo-body of the nation, birds can be carriers of viruses like H1N1. Economy folds into ecology and vice versa.

Flocks of birds are one major collective formation displayed, accentuated later by a shot of chaotic flight patterns as the extradiegetic music increases in tempo. The avian formations are juxtaposed with other collectives – crowds of people, packs of wolves and insect swarms. Each collective has an attached symbolism of their own. Following Canetti, we can call the human collectives represented "stagnating" crowds – "Its state has something passive in it, it waits" (34). This is evident if we consider the crowds coming out of the subway train, walking in the city streets, filing through the airport terminal or standing on a bus. Bodies are jammed together, yet individuals seem to go by his/her quotidian rhythm as an isolated monad. The crowd at the rock concert is more active, but the activity of such a stagnant crowd too operates via rhythms – people move when the camera comes close to them or in carnivalesque celebration.

Contrast this with the frenetic activity of the wolf pack or the insect swarm, prefigurations of the hordes of zombies later in the film. Wolves play a dominant role in Western political theology. Consider one of the opening statements of Thomas Hobbes's *De Cive* – "That Man to Man is a kind of God; and that Man to Man is an arrant Wolfe" (Latin "*homo homini lupus, homo homini deus*"). The wolf represents a form of prepolitical animality that lies suppressed beneath the mask of the human. Cannetti defines the pack as an elemental form of the crowd – "small hordes that roam about as groups of ten or twenty", characterized by "the fact that it cannot grow", and most importantly, a formation where the "individual can never lose himself as completely as modern man can in any crowd today" (93). No wonder then that wolves, animals that humans "knew well" and were impressed by "very early" serve as models of such elemental, prepolitical forms of association (97). In the conservative political theology that often predicates zombie apocalypses like *World War Z*, this "fall" into a prepolitical state reveals the lupine nature of humans.

Insect swarms, besides being perceived as vectors of disease and filth, represent a different form of alterity. Recently, there has been an affirmative representation of swarms as rhizomatic forms of decentralized intelligence.[2] Yet, a more negative connotation of swarms also persists – a collective formation that almost seems to move, attack or consume mindlessly by instinct, much like the insects frenetically consuming other beings in the opening sequence. Indeed, in the opening set piece of the film set in a Philadelphia boulevard, "crowds" of humans become "swarms" of zombies as the virus is transmitted trans-corporeally by the zombie bite.

The swarms of insects also prefigure how swarms of zombies create panic in Philadelphia's streets in the first set piece of *World War Z*. However, the opening sequence shows the variegated rhythms via which panic arrives on Western shores from elsewhere. Mediatic simultaneity again plays a big role here – besides the radio and television, we also have a shot of people glued to their iPhones as the tempo of the extradiegetic music accelerates. An interesting moment fuses media and animality in the clip. Around the minute mark of the opening sequence, we notice a still shot of beached dolphins taken from a television news broadcast. This is an example of embalmed time, the dead image showing still, bloodied animal corpses. What causes the dolphins to beach is a mystery, the newscaster's voice says. While cetacean beachings can be spectacular occurrences, such events flow under the radar when it happens "elsewhere", for instance, in the Sunderbans depicted in Amitav Ghosh's *Gun Island*. What raises the alarm in *World War Z* is that it is happening "here" in Euroamerican spaces with repeated regularity. The music too begins to rise in tempo as the length of the shots becomes shorter and shorter. As in *A Journal*, the first intimation of danger to hit "our" shores comes from the fringes of the nation's geo-body: its shorelines. Quotidian life continues with its regular, albeit uneasy, rhythms after this shot that jolt the public nerves. But increasing, simultaneous exposure to what is happening "there" and "here" by various media forms – accentuated by speeded-up montage and a cacophonous overlay of voiceovers – bring the disaster "home" and create a wave of something like panic. Soon, it mattered not from whence it came; but all agreed it was *come*.

Notes

1   Miasmatic theory held that outbreaks of plagues were caused by "bad" or "hot" air. It was popular till around the mid-nineteenth century when it was replaced by the germ theory of disease.
2   See Baishya for a discussion of the polyvalent representations of swarm imagery.

Works Cited

28 Days Later. Directed by Danny Boyle, 2002.

Anderson, Benedict. *Imagined Communities: Reflections on the Origin and Spread of Nationalism*. Verso, 2006.

Baishya, Amit R. "The Ethics and Politics of Postcolonial Animalities." *Postcolonial Animalities*. Edited by Suvadip Sinha and Amit R. Baishya. Routledge, 2020, pp. 48–69.

Bazin, Andre. "The Ontology of the Photographic Image." Translated by Hugh Gray. *Film Quarterly*, vol. 13, no. 4, Summer 1960, pp. 4–9.

Bishop, Kyle William. "The New American Zombie Gothic: Road Trips, Globalisation and the War on Terror." *Gothic Studies*, vol. 17, no. 2, Nov. 2015, pp. 42–56.

Boluk, Stephanie, and Wylie Lenz. "Infection, Media, and Capitalism: From Early Modern Plagues to Postmodern Zombies." *Journal for Early Modern Cultural Studies*, vol. 10, no. 2, Fall–Winter 2010, pp. 126–47.

Brooks, Max. *World War Z: An Oral History of the Zombie War*. Three Rivers Press, 2006.

Camus, Albert. *The Plague*. Translated by Stuart Gilbert. Vintage, 1975.

Canetti, Elias. *Crowds and Power*. Translated by Carol Stewart. Farrar, Straus and Giroux, 1984.

Cavarero, Adriana. *Horrorism: Naming Contemporary Violence*. Translated by William McCuaig. Columbia UP, 2011.

Cubitt, Sean. "Preface." In *Digital Contagions: A Media Archeology of Computer Viruses*, edited by Jussi Parrikka, 2nd ed. Peter Lang, 2016, pp. ix–xi.

The Dead Can't Dance. Directed by Rodrick Pocowatchit, 2010.

Defoe, Daniel. *A Journal of the Plague Year*. Edited by Paula R. Backscheider. W.W. Norton and Co., 1992.

Duffy, Enda. *The Speed Handbook: Velocity, Pleasure, Modernism*. Duke UP, 2009.

Ghosh, Amitav. *Gun Island: A Novel*. Farrar, Straus and Giroux, 2019.

Hobbes, Thomas. "De Cive." *marxists.org*. www.marxists.org/reference/subject/philosophy/works/en/decive.htm.

Kolb, Anjuli Fatima Raza. *Epidemic Empire: Colonialism, Contagion, and Terror: 1817–2020*. U of Chicago P, 2020.

Luckhurst, Roger. *Zombies: A Cultural History*. Reaktion Books, 2015.

Marx, Karl. *Capital*. Translated by Ben Fowkes, vol. 1. Vintage, 1977.

Night of the Living Dead. Directed by George Romero, 1968.

Pandey, Gyanendra. "The Long Life of Rumor." *Alternatives: Global, Local, Political*, vol. 27, no. 2, Apr.–June 2002, pp. 165–91.

Resident Evil. Directed by Paul W.S. Anderson, 2002.

Shelley, Mary. *The Last Man*. Wordsworth Classics, 2004.

Sontag, Susan. *Illness as Metaphor and AIDS and Its Metaphors*. Picador, 1990.

Virilio, Paul. *Speed and Politics: An Essay on Dromology*. Translated by Mark Polizzotti. MIT Press, 2006.

Wald, Priscilla. *Contagious: Cultures, Carriers, and the Outbreak Narrative*. Duke UP, 2008.

Winichakul, Thongchai. *Siam Mapped: A History of the Geo-Body of a Nation*. U of Hawaii P, 1997.

World War Z. Directed Marc Foster. Performance by Brad Pitt, 2013.

9

FORGETTING DIFFERENCE

The Plague in Hindi and Urdu Literature

Ishan Mehandru

Writing about Albert Camus' *The Plague* (1947), Edward Said notes that "true also, Arabs die of plague in Oran, but they are not named either, whereas Rieux and Tarrou are pushed forward in the action" (Said 175–76). Said rightly remarks that Camus, while talking about the plague and its effects in vivid detail in the Algerian town of Oran, does not name a single Arabic character. The doctor who is at the centre of this narrative is French, his friends are French, the journalist is French, and of course, the magistrate is also French. As Said notes, however, *The Plague* is still a novel about the deaths of Arabic people – their dire living conditions composing the backdrop of Camus' narrative – even if they remain faceless and nameless shadows for the French writer.

It is no surprise that the body of work available to Camus and succeeding contemporary writers systematically centres on European worldviews and knowledge systems when it comes to understanding the historical trajectories of such epidemics. Nukhet Varlik reasons that there remain large gaps in the scholarship about the plague with regard to its varied existence in the Ottoman Empire and the larger Asian continent. This is not only because within the European mind, plagues were discursively identified as originating from Asia but also because "disease" became a significant terrain over which the representation of oriental and specifically Muslim bodies was charted. Building on preconceived notions of Islamic "fatalism",[1] Muslims were thought of as unscientific, irrational and averse to hygienic practices (Varlık). These gaps contribute to the simplistic typification of certain communities and carry an eerie resemblance to contemporary biopolitical processes (consider, the Islamophobic panic constructed around the term "Corona Jihad" in India by mainstream news media in 2020).

The following chapter will attempt to measure these silences through turning to a differing set of discourses located in the fallouts of a spate of epidemics in early twentieth-century South Asia and specifically, the 1918 influenza pandemic.

DOI: 10.4324/9781003294436-13

Generally claimed to have arrived through the port city of colonial Bombay with the return of soldiers who were deployed to fight in the European trenches of the First World War, the pandemic death count is estimated between twelve to twenty million. This estimate is necessarily wide-ranging because historical records are scathingly limited, governed as this region was by a colonial administration that placed little value on the lives of their non-European subjects beyond economic exigencies (Spinney). By reading an Urdu short story and a Hindi memoir from within the same period, I look at other geographies and take seriously the multivalent effects of colonial history to argue for a political response to contagious phenomena that goes beyond the monoliths of precautionary measures and preventive isolation. A diversification of plague scholarship will not only help uncover non-Western histories of death and disease but demonstrate how these are dynamically understood as differing sites of power and production. Moving "beyond" therefore also demands moving through histories of caste, sexuality and religion that further complicate the business of living and dying. Borrowing from the Italian philosopher Giorgio Agamben and his critics, I will push us to think of the polyvocal histories of states of exception, where certain bodies are made antithetical to the public sphere and yet, prove necessary for its reproduction.[2] How do we declare those dead, whose lives we are only beginning to discover?

Fearing the Other

Rajinder Singh Bedi's short story "Quarantine" was given new life when countries began instituting lockdowns across the world due to the novel Coronavirus pandemic. However, the story itself does not mention the year or the name of the town where it takes place. Perhaps because, when it was first published in 1939, its premise was both widespread and self-evident. Between 1896 and 1921, over thirty million people died in the Indian subcontinent due to outbreaks of epidemics ranging from the bubonic plague and cholera to smallpox and influenza. The response in dealing with these diseases varied, but for a range of reasons – from apprehensions against colonial institutions to religious and caste-based affiliations – many people refused to report that they had been infected. The colonial government, on its part, did not institute a complete lockdown because the loss of labour would incur heavily on the British exchequer. Instead, it commissioned spies to report on families and households suspected of hiding infected members and implemented the "Epidemic Diseases Act" that allowed the government to restrict public movement and incarcerate anyone violating their directives (Spinney).

Translated across blogs, featured in podcasts and adapted for dramatized readings, this story begins by drawing an imagery of movement and stasis: "Like a thick fog that crawls over and blurs everything in the plains lying at the foot of the Himalayas, the terror of plague had spread all over" (Bedi and Singh). "Blurs" is an appropriate description for an epidemic that makes boundaries between disease and treatment uncertain, and for this story's narrator, Dr. Bakshi, the real terror of the plague is not only the threat of death but that of dying in state-enforced quarantine.

The Health and Safety Department put up gigantic posters everywhere instilling the fear of incurring the plague and warning citizens to be wary of rats, while also expanding their injunction to "no rats, no plague, *no quarantine*" (my emphasis). According to the doctor, families would often cover up instances of disease in their households for fear of being sent away to dreadful quarantine facilities.

It is perhaps for this reason that a translation was published in a blog called "Coronablues" with the following note from the translator:

> I have intentionally left the Hindi double honorific and somehow self-humiliating "Babu-ji" untranslated so as to introduce its specific cultural sense, without modifying it . . . "Babu-ji" is the equivalent of "mister" and "sir" at the same time. It marks the unshakable respect that Bhagu displays when he talks to a doctor. This usage has almost disappeared in contemporary India.
>
> *(Singh)*

While the closing claim in this preface can be subject to debate, the story also features William Bhagu, a sanitation worker, whose actions constitute another reason this narrative might feel resonant today. After waking up at three in the morning and drinking half a bottle of alcohol, Bhagu goes out to spray disinfectants in the town's drains. He is one of the few in the town that the doctor observes as "hardly afraid of the plague. Instead, he believed that if death is around, you cannot escape it, wherever you may go". Bhagu displayed, in the doctor's eyes, an unwavering commitment to helping people cope with the plague, by allowing families to stay indoors, carrying out their work and telling them ways to avoid falling sick. The veracity of his recommendations – which include consuming alcohol as a means of precaution – does not seem to bother the doctor. Instead, Bakshi finds himself inspired by Bhagu's efforts to aid the sick in quarantine. Bhagu was the only one who was not apprehensive of embracing the patients, motivating them to have faith in their eventual recovery and mourning the loss of those who could not make it with his tears. This intimacy with sickness is contrasted with the doctor's own regime of precautions, which he undertook with great discipline upon returning home from quarantine, as well as the distance he maintained while treating his patients. Seeing Bhagu's lack of care for self-preservation, the doctor asks, "Bhagu! Aren't you afraid of the plague?"

Perhaps a more accurate translation would be: "Bhagu! Aren't you *at least afraid* of the plague?" Fear seems like the common denominator in all the public responses to the epidemics mentioned earlier. Whether it is the colonial regime's fear for the loss of valuable labour, native fear for being incarcerated by alien invaders, upper-caste fear for mingling with the wrong caste, fear for the domestic privacy and purity of women across religions, or at the very least, the fear of confronting one's own mortality. However, Bhagu is a Dalit, recently converted to Christianity, and as a sanitation worker or a "lower-caste" person, was subject to deal with the unwanted aspects of urbanity even when the plague was not around. He belonged to the part of the town that is at its peripheries, the slums where nobody looked to counter the plague until Dr. Bakshi was inspired to do so by the sight of Bhagu's dying wife. Is fear an adequate lens to understand lives on the precipice of mortality, where vulnerability is an everyday phenomenon?

Bhagu is rendered as a "self"-less object since his actions are always oriented towards someone other than himself. When the doctor learns that Bhagu reported to help at the quarantine facility even though his wife was suffering, he scolds him for his "bravery". Later, as the infection dies down and the town recovers from the ravages of the plague, Dr. Bakshi is offered generous honorariums and felicitated at functions in lieu of his continuous treatment of patients as well as his proactive approach towards tackling the disease in the slums, beyond the government's quarantine facilities. On such occasions, the town's dignitaries heap praise and garlands on the doctor, who "looked this way and that smugly", with immense pride for his efforts and relish for the townspeople's gratitude. Towards the end of the story, he runs into a faint voice offering him a "congratulations" and turns to find Bhagu:

> "Oh, it's you, Bhagu bhai!" I could hardly speak. "The world may not know you, Bhagu, but don't worry, I know you. Your Jesus knows you . . ."
>
> My throat went dry. The image of Bhagu's dying wife and their child flashed before my eyes. It seemed my neck would break under the weight of garlands and my pocket would burst with the weight of my wallet. Despite receiving so much honour, I suddenly felt worthless.
>
> *(Bedi and Singh)*

Bhagu's labour is the story's subject only in as much as his presence proffers Dr. Bakshi the opportunity to evaluate his own self-worth. His status as a Christian South Asian is invoked only so Bhagu can pray to "Jesus" to forgive the sins of humanity and rid them of the plague. In addressing the doctor as "Babu ji" and referring to quarantine as "kontin" (another aural dimension of his character that the translation maintains), we are constantly reminded that for Bhagu, the prospect of treatment was always elusive, at a distance, and disfigured. The quarantine facility is the very "hell" his Christian priest told stories about. When a patient is mistaken dead and thrown in with the deceased to be burnt alive, Bhagu tries saving him but is unsuccessful. Bhagu's experiences confirm what the doctor can only narrate: "the plague was deadly but the quarantine was even deadlier".

Bhagu's labour is acknowledged within the story, albeit without an audience (in Bakshi's own words, the world does not know Bhagu), highlighting both how the exception comes into being and how it remains a diffuse phenomenon. Within the forgotten stories of epidemics in early twentieth-century South Asia, Bhagu's narrative remains doubly obscured. Bedi's story is therefore a fantasy beyond fiction: he narrates the experiences of a worker absent from archival recollection but negotiates another historical impasse – the reality of double neglect with a desire for being humbled in the face of one's active disavowal. His sentimental tribute to Bhagu offers a self-narration of compensatory regard that is itself unacknowledged, an exceptional occurrence invisible to the public sphere. In India, for instance, the number of dead during the 1896 epidemic was increased manifold, because of "the demand by the upper castes to have separate hospitals and their refusal to receive medical assistance from the lower caste peoples" (Mohan and Dwivedi). Bedi's story highlights that for workers such as Bhagu, the exceptional experience was notably normative – or rather, the normalcy Bhagu ensured in others was constituted by his own exceptional circumstances. Bhagu "allows" families to stay indoors because his labour precludes the possibility of publicly desiring safety. The plague does not germinate a state of exception: instead, exceptional circumstances afford the plague the opportunity to reach its pre-existing patients.

Fearful Desires

Kulli Bhat [translated as *A Life Misspent* (2016)] is not a text that centres itself around the plague, yet death haunts it throughout. As Suryakant Tripathi "Nirala" writes in the very beginning, it was not until Kulli Bhat's death that he was able to find a suitable subject for writing a biography. Published the same year as Bedi's "Quarantine", it was named after Nirala's friend and the inspiration behind the text. But in 2016, the translated title in English suggests something else entirely – whose life is misspent? Less a biography of someone else, the translator Satti Khanna suggests that Nirala gives us an autobiography, a memoir and reflection on his own life and misadventures, in relation to that of Kulli's. Already the demarcation between the self and the other, between one's life and another's death, is being rendered unstable.

From its beginning then, *Kulli Bhat* is an unlikely biography, with an unlikely subject and even when it deals with matters of mortality and greatness, Nirala declares that "the tone of the book is comic. It would be good if people did not take offence at it and thereby reveal their inadequacy as readers" (Nirala and Khanna, Preface). Why this disclaimer? Perhaps because Nirala wants to pull at the strings of the world of Hindi literature to which this memoir is addressed. Kulli is an unknown figure who lived in a rural out-of-the-way province, a corner of the country that not many are bothered with. Nirala is convinced that the only person who might have been able to truly understand Kulli's worth was the Soviet writer Gorky – an impossible prospect perhaps, and therefore, it would have been Kulli's destiny to die in relative obscurity. The memoir will save his friend from the doom of non-remembrance but, in detailing his life, also shine light on what is intentionally unseen by the world of Hindi literature (or the Hindi-speaking belt in Northern India). If Dr. Bakshi's chronicling of a sanitation worker offers a figure that is less human and more symbolic, Nirala's account of his friend constructs Kulli's humanity as the limit against which the nexus of sexuality, caste and religion visibly fails.

Much like "Quarantine", the plague in this memoir rages without chronological specifics that would otherwise make it useful for epidemiological research. Instead, the passing mention of different epidemics sets a structural background against which the organization of social life gets tested – first, to be reified and subsequently, to be rendered diffuse. Nirala begins his memoir by recalling the time he got married and "the plague was raging" in his family's village (Chapter 3). Keeping in mind the exigencies of an epidemic, his father-in-law had fetched his daughter with great haste, and this practical-minded approach left Nirala's family quite offended. As was custom, they had already abandoned house and were living in a nearby orchard to avoid the plague; however, this did not necessarily imply that rituals and ceremonies be conducted without proper regard. Nirala is sent to fetch his bride again and instructed to make sure that he is treated with great pomp and reverence as befits his caste status as a Brahmin.

The first time he visits his wife's village is also his first meeting with Kulli. If the purpose of Nirala's trip is to reinstate the proper order of things and reiterate the importance of custom and kinship, then Kulli's introduction makes this task trickier. It was "hard to tell" from the way he dressed if Kulli was Muslim or Hindu, but Nirala proceeds to accept his offer of a ride anyway (Chapter 3). At his bride's home, seeing his mother-in-law's reaction to Kulli, Nirala assumes that his new friend was an "untouchable", a Dalit, or someone who belonged to the lower end of the caste hierarchy. However, in his drive to defy "restrictions when they lacked all reason", Nirala accedes to a growing familiarity with Kulli (Chapter 6). In an episode of great confusion though, his self-perception as a social crusader is shattered when Nirala discovers that Kulli's desire for him is not rooted in social legitimacy but sexual intimacy. This rude awakening pushes Nirala to leave his wife's village behind and return to his studies. His wilfulness reassures the mother-in-law who, though "worried about the plague", is glad that he is thinking about the "future" (Chapter 8).

The plague's impertinence then, its disruption of tradition, becomes an occasion for Nirala to be sent on a mission to assert it more forcefully. But Kulli becomes a kink in the social structures that Nirala and his family inhabit, leaving things further unsettled. It is difficult to slot Kulli into this social order based on his appearance, difficult to specify his caste based on others' reactions and difficult to refuse his desires because they lack clear articulation. We leave Kulli confused and annoyed at Nirala's obtuse behaviour because neither of them clearly knows what the other wants.

The "future" is therefore muddied already. The onward-looking determination with which Nirala proceeds to maintain boundaries of reproductive normativity is cast by the disquieting shadow of his interaction with Kulli. A few years later, Nirala receives a telegram: "Your wife is gravely ill. Come immediately" (Chapter 9), though a more honest translation might be: "Your wife is gravely ill. Come to bid your last goodbyes". The influenza epidemic has reached India by this time. Nirala's father passed away the year before. By the time he reaches his wife, she too has succumbed to death. His cousin who had come to look after Nirala's wife is already sick and dies soon after. Back home, his uncle contracts influenza as well. He looks at Nirala and asks, "what madness brought you here?" Soon, his sister-in-law passes away and is followed by her nursing child:

> Words cannot describe how pitiful the scene was, how helpless, how tender. But I had no tenderness left after the death of my wife and my cousin . . . this

was the strangest time in my life. My family disappeared in the blink of an eye.
All our sharecroppers and labourers died, the four who worked for my cousin
as well as the two who worked for me . . . In whichever direction I turned,
I saw darkness.

(Chapter 9)

In a few short paragraphs, the deadly pandemic appears before us and leaves just as
quickly. It seems that by recalling the devastating phenomenon in this staccato and
blunt prose, Nirala foreshadows the manner in which historical archives and official
responses will eventually erase the flu's impact. As he passes by, the Ganga appears
swollen with bodies of the dead. He stares at corpses flowing along the turns of the
river, thinking "of the ascetic sadhus, sometimes of the ephemerality of the world"
(Chapter 9), when Kulli reappears in his life. The plague's devastation also marks
a traumatic point of tonal departure for the memoir, as the "comic" confusions of
their first meeting give into a more meditative strain in Nirala's authorial voice. His
relationship with Kulli takes on a new shape and as a "true friend", Kulli's words
offer great solace to Nirala's troubled heart (Chapter 9).

The disjunction between the two halves of the text (pre- and post-influenza
epidemic) is also marked by a shift in focus to the simultaneous growth of Kulli's
character. From an ostracized presence within the Brahmanical social order, Kulli
becomes a willing rebel. He is keen to set the stage for an anti-colonial movement by campaigning for the Indian National Congress; and in a bid to perform
social welfare, opens a school for "untouchable" children. However, this transition
does not affect his social status as much as heighten its peculiarity. Kulli marries
a Muslim woman (after seeking his friend's approval) and, in so doing, upsets the
gatekeepers of religious belonging whom even Nirala has begun to view with due
scepticism. The disturbing presence of a ravaging plague makes its way into the
foreground as Kulli's body becomes frail and weak. His saintly status as a social
reformer corresponds with a degenerating physical state – diagnosed with a "venereal disease" he lies on his deathbed.

With nobody willing to contribute to Kulli's medical expenses, this sorry state
of affairs causes great anger and disappointment in Nirala. But the conditions of
Kulli's death ["his genital organ is missing" (Chapter 15)] are resolutely amusing for
the rest of the village. The memoir has traced a circular journey: if at its beginning
Kulli was a troublesome sight for Hindu upper-caste masculinity, then towards the
end, he remains an uneasy outlier for a nationalist masculinity. His association with
"untouchable" children and a Muslim woman is a marker of his location in discourses of social marginalization, for this intimacy shatters the illusion of the public
space which is built upon forceful exclusions.

In 1868, the British government had introduced the Contagious Diseases Act
to regulate sexual liaisons between soldiers in the British cantonment and Muslim
and Dalit women. These laws enabled the colonial regime to bring the Muslim "public woman" under their surveillance, on the pretext of controlling the
spread of venereal diseases. Legal discourses such as these cast a longer shadow
on late colonial India while stigmatizing the "public woman", the "prostitute" or

the Muslim tawa'if (Waheed). Charu Gupta, in her study of instructional manuals written primarily for upper-caste and middle-class women in colonial North India, points out that the Dalit woman became a similarly constitutive footnote in the construction of a nationalist domestic space. Portrayed variously as "loud", "sexualized" and "dirty", the Dalit woman was shown to be a potentially corrupt influence on a virile nationalist masculinity (Gupta). While the rhetoric of general upliftment sits well within mainstream Congress narratives, the categories that need uplifting are simultaneously marked as the antithetical others or the disease carriers. Consequently, Kulli is pushed to the periphery of a respectable anti-colonial politics because his "evolution" does not provide a neat break from complicated histories of exploitative inter-relatedness.

Deceit and Difference

When he first comes to fetch his bride, Nirala's mother-in-law relates a tale of a mythical demon who fooled a God by pretending to be a "well-educated Brahmin" (Chapter 5). Her intent is to forewarn her son-in-law against Kulli's deceitful nature. However, Nirala's memoir suggests otherwise. He takes us further down memory lane to the time of his sacred thread ceremony that would confer his status as a Brahmin progeny. His father had forbidden him from remaining friends with a family of four children whose caste status is questionable, but Nirala chose to ignore his father's advice and risk communal excommunication by being a part of the ceremony and continuing to share food with his friends. Nirala's firm faith in a proto-nationalist vision that wishes to leave behind unreasonable "restrictions" is the presumed basis of his friendship with Kulli. Even though it will be Nirala who is surprised and taken aback by Kulli's desires, it was always the former who was being deceitful.

In her critical introduction to postcolonial theory, Leela Gandhi writes of the dilemma of "post-coloniality". The independent nation-state has to contend with "its political and chronological derivation from colonialism, on the one hand, and its cultural obligation to be meaningfully inaugural and inventive on the other" (Gandhi 6). The "neat break" that Kulli denies through his continuing closeness with the exceptional undercurrents of a nationalist imaginary makes him an ambiguous and troubling site for the Hindi-speaking world (Nirala and Khanna, Chapter 2). Even while its presence gets recorded in the form of a memoir by his poet-friend, Kulli's body does not conform to the collective deceitfulness where the end of colonialism implies the emergence of a promised "inaugural" future.

Returning to Bedi's story in the light of the ongoing Coronavirus pandemic is another way through which we might helpfully disrupt the myth of the future that had supposedly been invented anew. The Epidemic Diseases Act that compelled doctors to inform authorities about new infections, for instance, was put to use by the Indian government recently to clamp down against dissenters protesting their majoritarian legislations.[3] The continuity between a colonial regime and its decolonized progeny undercuts any easy understanding of linear progress while also positing a complicated history of differing exclusions. While Bedi's story attempts a fantastical reconciliation between the centre of the public sphere (the doctor decorated with accolades) and what it unsees (the undesirable yet necessary labour of the sanitation worker), it really brings to fore the narrative anxieties of Bakshi's guilty outburst. His account of Bhagu does not penetrate the lives we continue to ignore in our concern for health and safety but prescriptively conjures a figure whose miseries outline the spaces Bakshi occupies. If the fear of a plague that spreads like a fog renders normative distinctions unstable, then the portraiture of Bhagu's "sacrifice" helps reinscribe these boundaries.

In this chapter, I read a couple of texts to argue that experiences of death and disease are oriented differently along communal, gendered and caste-based lines. While tackling epidemics pushes us towards adopting regimes of exception, such measures operate endlessly in many instances. For instance, responding to Agamben's recent comments on the measures adopted by European governments to counter the ongoing pandemic, Shaj Mohan and Divya Dwivedi argued that "India has for long been full of exceptional peoples, making meaningless the notion of 'state of exception' or of 'extending' it". Their own suggestion is that the experience of vulnerability produced in the throes of a pandemic will enable us to "attend to each life as precious" – where we consider the "non-exceptionality of exceptions" (Mohan and Dwivedi). Merely discovering new texts and new terrains of experience does not necessitate the route towards justice, as much as enable us to see how violence is reproduced. How do contemporary notions of distancing and nearness, intimacy and untouchability, and sanitation and pollution change when we read these texts? How does the act of translation help us in foregrounding culturally diffused perceptions of death and treatment? It is interesting, for instance, that Rajinder Singh Bedi's story is published as "Quarantine" and "Plague and Quarantine" across different platforms. It should remind us that for a sanitation worker such as Bhagu, the difference between the two is not as rigid – what saves some people, kills others.

Notes

1   Consider Daniel Defoe, *A Journal of the Plague Year* (1722): "Then he proceeded to tell me of the mischievous consequences which attended the presumption of the Turks and Mahometans in Asia . . . and how, presuming upon their professed predestinating notions, and of every man's end being predetermined and unalterably beforehand decreed, they would go unconcerned into infected places and converse with infected persons, by which means they died at the rate of ten or fifteen thousand a week, whereas the Europeans or Christian merchants, who kept themselves retired and reserved, generally escaped the contagion".

2   See Agamben, *State of Exception*; Mbembe, *Necropolitics*; Weheliye, *Habeas Viscus: Racializing Assemblages, Biopolitics, and Black Feminist Theories of the Human.*

3   See Ajoy Ashirwad Mahaprashasta. *Outrage as Adityanath Govt Uses Epidemic Diseases Act to Arrest CAA Dissenter*, 27 Mar. 2020. https://thewire.in/rights/ashish-mittal-epidemic-act-uttar-pradesh. Accessed 9 Dec. 2020.

Works Cited

Agamben, Giorgio. *State of Exception*. University of Chicago Press, 2005.

Bedi, Rajinder Singh, and Madhu Singh. "Quarantine★ (Translation: Rajinder Singh Bedi)." *Coronablues*, n.d. https://coronabluescollective.wordpress.com/2020/07/11/quarantine/. Accessed 9 Dec. 2020.

Gandhi, Leela. *Postcolonial Theory: A Critical Introduction*. Cambridge UP, 2019.

Gupta, Charu. "(Mis)representing the Dalit Woman: Reifying Gender and Caste Sterotypes in the Hindi Didactic Literature of Colonial India." *The Indian Historical Review*, 2008, pp. 101–24.

Mbembe, Achille. *Necropolitics*. Duke University Press, 2019.

Mohan, Shaj, and Divya Dwivedi. "On Pandemics. Nancy, Dwivedi, Mohan, Esposito, Nancy, Ronchi." *European Journal of Psychoanalysis*, 8 Mar. 2020. www.journal-psychoanalysis.eu/on-pandemics-nancy-esposito-nancy/. Accessed 5 May 2021.

Nirala, Suryakant Tripathi, and Satti Khanna. *A Life Misspent*. Harper Collins, 2016. Ebook.

Said, Edward. *Culture and Imperialism*. Knopf, 1994.

Singh, Madhu. "Quarantine★ (Translation: Rajinder Singh Bedi)." *Corona Blues Collective*, 11 July 2020, Blog Post. Accessed 30 Oct. 2021.

Spinney, Laura. "Vital Statistics: How the Spanish Flu of 1918 Changed India." *The Caravan Magazine*, 18 Oct. 2018, Internet. https://caravanmagazine.in/history/spanish-flu-1918-changed-india. Accessed 5 May 2021.

Varlık, Nükhet. "Rethinking the History of the Plague in the Time of Coronavirus." *Alwaleed Webinar*, 29 May 2020. Video. https://islamicstudies.harvard.edu/news/rethinking-history-plague-time-coronavirus-n%C3%BCkhet-varl%C4%B1k. Accessed 5 May 2021.

Waheed, Sarah. "Women of 'Ill Repute': Ethics and Urdu literature in Colonial India." *Modern Asian Studies*, 2014, pp. 986–1023.

Weheliye, Alexander G. *Habeas Viscus: Racializing Assemblages Biopolitics and Black Feminist Theories of the Human*. Duke UP, 2014.

10

THE PERIWIG MAKER AND DEFOE

A *Déjà vu* Upon the Present

Sanghita Sanyal

Since the end of 2019, as the world is shaken to its core, due to the raging Corona-virus pandemic, we have had more reasons than one to go back into history and dig out records and perceptions around epidemics and their causes, immediate impacts and after-effects. When humanity is threatened by a mass-destructive wave then such categorical information supply us with a rich, empirical, data-driven resource about a past, which helps to negotiate with the present and shape a future from the debris of a fraught civilization. That is why, all over history, writings and records on pandemics are newly getting revived, their significance is realized afresh, because they start to make more sense, with respect to our current situation. Then, it feels utterly bizarre to see how history repeats itself each time, and humanity finds out plausible ways to negotiate with it.

One such text that has widely been re-read during the past two years is Daniel Defoe's *The Journal of the Plague Year* (1772) that vividly records The Great Plague of London in 1665 and has been the focus of many critical readings and popular cul-ture adaptations. One such manifestation has been *The Periwig Maker* ("*Der Perück-enmacher*" – 1999) a stop-motion puppet animation film, scripted and designed by Steffen Schäeffler. This chapter examines a close analysis of the film and its theme as a part adaptation of the "pseudo-historical" novel of Defoe as it is considered to be. Also, this chapter would attempt to connect the film and Defoe's text to nar-rate the historical pandemic (both fictional and historical) vividly and play with the imagination and reality so skilfully that we start to understand the various global crises induced by COVID-19 almost in the manner of a *déjà vu* or precognition. In this context, I would also refer to some articles like Maximillian E. Novak's "Defoe and the Disordered City", F. Bastian's "Defoe's *The Journal of the Plague Year* Revisited", W. Austin Flanders' "Defoe's *Journal of the Plague Year* and the Modern Urban Experience" and a few other critical interventions to justify how much real

DOI: 10.4324/9781003294436-14

and fictional Defoe's account was, and through the film in focus, how both became vital interferences in shaping current studies in pandemic literature.

The Periwig Maker (1999)

The Periwig Maker, a short film in English that is set in 1665 London, edges on the Gothic – its script and dialogue are uncannily similar to what we have been seeing all over the media every day since COVID-19 hit the world as one of the biggest blows to humanity. The pandemic reminds us that every day we faced a newness of experience that we never had, but shortly after, we realized that it was all known through human history. So, in a way, although the pandemic is like a never-before experience, yet it is like a *déjà vu*, rattling us with a number of questions that are ubiquitous and still remains unanswered. As Schäeffler himself notes,

> Besides its story about the plague and how every epidemic changes people's behaviour, *The Periwig-Maker* asks some philosophical questions. It deals with the problem of responsibility for other people and for yourself: can you do wrong, when you do nothing.[1]

The film in focus, set in London, September 1665, portrays this moral question and its psycho-emotional repercussion graphically through a periwig maker who shuts himself indoors for days and saves himself from the plague. However, he watches the dead bodies around his home and neighbourhood being carried out with a kind of dispassion out of helpless acceptance which is only possible when humanity's very existence is threatened and no one knows what awaits.

He diligently records them and his views and thoughts in a journal. He notes in his narration: "death bells tolling night and day, the plague rages dreadfully and the weekly bill of mortality must be higher than ever".[2] Things are worse when the periwig-maker watches from his window that a small girl-child in the closest home across the street, is left all alone and helpless, as her plague-hit mother's dead body is carried out by the morticians. With no cortège to accompany, as the body is being taken away, the child tries to go closer to her mother when one of the men pushes her away. The child is worn, perhaps hungry when she intently tries to escape the home and seeks help from the periwig maker, peeping through his window, time and again. He escapes the situation with the same dispassion mingled with fear that is everyman's essence of dilemma and moral tribulations at that time, but his attention is fixed to the thick hair of the girl, each time he sees her, beyond the window.

In the next few scenes, one of the men eventually catches hold of the little girl and shuts her off in her home by putting wooden bars as deadbolts, so that the girl cannot escape; in a way, the girl is left to die there alone finally. Among the various subtle images, that of rats running around the dark alley is very evocative, brilliantly symbolic, signifying death looming large, in its miniscule yet sure footsteps. At night, the narrator-periwig maker has a vision like a precognition that the child stands at a distance and in a tone of accepted doom tells him about her imminent death: "Are you disturbed by me, then I'll go home and die there". The haunted tone of the words sounds like some eerie voice of conscience that can plague an individual from within. Her words are ringing with irony, as the conscience of the man is only thinking of her thick, red hair. In the morning, he again watches from his window, this time the push cart is carrying away the child now dead, to the cadavers' dug hole.

What follows is evocative of man's contradictory self that often denies what can be termed as human. The periwig maker, who has never stepped out of his home to escape the plague, ironically, is seen to go to the cadavers' pit where there are heaps of plague-hit dead bodies. He steps down the ladder, into the hole and unfurls the body of that child only to cut her hair, so that he can make a periwig out of it. The top shot of this trench with the child's body among the heap of corpses and the wig-maker's unscrupulous attempt to cut the red hair remains one of the creepiest scenes of the film – as if the detached world (viewers), sees from outside, how low a human can stoop!

The periwig maker is seen next at his working desk, weaving a wig and coughing. The film closes with a note of ambiguity – with the view of the man sick on his bed, with a red-haired peruke on his head, with his wide eyes listlessly looking, lost and reflecting a mind "addled by encroaching madness or disease".[3] At this point, the narrator continues to sit on his bed and brood, while a voice like oracle says:

> so in the plague it came to such violence that the people sat still looking at one another and seemed quite abandoned to despair – but the near-view of death would soon reconcile men, one to another so that another plague year would reconcile all differences; and close conversing with death would scum off the gall from our tempers, remove the animosity among us and bring us to see with different eyes than those with which we looked on to things before.[4]

This long speech feels precarious and ironic. On the one hand, it surely rings of an optimism about how death is a great leveller, and how it brings all to a rung of equivalence, as humanity suffers to realize, that nothing else matters more than the sheer desire to live and the fear to die. Human beings, in their selfish urge to survive, have to give in finally to the deepest conscience that plays within, and wreaks the soul. The periwig maker is showing clear signs of madness and this narration of realization comes as an irony at this hour when he has lost his mind.

Defoe's Novel: History Versus Fiction

The periwig maker who is the film's protagonist and narrator is cast with close resemblance to H.F., that is, Defoe's narrator. As a visual adaptation of Defoe's novel, *The Periwig Maker* can also be perceived as a newly emerging pandemic-captivity narrative, as a sub-genre of trauma literature, where the trauma inflicted upon humanity may not have a political grounding, but is completely based on natural (or man-made, medical) calamity or catastrophe. Like every such corpus of literature that records disturbance, suffering, anxiety, hopelessness, dejection and even hopefulness too, this kind of redolent texts would reflect the dichotomy of life during the catastrophe from various planes and angles and feature-rich ironies of life, like free existence within the space of home, the anxiety of contagion and death, the comfort of home, the anxiety of profession and subsistence and such other contradictions. They would open up a layer of deep psychological repercussions that come from being captive, claustrophobic and panic-stricken about both life and death. In them, everyday life, of rich or poor, is as dark and scary as the dimension and unfamiliarity of death is.

Although Daniel Defoe had experienced the 1665 plague of London as an infant, his fiction in the form of a journal was written almost about 55 years after the historical devastation, specifically when the Plague revived in 1722, around Marseilles and spread considerably, despite strict precautions. The *Journal* serves as a ubiquitous pandemic narrative besides Samuel Pepys' *Diary* and Gibbons' *History*, offering "a different view of human life under the stress of the plague", to quote M.E. Novak from his essay "Defoe and the Disordered City" (241). Despite its historical accuracy questioned and efforts made to establish it more as an adapted historical account than a fictional narrative, *The Journal of the Plague Year* recounts and gives a kind of magnified validity to the human sufferings by describing it objectively as well as like an insider experiencing it (like H.F.'s own personal account) and the events have true bearings, far from being imagined. Contextually, we can also quote W. Austin Flanders from his article "Defoe's *Journal of the Plague Year* and the Modern Urban Experience":

> Dread and anxiety are the central emotions examined in the work. In the early pages of the *Journal* Defoe discusses the alternations of hope and fear that beset Londoners after the first threat of plague and conveys a growing sense of insecurity as the plague visibly worsens. One does not have to have lived under a threat of plague to empathize with this feeling; it is a principal emotional condition of city life and is widely exploited in popular literature written for the now pervasive urban mentality.
>
> *(331)*

It packs the psycho-emotional stress more accurately in between the lines, which constitutes a subtle history of human suffering behind the mere statistics and its later adaptations, *The Periwig Maker* being one of them completely lives up to what Flanders notes. It was said, when plague struck, "The Father abandon'd the Child, and the Son the Father; the Husband the Wife, and the Wife the Husband" (Novak 241). Death looms too big on the city in complete disorder and is reflected everywhere, as Defoe caught in everyman the "death in his face" (*JPY* 74) we identify that in Schäeffler's film too. Death is not just in the fearful, resigned eyes of the child, but also in the unblinking wide, ocular eyes of the periwig maker, that catches the insecurity and anxiety of captivity and death even in the most economic rhetoric of the short film.

Defoe notes in his *Journal*, "there was no other way of Burials" which is portrayed through the cadavers' pit in the film. Audiences in the post-2020 world would find it like a precognition as our own experiences of the COVID-affected corpses wrapped in unidentifiable, inaccessible plastic would be taken in bulk to the specially constructed crematoriums. Terror strikes those who are living. It is the sheer imagination of the "indecency" and undesirability of such painful death and the failure to bid a fitting farewell to the dead that injects fear and an epiphanic moment, which Defoe cogently verbalized as follows:

> the burials in the plague pits were full of Terror, the Cart had in it sixteen or seven- teen Bodies . . . the Indecency much to any one else, seeing they were all dead, and were to be huddled together into the common Grave of Mankind, as we may call it, for here was no Difference made, but Poor and Rich went together.
>
> *(55)*

It is this objectivity in H.F. that Novak observes that makes him probably "the first fictional narrator whose sympathies embrace even the swarming poor of the city" (241) and points, "what distinguishes Defoe's narrative is its remarkable concern for the ordinary man and his anguish as the city struggled to survive". He claims "no narrator in realistic prose fiction before H. F. reveals this type of general sympathy for the human condition" and in that way "experience to have the kind of combination of sympathy and detachment to be found in H.F" through whom "Defoe wanted to spread feelings of hope and charity" (250), exactly like the final words in the film, quoted earlier in this chapter.

As debates proliferated about the authenticity of Defoe's accounts, especially because of the very hazy identity of a mysterious narrator H.F. who, as F. Bastian stated in his article, was none other than his uncle Henry Foe,

> who was an unmarried saddler, of Northamptonshire origin, who lived Botolph, Aldgate, on the north side of the High between the parish church and Whitechapel Bars, London throughout the Plague, serving for a while in the precinct in which he lived.
>
> *(158)*

However, drawing upon F. Bastian's article, we cannot discount his words of conviction:

> Fiction implies the invention of incident and the creation of character. We have seen that the characters and incidents once confidently asserted to be the products of Defoe's fertile imagination, repeatedly prove to have been factual. Some residue of invented detail there certainly must be in the *Journal,*

but it is small and inessential. It is of course true that all fictional writing must grow from the real or vicarious experience of the writer, but the essence of creative writing is the transmutation of this experience. Defoe, in the *Journal* at least, constantly strives towards the factual. The *Journal* thus stands closer to our idea of history than to that of fiction. Many confident judgements have been the real character of the *Journal of the Plague Year*, ranging from "authentic history" to "absolute fiction". In the end we cannot greatly improve upon Sir Walter Scott's opinion that it was "one of that peculiar class of writing which hovers between history and romance".

(172–73)

This long explanatory defense justifies where exactly lies the significance of the two texts in our contemporary context.

The Universality of Suffering

With mostly black-and-white scenes, and the incorporation of a few coloured ones signifying the warmth of home catapulted against the dark, filthy, blind alleys; the shut doors and windows, silence and emptiness, minimal exchange of thoughts between men, their ominous gestures and nods, screams of a child, the gravediggers, the child peeping through the window, the singular blotch of ink expanding itself, an empty boat tied to the bank of the dark waters, the mound of dead at the far edge of a city, are sinister and evocative registers of humanity's suffering and helplessness in the face of imminent death; and that feeling is now no more limited to historical records or are figments of fictions – it is a reality we have been living. A constant fear of falling sick, panic over symptoms, long hours of brooding over the menacing chances of contracting the disease which would mean death, depression and claustrophobic reactions to be locked inside home blend with the sheer anxiety of how to survive and subsist while one is still clinically alive. Man is feeling death every moment and instead of relishing the blessedness of being alive, life at a point feels to be a burden, where death is surer and perhaps therefore, easier. The film raises these questions as the periwig maker eventually shows signs of psychological trauma and breakdown and goes out to get the child's hair, driven by the sheer suicidal urge to subsist and live, in hindsight, losing his humane essence. Yet the final soliloquy-like words that are perhaps his resounding conscience ring of a hope that through this phase, man would realize the significance of life and learn to see things differently.

To conclude this chapter on how Defoe's novel *The Periwig Maker* churns ripples into our contemporary COVID-affected life in the clearest of terms, Daniel Gordon's observation seems notable in his article "The City and the Plague in the Age of Enlightenment", where he says that not all calamity might be recorded with as much intensity and earnestness and he gives example of how Europe failed to record much of the influenza pandemic of 1918–19, "which killed more than twenty millions" because perhaps although modern literature drew attention to disaster, it could not "accommodate too many paradigms of evils at once" (69). However, on the other hand, we may also choose to derive from Felix Vodička's theory of "concretization" as summarized by Robert Mayer in his article "The Reception of *A Journal Of The Plague Year* and the Nexus of Fiction and History in the Novel" that somewhat refutes this point of Gordon. He explains:

> For Vodička, concretization is "the reflection of a work in the conscious-ness of those for whom it is an aesthetic object". He clearly thinks of such reflections-of which there can be many, although the nature of any concre-tization is controlled both by "the properties of the work" itself and by "the period's literary requirements"-largely in terms of the application of prevail-ing "literary values".
>
> *(532–33)*

Mayer quotes Vodička further "that after a certain hesitation caused by the nov-elty of the work, it is accepted into literature in a certain concretized appearance" which endures until "a new concretization is recorded and publicized".

If we superimposed this observation on Defoe and Schäeffler's film, the latter, by drawing completely upon the former, re-/concretizes each other in the con-temporary context of suffering, anxiety as well as hopefulness, where literature and film reflecting similar or same turmoil and tribulations and insecurities rise way beyond their singular historical/aesthetic value. It is more like a psychic identifica-tion with fellow sufferers across time and space.

Notes

1 Schäeffler, Steffen. www.awn.com/oscars01/animperiwig.php3. Accessed 20 Jan. 2022.
2 Schäeffler, Steffen. *The Periwig-Maker*. Film. Germany: The Mills Studios. 1999. www.youtube.com/watch?v=DpLo7DW8hwM. Accessed 10 Dec. 2021.
3 From an anonymous viewer's comment. https://letterboxd.com/film/the-periwig-maker/details/. Accessed 20 Jan. 2022.
4 *The Periwig-Maker*. Film.

Works Cited

Bastian, F. "Defoe's *The Journal of the Plague Year* Revisited." *The Review of English Studies*, vol. 16, no. 62, May 1965, pp. 151–73. www.jstor.org/stable/513101. Accessed 10 Jan. 2022.
Defoe, Daniel. *A Journal of the Plague Year*. Hatchett India, 1999.
Flanders, W.A. "Defoe's *Journal of the Plague Year* and the Modern Urban Experience." *The Centennial Review*, vol. 16, no. 4, 1972, pp. 328–48. www.jstor.org/stable/23737835. Accessed 12 Jan. 2022.
Gordon, Daniel. "The City and the Plague in the Age of Enlightenment." *Yale French Stud-ies, Exploring the Conversible World: Text and Sociability from the Classical Age to the Enlight-enment*, no. 92, 1997, pp. 67–87. www.jstor.org/stable/2930387. Accessed 10 Jan. 2022.
Mayer, Robert. "The Reception of *A Journal of the Plague Year* and the Nexus of Fiction and History in the Novel." *ELH*, vol. 57, no. 3, 1990, pp. 529–55. www.jstor.org/stable/2873233. Accessed 10 Jan. 2022.

Novak, E. Maximillian. "Defoe and the Disordered City." *PMLA Journal*, vol. 92, no. 2, 1977, pp. 241–51. www.jstor.org/stable/461944. Accessed 20 Jan. 2022.

Schäeffler, Steffen. *The Periwig-Maker*. Film. The Mills Studios, 1999.

———. *Comments on the Periwig Maker*. www.awn.com/oscars01/animperiwig.php3. Accessed 20 Jan. 2022.

———. *The Periwig-Maker*. Web Comments. https://letterboxd.com/film/the-periwig-maker/details/. Accessed 20 Jan. 2022.

IV

Fear, Disaster and Dystopia

11

PESTILENCE, DEATH, FEAR AND A TESTIMONY OF FEMALE OUTRAGE

The 1897 Bombay Plague in the Writing of Pandita Ramabai

Subarna Bhattacharya

In the historiography of colonial India, medical catastrophes mark an important area of study. There were several outbreaks of epidemics in colonial India since as early as the seventeenth century, cholera and smallpox being the most reported. Among these outbreaks of epidemics, the plague that happened in Bombay in 1896–97 is noteworthy, especially because of the deep anti-colonial, anti-imperialist sentiments it triggered. In the earlier instances of epidemics, state interventions had always been minimal. Firstly, there was the generally non-interfering attitude shown by the State, fearing the public opposition that it may arouse, and then, there was also the reluctance to spend on public health. However, during the Bombay plague years, the colonial government launched a series of stringent measures to control the spread of the epidemic, which resulted in far-reaching racial, caste and communal tensions in the colonial subjects. The British medical journals and public health reports of the time abounded with entries on the 1896–97 Bombay plague, enumerating the rising mortality rates and the preventive measures that the plague committee implemented. However, in order to understand the stark complexities that the situation gave rise to, one probably needs to consider reading some of the other writings, beyond the official reports, which sought to textualize the histories of the time.

A reference to the dreadful scourge occurred in many contemporary Western narratives on India. Among them, a significant one was by George Lambert, an American Mennonite missionary traveller who happened to visit India, in 1897, to oversee the relief operations of his organization. His book called *India: The Horror-stricken Empire* (1898) portrayed how the country, during 1896–97, was devastated by multiple natural disasters one after another – the famine, the plague and the earthquake. Talking about the plague, Lambert said Bombay looked like a city gripped with fear. The streets, now, at night-time, looked like a deserted village. A city, which used to be as noisy at night as it was during the daytime, was suddenly put to a dead sleep, with rows of empty houses, marked on their gates with the dreadful plague

DOI: 10.4324/9781003294436-16

mark, notifying that the disease had claimed lives residing in them. Sometimes, fire burning in front of a door indicated the presence of the disease in the house, and in some places, the shanties were deliberately burnt down to prevent spread. Lambert's Western gaze analysed the whole crisis as a problem primarily caused by heathenism and primitivism. Praising generously the Empire's capacity for good governance, he saw even the colonial government's most coercive plague control measures as necessary to combat the ignorant and unruly behaviour of the natives. Thus, like most missionary writings on colonies, what lies embedded in Lambert's evangelical text, narrativizing the crisis, is certainly a discourse of race and imperialism.

In such a context, when most textualized accounts of the Bombay plague came in the form of testimonies marked by Western imperialism, Pandita Ramabai's writing on the Bombay plague is an interesting subversive reading of the chilling history of the time. Ramabai, a firebrand women's rights activist and a social worker of contemporary Maharashtra, was already carrying out rescue operations for famine victims, when the plague broke out in 1896. In 1897, she wrote a letter to *The Bombay Guardian* fiercely criticizing the actions of the colonial government.[1] As a bold condemnation of the colonial government's handling of the plague crisis, the "Letter" enumerated some unnerving details of the women plague victims' plight and miseries; how, often with no special wards for women, the public hospitals and segregation camps were places which, instead of protecting the women patients' modesty, were actually exposing them to sexual threats. Such an accusation on the government's plague management system created an immediate furore. Soon more controversies sparked surrounding the "Letter", which eventually had far-reaching implications. Understandably, the nationalist tone of the "Letter" was not looked upon favourably by the imperial State, and it brought on her charges of sedition.

The Bombay plague years offer an interesting historical reading particularly because the historiography is formed of conflicting narratives. The narratives countered each other through contrary pictures of the time they sought to archive. While Western missionary writings, such as Lambert's, in spite of being evangelical texts, implicitly served the agenda of the Empire, Ramabai's writing, in the "Letter", added to the time's nationalist narrative. Reading George Lambert's book, *India: The Horror-stricken Empire* and Pandita Ramabai's "Letter", as positing two contrary positions in the colonial historiography of the Bombay plague years, my efforts, here, are to reflect on how this agonised time of sickness, disease and death was also, simultaneously, a political terrain of coercion and resistance.

Furthermore, it is worthwhile to analyse how missionary writings of the time, while negotiating "otherness" in colonial contexts, constituted imperialist discourses on race. During the Empire, missionary travels were important sites of cross-cultural negotiations, constructing what Mary Louis Pratt calls a "contact zone" (Pratt 7). Anna Johnston, in her book, *Missionary Writing and Empire, 1800–1860*, argues how missionaries, working in the colonies at the time of the Empire, were caught between the twin axes of imperialism and religion. According to her,

> Missionary texts are crucial to understanding cross-cultural encounters under the aegis of empire because they illuminate the formation of a mode of

mutual imbrication between white imperial subjects, white colonial subjects, and non-white colonial subjects.

(Johnston 3)

Lambert, in his book, was clearly writing for a religious audience as well as an imperial audience. In this respect, it is important to view Lambert's ambiguous position in the colonial cultural context of India, and understand how, in his text, he negotiates between his imperial and religious interests. Probably, the best way one can do this is to look closely at the places where the book talks about Ramabai.

Interestingly, Lambert's book has a substantial section on Ramabai and her social work during the famine of 1896–97. She, according to him, was an ideal example of an Indian Christian convert, dedicated to humanitarian work, prompted by her missionary lessons. In the book, he reproduced two famine letters written by Ramabai, in 1897, to make his case. The said letters speak highly of the missionary help that she received in conducting her social work during the famine, and even, speak appreciatively of the benevolence of the colonial government towards its subjects. It is curious enough to find that, at one point in the book, though Lambert referred to Ramabai's indignation about the lack of safety of the women, in the government hospitals and segregation camps, he did so in a very cursory manner. He dismissed her charges as one single incident, something which alone cannot or should not tarnish the otherwise impeccable image of the imperial government. It is important to mention here that there is no reference to the plague letter she wrote to *The Bombay Guardian* in May 1897, which caused her charges of sedition.

Ramabai's nationalistic position had always been a problematic one to her fellow nationalists, due to her conversion to Christianity. In the context of colonial India's brewing nationalistic fervour, it is hardly surprising that her association with the Western missionary societies was not viewed favourably by her fellow nationalists. Being a colonized subject, her embracing of the religion which belonged to the "rulers" and her dismissal of her Hindu Brahmin identity were seen as a kind of betrayal that gave her a marginalized position in the nationalistic discourse of the time. To her Western supporters, though, she was an iconic image of an Indian Christian missionary, even with them, her resistance to the hegemonic structure of Western imperialism had, on more than one occasion, been a reason for her alienation. Ramabai's position, therefore, was a complex one. On the one hand, was her nationalistic identification with Indian cultural Hinduism, and on the other hand, was her commitment to serve as a Christian missionary. As Meera Kosambi rightly points out,

Ramabai was uniquely located within the turbulent confrontation between British imperialism and the traditional Hindu culture of Maharashtra (the Marathi-speaking region in Western India, then partly subsumed under the Bombay Presidency).

(Kosambi 194)

Locating Ramabai's "Letter" in the contested historiography of the Bombay plague years, the following sections, thus, will, first, discuss the complexities and ambivalences of the time, through the politicized narratives it produced; and second, through a discursive reading of the "Letter", this chapter will try to examine Ramabai's complex identity position and how that throws light on her deviant life.

1896–97: A Politicized Terrain of Conflicting Discourses

Amartya Sen, while discussing "the relevance of positionality in the objectivity of observations and the knowledge they yield", in "On Interpreting India's Past" (the Abha Maity Memorial Lecture), said,

> the objectivity of an observation or an analysis can be judged not only in uncompromisingly universalist terms (what Thomas Nagel has called "the view from nowhere" in his perspicacious exploration of the demands of objectivity), but also with reference to identified "positional" perspectives – as the view from a specified and delineated somewhere. Positionality can influence both (i) observation of events seen from a particular position, and (ii) the overall assessment of an event, from a particular perspective, taking note of different observation.
>
> *(Sen 12)*[2]

In understanding the historiography of the Bombay plague years of 1896–97, Sen's idea of "positionality" seems relevant, considering how the historicized narratives of the time were built on conflicting discourses, and how they offered identifiable "positional perspectives" of the history of the time. Among the plague writings that the time produced, Western missionary accounts formed a substantial part. Lambert's *India: The Horror-Stricken Empire*, for instance, was a detailed survey of the time of triple calamities – that of plague, famine and the earthquake. Beginning as a philanthropic project, the book was a curious blend of religious writing, geographic and ethnographic travel account across famine and plague-stricken places and scientific data mining on epidemicity of diseases like plague. Although it stated its purpose as solely philanthropic, originating in the American Mennonite missionary organization's handing over the responsibility of overseeing the relief distribution work to him, it was far more complex than that. His commentaries, describing his travels across the famine and plague-ravaged districts, were laced with serious racial overtones. Throughout the book, Lambert maintained an ambivalent position in narrativizing the events, moving his "positionality" frequently from the point of a philanthropist/neutral observer to an overt sympathizer of Western imperialism. Amidst his eyewitness descriptions of the catastrophe and countless images of helplessness and suffering, what he repeatedly saw as the reason for the calamities was the ignorance of the natives and their heathen lifestyles. According to him, it was "the uncleanliness of the inhabitants" and "the ignorance of the simplest laws of health [that] has caused a frightful amount of suffering and woe"

(Lambert 348–49). Images of filth abounded in his descriptions, at the end of which he remarked, "Do you wonder India should be visited with sickness and plague?" (Lambert 363). In his view, the colonial government was simultaneously fighting two battles, one against the contagion and one against the ignorance and superstitions of the natives, and that the plague committee's task force was actually doing a commendable job in spite of the strong native resistance:

> Indeed there is no other government on the face of the earth that has done so much for the development of a colony as has the British government in India, all the vituperations and slanders of foreign prejudiced jingoists and howling maledictors to the contrary withstanding.
>
> *(Lambert 74)*

To describe the position Lambert took here, one may use Anna Johnston's term, "surrogate imperialists" (Johnston 6). According to Johnston, although missionaries were not directly a part of the Empire's administrative machinery, missionary texts were abundant proofs of their surrogacy. The religious propagandism of the texts was built purely on a binary between Christianity's high moralism and intellectualism and heathenism's moral and intellectual depravity, which itself acted as a justification for colonialism and also, evangelization. Textual descriptions of native ignorance and moral lawlessness were a significantly recurrent trope used to legitimize the colonial missionary projects. This, in case of Lambert, was especially true, considering his textual images of the plague. In citing innumerable examples of how the native Indian population callously allowed the plague bacilli to multiply by indulging in ignorance and unhygienic living, what he actually textualized was a binary construct of an unenlightened heathen "self" and an enlightened Christian "self". Needless to say, by doing so, not only did he justify the need for the native population's evangelisation but also participated wholeheartedly in the larger imperial discourse by echoing the agenda of the Empire.

Lambert's writing was pedagogic in intent, keen on instructing the Western audience about why and how the country fell into the grip of the two calamities, famine and plague. And in his account of this "why" and "how", what strikes as a circulating trope is a logic of difference and the construct of two contrary absolutes – a Christian emancipated "self" and a dark heathen "other". Actually, such a binary was the staple of colonial thinking, the principal orientation around which almost all colonial discourses developed. To argue how colonialism operated on binaries/differences, Frantz Fanon in *The Wretched of the Earth* has described the colonial world as a "Manichean world", saying that "This world divided into compartments, this world cut in two is inhabited by two different species" (Fanon 39–41). That is to say that, in colonial contexts, one important marker of the binary was undoubtedly "race". But in cases of missionary writings like Lambert's, there was an interesting discursiveness in the construction of this binary, as the logic of difference formulated itself around multiple ideas – that of race, religion, knowledge, scientific knowledge and even morality. Especially, the ideas of race, religion and knowledge/scientific knowledge occupied interchange-able positions in Lambert's narrative. Aligning Christianity and Western science on one plane and heathenism and ignorance of the East on the other, he commented that a plague epidemic was always more likely to happen in non-Christian places. To accentuate this geographical positioning of the disease, he further argued that by the beginning of the eighteenth century the disease had disappeared from Europe and that, "Constantinople, the hotbed of Mohammedanism filth and disease, continually served as a gateway for the plague to re-enter Europe" (Lambert 346) through its eastern corridor. Here, it is interesting to note how Lambert used progress of Western science to explain Christianity's glorious success over other religions. Talking about particularly the context of colonial India in the plague years, he said, "It is a significant fact that comparatively very few native Christians died of the plague" (Lambert 399). Adding to his point further, he remarked that there are reasons why Christian missionary field workers, in spite of their daily exposure, were successful in evading the disease. If one reason for this was their scientific temperament, the other was the efficacy of their religion and their faith. He concluded his argument saying, "God speed the day when Christian civilization and its beneficent influences shall bring happiness and health to the benighted lands of earth" (Lambert 349).

In the book, the survey of the calamitous situation was dotted with a few letters and reports by other missionaries, which Lambert seemed to have included with the purpose of authenticating his work. These letters and reports were to bring alive the most adverse ground realities which the Western missionaries were fighting from day to day with their utmost zeal and goodwill. Amidst an all-Western list of missionaries, the only Indian who found mention was Pandita Ramabai. The book extensively talked about Ramabai's relentless social work during the days of famine and plague. She, in Lambert's view, was an ideal native Christian convert, who prompted by the Christian teaching of benevolence, dedicated her life to the upliftment of her people. She, by her work, had set an example through which the West's evangelical missionary projects in colonial countries like India stood justified. Not only did Lambert pay a visit to Ramabai's home for widows in Poona and wrote about it but he also published in his book, Ramabai's own written accounts of her tours in the famine-stricken districts of Maharashtra and Central India, rescuing women and young girls with the help of the Western missionaries. Clearly, Lambert made his case here by projecting Ramabai as one of those dedicated missionaries he knew closely, who were active on the field during 1896–97 famine and plague and showered praises on her for her selfless service. Through her he brought to his readers the struggle and hardship of missionary life, the steadfastness of the mission against all possible odds. Now, one of these odds, as Ramabai enumerated, was the laxity and callousness of the colonial government. In her account of the famine, she more than once had raised questions about the British government's negligence of law and order and the unsafe conditions of the Poor Houses where young girls were often exploited by the military and the soldiers. This, however, to

Lambert wasn't as much a matter of concern and he clearly dismissed them as "stray incidents". To put it in his words,

> that although utmost arrangements in hospitals were done by the management to separate male patients and female patients, separate patients by their castes, still some stray incidents happened, of which, Ramabai complained about in a letter.

> *(Lambert 381–82)*

Even the plague letter of Ramabai, published by *The Bombay Guardian*, was only passingly mentioned, although the *Letter*, since its publication, had been much of a subject of talk. It is therefore hardly possible to overlook the fact that Lambert chose to conveniently position Ramabai in his narrative, portraying her as a model Indian Christian missionary, and ignoring completely her identity as a leading female nationalist of her time. Surely, her criticism of the colonial government, as a nationalist, was a clash of interest within the imperialist framework of his writing.

Pandita Ramabai's *Letter*: An Act of Defiance, an Expression of Strength

Ramabai's life, from her childhood, was one marked by non-conformities. She was the daughter of an erudite Sanskrit scholar, Anant Shastri Dongre, who was ostracized by his fellow Brahmins for his decision to educate his wife and impart her knowledge of Sanskrit. Thus, ousted by the Brahmin community, the family led a modest living in a forest where Ramabai's father ran a residential school for boys. Growing up outside the confines of a patriarchally regulated community, her childhood was an unusual one for girls of her time as she was given her first education and taught in Sanskrit by her mother, Lakshmibai Dongre. Her younger days were spent fighting poverty and travelling incessantly across the Indian subcontinent, trying to make a meagre living by reciting sacred stories and teaching Sanskrit "shlokas". Quite early in her life she lost both her parents, and even her older sister, whose early and unhappy marriage had turned her father against getting Ramabai married, again something contrary to the conventions of the time. A deviant life mostly of travelling and teaching, which were her means of earning livelihood, took her to Calcutta in 1878, where, just at the age of 19, her public appearances and scholarly debates in the erudite Sanskritic circles of Bengal earned her the titles "Pandita" and "Sarasvati". Lecturing widely across the Bengal Presidency about the importance of women's education, Ramabai was, by then, already a public figure, campaigning for gender equality and women's right to education. Contemporary newspapers, like *The Bengalee* and *The Deccan Herald*, were celebrating her as discernibly the time's most prominent female voice in social reform.[3]

Ramabai's work towards women's education was further strengthened when she was invited by the colonial government to testify before the Hunter Commission on Education. The *testimony* powerfully articulated the need for the government to focus on women's education with the aim of producing female teachers, female inspectors of schools and women doctors, especially with specialization in Gynaecology. Clearly, she was pointing at the current female mortality rates during childbirths, underlining the colonial government's lack of intention in matters of women's welfare. The *testimony* was translated from Marathi to English for a wider circulation in England and is said to have led to the formation of the "National Association for Supplying Female Medical Aid to the Women of India", commonly known as the Countess of Dufferin Fund. Ramabai's vocal criticism of the colonial government's non-interventionist policy is found in her other writings as well. In her book, *The High Caste Hindu Woman*, she sharply criticized the government's stand in matters relating to the Hindu laws and its gender injustices and called it opportunistic, self-serving and a kind of appeasement politics.

Thus, even before the incident of the plague letter, there had been instances when Ramabai's feminism had been in the form of a blunt critique of the imperial policies. Her feminist position was one of multiple contestations, where, if, on the one hand, she was fighting the patriarchy of the Hindu laws, on the other hand, as a nationalist, she was acting as a vocal critic of the colonial government's patriarchal stands. To borrow from Inderpal Grewal's writing on her, she, thanks to her incessant, almost nomadic travelling experiences throughout her early years, was able to form "her own 'fuzzy' sense of community since she saw women from different regions in India as connected by a common exploitation" (Grewal 184), under colonial rule and Hindu patriarchy. The feminist, reformist position that Ramabai owned was a clear and distinct one, and in that she refused to get overcast by her Christian missionary identity. The context of her work towards the upliftment of Hindu women was a complex one as it was a time when Indian women were being seen as an object of missionary and colonial benevolence. Gender justice was being centrally used as a moral reason for imperial missionary projects, and Indian Zenana was attracting a lot of Western feminist participation in women's welfare work, especially through missionary enterprises. After her conversion to Christianity, Ramabai's association with the Western missionaries brought her close to the time's missionary discourse surrounding the Indian zenana. She was being seen by her Western sisters as just the perfect native counterpart of the Western missions. However, on multiple occasions, Ramabai had adopted an independent stand, dissociating herself from her missionary bondage, which had become the reason for an uneasiness and strain in the relationship. That she strictly disallowed her Indian nationalist identity to be subsumed by her identity as a Christian missionary, working under the aegis of the Western missionary organizations, naturally was not looked upon favourably by her Western sponsors. The plague letter was one such occasion when Ramabai, by taking a fierce nationalist stand, not only outraged the colonial government but also provoked the ire of her Western missionary sympathizers.

The plague letter was published by the liberal newspaper, *The Bombay Guardian* on 18 May 1897, as a "Letter to the Editor". The epidemic had spread from

Bombay to Pune, and Ramabai was instructed by the city magistrate to evacuate her Pune shelter home, Sharada Sadan. By then, Ramabai had already started another shelter home for famine victims in Kedgaon, near Pune, and when the order of the city magistrate came, she had to shift the inmates from Sharada Sadan to Kedgaon. It was at this time that the most unfortunate incident happened to one of the widows sheltered in Sharada Sadan, reporting which Ramabai wrote in the newspaper, alleging the Government Plague Hospital and levelling charges of negligence and even, malpractices against the authorities. According to the incidents described in the *Letter*, the young girl had reported high fever and, under suspicion of plague, she was placed under quarantine in Pune's Sassoon Hospital. When, even after 6 weeks, she was not released, Ramabai went to enquire about the girl. Initially, the girl was reported to be dead and afterwards, by some other sources, reported to be alive, but "kept" by a watchman of the hospital. The hospital authorities took no cognizance of the matter and in spite of an earnest search conducted by Ramabai herself, the girl was never found. With a heavy heart, Ramabai wrote,

> I shall never let a girl come alone to this dreadful place while I have a little strength in me. God help the young women who may be obliged to come to such a place as this and may He open the eyes of our City Magistrate and his colleagues to see the evils resulting from their heartless unjust rule.
>
> *(Kosambi 233)*

The "Letter" also laid bare the real conditions of the plague hospitals and segregation camps in terms of insufficient infrastructure and lack of provisions. Complaining about the complacency of the higher authorities regarding the appalling cases of mismanagement, she said, "The City Magistrate, with other people living in style, know very little and care less for the hundreds of poor unfortunate victims of their careless rule" (Kosambi 232). The "Letter" provoked unthinkable repercussions such that it was read out in the British Parliament, House of Commons, 2 months after its publication. The colonial government charged her with sedition and pressurized her to make a public statement of the withdrawal of the "Letter".

As much as the unapologetic "Letter" enraged the colonial government, it upset Ramabai's missionary friends of the West, and it is important to examine the reasons underlying this. Sister Geraldine, Ramabai's godmother from St. Mary's, the Virgin, England and Dorothea Beale of Cheltenham were perhaps the strongest and most vocal critics of her on this occasion.[4] It is interesting to think that the "Letter" expressing concern about women's issues found no sympathy in the missionary quarters of the West, when most Western missionary writings of the time recurrently had images of downtrodden Indian women as victim figures, circulated almost as a trope. Indira Ghose, while talking about philanthropic travelling of Western women to nineteenth-century colonial India, says, "the degraded condition of Indian women is a topos that runs through women's writing on India throughout the century" (Ghose 107). Graphic descriptions of Indian zenana, as enslaved by the Indian patriarchal society, flood Western missionary writings of

the time. These were undoubtedly aimed at adding a moral compass to missionary organizations' zenana work, which Anna Johnston claims was "transforming
imperial projects into moral allegories" (Johnston 13). The projects, though apparently standing for Western feminism's formation of eastern sisterhood, carried
very much in them an intrinsic sense of Western cultural and moral superiority,
which even meant ignoring the work of the Indian female reformers for the Indian
zenana as valueless. It is not surprising, therefore, that Ramabai's concern for the
safety of Indian women, expressed in the "Letter", did not get any Western audience, and was deemed as "unnecessary" by Sister Geraldine or dismissed as stating
"a stray incident" by George Lambert. The "Letter", through its wide publication,
effected a significant rupture in the imperial narrative of benevolence, floated
by the political machinery of the Empire and the missionary organizations alike.
Gayatri Chakravorty Spivak has famously described the time's Western projects of
benevolence as "white men saving brown women from brown men" (Spivak 284).
Ramabai's notorious "Letter" seems a subversion of that idea, in the sense that it,
as if, textualized an urgency to "save brown women from white men and white
women".

Conclusion

The Bombay plague years were, thus, a politically eruptive time when the context
of an epidemic had proved itself to be an ideological battleground. In the colonial
times, sickness and disease had been recurrent tropes in colonial constructions of
difference. On the one hand, the idea of fighting the epidemic through the scientific rationale of medicine and treatment, as against arbitrary heathen practices,
was being exploited as a useful political agenda for the Empire, on the other hand,
a slightly different version of the same idea was also being used by Western missionary organizations to intervene and gain further entry within the Indigenous
communities. In that respect, missionary writings, like George Lambert's *India: The
Horror-Stricken Empire*, with their loads of vivid visuals, of the pestilence, death and
sufferings of the native population, were contributing significantly to the construction of a particular image of "heathen suffering". Calling this process "pathologiz-
ing heathenism", Esme Cleall, in *Missionary Discourses of Difference*, describes how
"Sickness became part of the 'spectacle of heathenism' and was represented in missionary writing by crowds of sick, emaciated or dehumanized bodies" (Cleall 79).
In his book, Lambert's pictorial descriptions and photography of starved, mutilated
and dying figures of natives, were certainly embodied specimens of this "spectacle of heathenism". Needless to say, the textual proliferation of such spectacles
helped immensely the ideological propaganda of Western imperialism, during the
plague years. And written in the context of such a fierce ideological struggle that
the time was witness to, Ramabai's plague letter was a remarkable testimony of
nationalist resistance and a powerful female voice, challenging imperialist hegemonic dominance.

Notes

1   The said letter was a "Letter to the Editor" written by Pandita Ramabai to *The Bombay Guardian* on 18 May 1897, from the Government Plague Hospital, Poona. It has been included as *Selection 5: About government provisions during plague epidemic, 1897* in Meera Kosambi's *Pandita Ramabai. Life and landmark writings.* All quotes from the "Letter" are from this book.

2   Amartya Sen's "On Interpreting India's Past", published in *Nationalism, Democracy & Development. State and Politics in India*, edited by Sugata Bose and Ayesha Jalal, was first presented as Abha Maiti Memorial Lecture at the Asiatic Society in Calcutta.

3   The contemporary English newspaper, *The Bengalee*, published every Saturday from Calcutta, closely followed Pandita Ramabai and her achievements as a pioneering female social activist of the time. The newspaper regularly published reports covering Ramabai's lectures in educational institutions, her public speeches like her "testimony" at the Hunter Commission and, even, her travel to England with her daughter.

4   Sister Geraldine, of Community of St. Mary the Virgin, Wantage, Ramabai's godmother and Miss Dorothea Beale, of Cheltenham, wrote several letters criticizing Ramabai's plague letter, which can be read in a compilation called *The Letters and Correspondence of Pandita Ramabai*, edited by A.B. Shaw.

Works cited

Cleall, Esme. *Missionary Discourses of Difference: Negotiating Otherness in the British Empire, 1840–1900.* Palgrave Macmillan, 2012.

Fanon, Frantz. *The Wretched of the Earth.* Grove Press, 1963.

Ghose, Indira. *Women Travellers in Colonial India: The Power of the Female Gaze.* Oxford UP, 1998.

Grewal, Inderpal. *Home and Harem. Nation, Gender, Empire, and the Cultures of Travel.* Leicester UP, 1996.

Johnston, Anna. *Missionary Writing and Empire, 1800–1860.* Cambridge UP, 2003.

Kosambi, Meera. "Multiple Contestations: Pandita Ramabai's Educational and Missionary Activities in Late Nineteenth-Century India and Abroad." *Women's History Review*, vol. 7, no. 2, 1998, pp. 193–208.

———. *Pandita Ramabai: Life and Landmark Writings.* Routledge, 2016.

Lambert, George. *India: The Horror-Stricken Empire.* Mennonite Missionary Co., 1898.

Pratt, Mary Louis. *Imperial Eyes: Travel Writing and Transculturation.* Routledge, 1992.

Sen, Amartya. "On Interpreting India's Past." *Nationalism, Democracy & Development: State and Politics in India*, edited by Sugata Bose and Ayesha Jalal. Oxford UP, 1998, pp. 10–35.

Shah, A.B. *The Letters and Correspondence of Pandita Ramabai.* Maharashtra State Board for Literature and Culture, 1977.

Spivak, Gayatri Chakravorty. *A Critique of Postcolonial Reason: Toward a History of the Vanishing Present.* Harvard UP, 1999.

12

PANDEMIC AS A DISASTER

Narratives of Suffering and "Risk" in *Twilight in Delhi*

Sumantra Baral

The influenza flu of 1918 holds the unfortunate reputation of being known as "forgotten pandemic, lost in the archives amidst records of the Great War, the armistice, and the new era of modernity ushered in by these cataclysmic events" (Hovanec 1). Its destructive impact, however, at that time was felt magnanimously throughout the globe, especially in India. Between 1918 and 1920, the pandemic broke out in India and the country became part of the global infection which was known as Spanish Flu. This pandemic was responsible for killing almost 17–18 million people in this country alone which was also statistically the most among all other countries. Spanish Flu was localized semantically as the Bombay Influenza or Bombay Fever in India as Bombay (modern Mumbai) became the nautical intercontinental transaction port which involved Europe, especially during the First World War. Among the three waves of this pandemic, the second one was the deadliest which affected the younger people in the age group of 20–40 most severely.

1918 influenza flu had an enormous impact on the socio-economical public sphere of colonial India. David Arnold observed how the Ministry of Health in London acknowledged that the "total mortality in India in the month of October 1918" was "without parallel in the history of disease" (183). Arnold questions our exercise to revisit this pandemic by asking "what exactly are we seeking to investigate and by what means can we recuperate that 'forgotten' past?" (183). This chapter is an attempt to investigate the erasure of this event from history and how and why Ahmed Ali revisited this historical event through his novel *Twilight in Delhi* (1940).

Influenza Flu and the Politics of Its Erasure

In *Twilight in Delhi*, while the realist aspects have been read with critical attention, I would like to focus on the realistic treatment of 1918 Iinfluenza flu which impacts

DOI: 10.4324/9781003294436-17

the proceeding of the novel greatly and influences the lives of the characters, from the purview of what Sourit Bhattacharya defines as "Catastrophic Realism" in his *Postcolonial Modernity and the Indian Novel: On Catastrophic Realism*. For Bhattacharya, catastrophic realism is an aesthetic framework of postcolonial modernity. It defines catastrophes and acknowledges the co-existence of different registers (catastrophes, disasters and so on) where "realism is capacious and expansive, manufactured by the demands of history and society, of catastrophic modernity and modality" (19). In Ali's novel, the pandemic of 1918 demands from the narrative style (realism) the expansive contours of history and society, the gap in its representation from literature and culture and also the modalities of the new treatment. This will provide us with an addition to our understanding of this long-read novel from the perspective of disaster studies.

In the post-pandemic era, specifically in the 1920s, the effacement of the 1918 Influenza flu from Indian culture and literature problematizes how Indian history in the early twentieth century was crafted with selection and rejection of events which constitute our understanding of nationalist discourse. The result of this abandoned attention towards the pandemic was very much affected by the last phase of the First World War. By 1919, most of the Indian soldiers had returned home. Bodies and minds wounded with bullets, gunpowder and shell shocks, their experience in fighting as allies for the liberation of other countries gave birth to a strong sense of freedom in their consciousness. This ardent spirit and taste for freedom overpowered the pandemic-centred time. The year 1919 was also a time of transition of realization and anger out of disillusionment of the so-called Imperial "co-operation".

> For Gandhi and the wartime Indian politicians, however, 1919 was a year of British betrayal in India: the constitutional reforms they had bargained for since 1914 were not realised. Yet as national leaders, their war on the home front had accelerated and heightened their calls for self-government, laying the foundation for India's freedom from colonial rule within thirty years.
>
> (Morton-Jack)

An era dominated by Gandhian sensibility and his Nationalist manifesto to liberate India from the Raj along with the publication of works like *The Story of My Experiment with Truth* (1925) which explored his life from early childhood to 1921 and was published weekly from 1921 to 1925, wrought an ambience very different and unexpected in post-pandemic India. The event of the Jallianwala Bagh massacre, also known as the Amritsar massacre (1919) which took place right in the middle of the pandemic, made the situation grave. In the month of April 1919, a large but peaceful crowd gathered on the premises of Jallianwala Bagh to protest against the arrest of two national leaders, Dr. Saifuddin Kitchlu and Dr. Satya Pal. Brigadier-General R. E. H. Dyer enveloped the crowd with his army, blocked the exit route and ordered to fire till they were out of ammunition. One thousand people were killed and over 1200 were injured that day.

This incident shocked the nation from all corners. Rabindranath Tagore rejected the knighthood conferred on him as a protest against this inhuman act. It was an eye-opener for the nationalists. The ineffective inquiry along with the initial accolades for Dyer generated

> a strong sense of disillusionment and disenchantment which raised questions to the imperial policies. Gandhi who at the beginning of the war sided with Britain with troops and goods, "I tender my support to it with all my heart" (Morton-Jack), now called for the Non-cooperation Movement.
>
> *(1920–22)*

All these post-World War developments in conjunction with the rise of Nationalist efforts to end the Imperial regime became responsible for the lack of attention and importance of this pandemic in the crucial phase of colonial history of India. India's freedom struggle, rather than the pandemic, the loss in Jalianwala Bagh, rather than the loss in pandemic, became part of Indian history of that decade and after. The prime focus of the Age was to uphold the anti-colonial agenda with Nationalist consciousness where the event of 1918 influenza remained stacked in papers and journals. Like Mir Nihal in Ali's novel, so also for Mahatma Gandhi, the epidemic was also an evidence of God's punishment of Western civilization for its colonialism. Gandhi's interpretation of natural catastrophes as God's will was vehemently criticized, even by some of his own followers. Most importantly, Gandhi's role as a recruiting agent for the British Army in the First World War tore him apart emotionally and spiritually, resulting in the prolonged deterioration of his health due to diarrhoea which many believed to be caused by the Flu. This caused his indifference to the raging pandemic that was going around him even when Harilal Gandhi, his eldest son lost his wife and a child to the Flu. Even in his autobiography, he does not mention this pandemic. Jawaharlal Nehru, too, does not refer to it in *The Discovery of India* (1946). It is understandable that diarrhoea exhaustion, nervous breakdown due to existential crisis and piles surgery were responsible for Gandhi's ignorance but considering his role and stature as one of the most important leaders India has ever seen, it is quite inadmissible. Though Gandhi was ignorant and indifferent to the pandemic, for Dinshaw Mehta, his personal physician, the impact of the pandemic was deadly and severe as he gathered his thoughts and wrote a letter to *The Times of India* in 1919. What he lamented the most is the government's "criminal neglect towards mute and meek masses which could be pleaded before the Bar of Humanity" (Singh 39). Another irony is that "like Nehru, Gandhi never associated the 1918 pandemic with the cost of colonialism" (Weber and Dalton 39) which puts forth more questions and concerns.

The millions of deaths caused by the pandemic ceased to be a part of the national history of India in ways war casualties did.

> When we fail to read for illness in general and the 1918 pandemic in particular, we reify how military conflict has come to define history, we deemphasize

illness and pandemics in ways that hide their threat, and we take part in long traditions that align illness with seemingly less valiant, more feminine forms of death.

(Outka 2)

The massacre was easier to see, the violence and obnoxious imperial mass execution were too diabolical to ignore which sharply contrasted with an invisible virus, killing common man which ultimately became a matter of everyday and of no greater value. A death for the liberation of this country mattered way more than a death by the Flu. Such was the spirit of the time.

Pandemic, Literature and PWA

In the 1930s, however, a few authors began to look back on 1918 in a different light. This resurgence of interest in the Flu during the 1930s may have been influenced by new developments in virology and influenza research. "The field of virology was then in its infancy, having been created in 1926 when Thomas Rivers defined the difference between bacteria and viruses" (Hovanec 2). India in the 1930s, however, was going through a transitional phase in its history, politically and aesthetically, which was welcomed with the call of decolonizing not only the country but also the way the country thinks. To construct the change and the novelty that it coveted, it was important for the agents to look back at the history of this country for method and contents. While there were not so much in methods as was anticipated, history was kind to provide with contents for this new cause. 1918 Bombay Fever was among those contents in India's colonial history to which Ahmed Ali looked back and used in *Twilight in Delhi*, a novel also of transition and change. The Flu appeared not only as a reminder of colonial subjugation but also as an agent of change lost in the national history that made an impact not only geographically, sociologically and economically but also in the domain of literature.

In India, the notion of the "progressive" has been synonymously perceived with the Marxist ideology of social change. The notion of progressive or the reception of it goes back to the emergence and construction of the Progressive Writers League and later Progressive Writers Association in 1933. In 1932 from Lucknow, with the publication of *Angarray (Embers)*, a short story collection of four progressive writers – Sajjad Zaheer, Mahmuduzzafar, Ahmed Ali and Rashid Jahan, a revolt was announced against the twin problems of the contemporary time – the first was fundamentalism and orthodoxy and the second was colonialism. *Angarray*, though planned for the revival of Urdu Literature from the clutches of escapism and conformity, was declared controversial for the choice of narratives and description and was banned under section 295A of the Indian Penal Act. In December 1933, the then United Provinces Government seized all the printed copies and set them on fire as the Government held that the book "intended to outrage religious feeling by insulting its religion or religious beliefs". If we notice the points the Progressive Writers made in their official manifesto, we find a continuous emphasis on rationalism, scientific thought and social awareness. The second emphasis was on the choice of subject and the common people, their problems, hunger, poverty, oppression, revolt and many such issues. A shift in focus from transcendentalism to materialism is clearly evident. Ahmed Ali's essay "A Progressive View of Art" furthered the agenda of this radical movement. Ahmed pointed out:

> The artist communicates his feelings through images, or symbols. In order to be really expressive of the artist's feelings they should be accessible to the audience also, for the artist does not create merely for himself. It is, therefore, necessary that the images or symbols should not be arbitrary as those of many occidental artists and writers have been in the present society. They should be accessible to the public; otherwise, that contact between the artist and the public will never be established which leads to the state in which the public also start sharing feeling of the artist, and a right communication of which leads to stimulation.
>
> *(68–69)*

Even though PWA was functioning and proving to be effective in Indian soil, its root, however, stretched to Europe. Their association with the Bloomsbury circle especially how Zaheer and Mulk Raj Anand bonded on a personal level and their attendance at "International Writers for the Defense of Culture" Congress in Paris in 1935 influenced the movement on a larger scale and the movement got a Western tinge. Ahmed Ali wrote:

> The main figures of the movement then, in 1932–33, had shared a love of sombreros, bright shirts and contrasting ties, collecting candlesticks and gargoyles, Bach and Beethoven, and an admiration for James Joyce and D.H. Lawrence and the New Writing poets, as well as Chekov and Gorky. Whereas we were ardent nationalists and anti-British, Marxism was not a ruling passion, through a progressive outlook was inherent in the revolt; and as the group expanded, leftist leanings, vague in some and pronounced in others, did became apparent, for there seemed no other way out of the social and political morass.
>
> *(36)*

Ahmed Ali identified himself and his peers as nationalists but the very idea of nationalists at that time was complicated. The grand Nationalist consciousness, the very character of India as a nation focused on pastoralism and mysticism and engaged in revivalist ideals to decolonize its sensitivity around the globe. In this enterprise to constitute a character of novelty, the nationalist art and literary practitioners discarded the contemporary struggles and problems. The emergence of PWA was to critique this tradition as a representative canon. Ahmed Ali's notion of nationalism therefore appears as an alternative nationalism indicating the fissures in the grand one which makes them not nationalists but nationalitarians. "The primary agenda or task of nationalitarians is to criticise nationalists for conflating independence with freedom and for not undertaking the radical social and economic restructuring that would mean real freedom" (Gopal 14). Gopal writes:

> Nationalitarians, such as the founders of the PWA, do see the moment of independence as one with revolutionary potential; the postcolonial era must bring with it "a wholesale reconstruction of society" (5). If for Nehru, despite cautionary disclaimers, "the past is over and it is the future that beckons us now", the PWA manifesto eyes the future with a radical sense of the present and its challenges.
>
> *(14)*

Twilight in Delhi and Realism

Published three years before the Great Bengal famine of 1943, Ahmed *Ali's Twilight in Delhi* is a trendsetter of the Progressive and Realist mode of writing which would become the marker of literary representation of the entire decade of the 1940s in India. One of the founders of the Progressive Writers Association, Ahmed Ali's essay "A Progressive View of Art" which unofficially became the manifesto of this movement, defines progressiveness as "a constant becoming – a continuation which never comes to an end. The moment it is labelled . . . it ceases to be 'progress' and comes to an end" (Zaman 24). Posited in the background of the newly made capital of India – Delhi, the novel records the impact of the 1918 influenza flu, popularly known as Bombay Fever (which throughout the world claimed over 50 million lives and in India 10 to 20 million lives), in the life of old Delhi. Twilight, the keyword in the title of the novel suggests not only scenic beauty but also a kind of precarity. Twilight indicates in-betweenness and liminality – the position of Delhi between two languages – English and Urdu and two empires – Mughal and British. Twilight serves as an anaesthetic expression of the miserable life of people living in Delhi during the pandemic. Twilight which usually hints at the situation between day and night here posits itself between life and death, tradition and change, orthodoxy and progression. All these issues are summed up in the narratives of Ali whose novel was heaped with praise by none other than E.M. Forster in London from where his novel was published by Hogarth Press.

The novel touches upon so many issues of the time ranging from nationalism, progressive writing, protest against orthodoxy and fundamentalism, love, marriage, pining, death and influenza flu. Asghar loses his wife Bilqeece to the pandemic as she catches the fever. Ahmed Ali's realist details of the whole scenario bring shivers down the spine. The descriptions are naked and cold as are the bodies. The graveyard became full with those bodies.

> A new cemetery was made outside the city where people buried relations by the score. The Hindus were lucky that way. They just went to the bank of the sacred Jamuna, cremated the dead, and threw away without a shroud

or cremation. They were mostly the poor. Yet in death it was immaterial whether you were naked or clothed or burnt or thrown away to be devoured by vultures and jackals.

(Ali 169)

Ali also points out the ritualistic difficulty in dealing with the dead bodies. As for Hindus bodies are burnt, for Muslims bodies are covered in shrouds and buried in graves. In this difficult time amidst the pandemic, poverty has given birth to the profession of shroud-stealing. "The people had discovered new and newer ways of procuring bread" (Ali 170). It was not only the shroud thieves but also the grave diggers and the cloth merchants or banias who took full advantage of the situation. With the number of dead bodies increasing every hour, the importance and requirement of the gravediggers exceed the limit. They were able to make a good living and fortune out of this situation.

They raised their wages from two rupees to four and from four to eight, and even then, grumbled and complained. They did not bother to see that the grave was properly dug deep enough or not. They had so many more to dig. If someone protested, they only said:

'Dig for yourself, then. This is the best that we can do.'

(Ali 170)

In the other part of the city, the cloth merchants or banias increased the price of line cloth, the primary material to make winding sheets. They exploited the sentiment of loss and mourning by hiking the price of those sheets. If someone protested, they replied:

One should not think of expense regarding a winding-sheet. After all, this is the last time that you are going to spend on the deceased. He must have given you so much comfort in life, and may have even spent on you. You should not really grudge him a decent burial . . . But if you cannot afford, well, then buy a cheaper winding-sheet . . .'

'But, of course, the cheaper shroud would be so thin that one could see the naked body through it; and the person would starve, but spend a little more to give his dear one a decent shroud.'

(Ali 171)

One can definitely relate the politics and money-making agenda behind the shroud to Munshi Premchand's short story "The Shroud" (*Kafan*). On the other hand, the Ghassals (or, Gassaal, one who professionally washes the dead bodies before burial) have started to charge more. Ali shows how religion is turned into profit-making profession in desperate times:

They charged a high sum for having performed this virtuous deed, and departed for the next, from morning till night, from sunset till dawn, stroking their pious beards, feeling their deep purses that were filled with silver and gold, muttered the name of God, and massaged their bellies with satisfied yet greedy hands.

(Ali 171)

What the novel does miss in depicting the epidemic is the medical intervention. There are hardly any narratives dealing with any prophylactic measures taken either by Government, locais or even in the household of Ashgar when Bilqueece dies. Though the doctor tried his best, it was not enough. But there is a reason for this. As bacteriology was still young, people had no other choice but to rely upon their immune system. Every time a new pathogen appears in the environment, it announces a great threat to immunity and the body. As a reason people turned to God for prayers and Azaans. The situation is very similar to the worship of Goddess Manasa, Olabibi, Bonobibi, Sitala at the time of cholera or smallpox epidemics in Bengal. The Bible also holds plague as the punishment of God. Mir Nihal equates the outbreak of influenza as the revenge of nature:

Nature herself was rebellious and seemed angry with the people of Hindustan. Hundreds and thousands of Indians had been killed in the war, acting as fodder to German guns. But not content with this and, as it were, filled with anger against the inhumanity of man, Nature wanted to demonstrate her own callousness and might. Influenza broke out in epidemic form, and from the houses in the mohallah and around, heart rendering cries of lamentation and weeping began to rend the air.

(Ali 169)

The invasion by the English of the territory of Delhi becomes analogous to the virus of Influenza, a foreign pathogen claiming the native colonial body. The virus appears to be an unwanted excess. What this residual corporeal other does to the body, imperialism does to India, especially Delhi. "Charting brief histories of disaster and postcolonial studies", Anthony Carrigan argues "for a decolonised disaster studies where the epistemological and cultural practices of a catastrophe-based text, especially from the Global South, would be read politically through their links with the histories of colonialism, imperialism, and current forms of global capitalism" (Bhattacharya 48).

When *Angarrey* was published in 1932, its agenda was to critique the ongoing fundamentalist orthodoxy and nationalist revivalist ideals of this country as a method of not only decolonization but also denationalization. Their realist narratives of inequality, suffering, communal tensions, the lives of common man in the transition between two empires – Mughal and British stand solidly against the nationalist's narrative of escapism and pre-capital rustic unity and harmony. S. S. Zaheer, the general secretary of All-India Progressive Writers' Association, argued:

The need for organizing the progressive writers' movement in India was being felt by many of us for the last two or three years. In many parts of India

groups of writers, mostly young, were feeling the need of making a break
with the supine and escapist literature with which the country was being
flooded; of creating something more real, something more in harmony with
the facts of our existence today something which will make our art full-
blooded and virile.

(48)

The intention of "creating something more real" is what Gopal defines as "critical
realism". According to her,

The formation of the All-India Progressive Writers' Association was pivotal for
the building of a critical spirit for decolonisation, as opposed to the bourgeois-
nationalist discourses of harmony and inclusion. This critical spirit was the
product of the country's particular late-colonial historical conjuncture.

(20)

Pandemic as Disaster and the Narratives of "Risk"

A virus is always present no matter whether human civilization exists or not. Just
the presence of a virus does not create a pandemic or epidemic. It is the involvement of human beings with a virus on a massive scale that qualifies as epidemic
or pandemic. When the immune system fails to fight back against the invading
virus, some major symptoms such as flu and fever start to develop. The gradual dissemination of the communicable disease in the mass and the failure of the existing
medicine to combat the virus result in the multiplication of death. This creates an
omnipresent threat of death in family and society that forces one to get used to the
habit of isolation.

Rob Nixon identifies epidemics and pandemics as "slow" or "attritional" disasters. According to him, these "slow" or "attritional" disasters "overspill clear
boundaries in time and space (and) are marked above all by displacement – temporal,
geographical, rhetorical and above all technological displacements" (7). On the
other hand, Mark D. Anderson established a relation between the nature of disaster
and the nature of writing style produced with it. "Disaster narratives that arise following a single powerful event. . . often mirror existing forms and draw on latent
political narratives to endow the event with social meaning" (22). Pablo Mukherjee explored "a radical shift of literary modes between the gothic, the realist, the
autobiographical, and the historical; and an unevenness of style" (Bhattacharya 46).
For Mukherjee, "disaster environments" in turn demanded "disaster styles" (24).

Historical and anthropological studies have found two common elements embedded in catastrophes regardless of their nature, culture and geographical change. The
first one is "danger" and the second one is "risk". Robert Paine opined that we are
the ones who construct risk between ourselves but danger, it is out there. This led
him to the no-risk theory. In his "Danger and the No-Risk Thesis", he argued that
the perception of risk is culturally constructed which functions under the paradigm

of cultural contexts and logic. "The no-risk thesis is one of cognitive repression of risk", Paine continues, "It implies the preclusion of doubt and the effective elimination of ambiguity. It means the effective shutting out of perceptions of the world, and of what is or is not possible, that others may hold" (69). On the other hand, Ulrich Beck, a German sociologist and social scientist, identifies "risk" as a major characteristic of this time when the world has moved towards second modernity. Reading pandemics and epidemics in literature and history of the past must not be just read as the consequences of modernity but also as how they metamorphosed into a bigger, stronger and global threat. In the twenty-first century, catastrophic writing, therefore, cannot be read just as narratives of pain and suffering, victory and overcoming the odds but the narratives of "risk" (Global Warning, Nuclear War) that quietly lurk underneath the narratives, which are linguistically absent for which we are not yet ready. In the words of Maurice Blanchot:

> We are on the edge of disaster without being able to situate it in the future: it is rather always already past, and yet we are on the edge or under the threat, all formulations which would imply the future – that which is yet to come – if the disaster were not that which does not come, that which has put a stop to every arrival. To think the disaster (if this is possible, and it is not possible in as much as we suspect that the disaster is thought) is to have no longer any future in which to think it.
>
> *(1)*

This notion of "risk" is helpful to contextualize my explanations for the erasure of the 1918 pandemic from Indian history, the oblivion of national leaders like Gandhi and Nehru and its lack of representation in literary domain. Stretching out a bit from Paine's distinction between danger and risk, a possible explanation of this buried pandemic lies in its perception of people as danger but not risk. The contemporary media coverages also reported the situation in this light as if personally no risk was involved. Individual narratives of suffering were missing. There were only precautions and statistics.

As I have already referred to Gandhi's association and responses regarding this pandemic that he found this pandemic as a danger and of no risk. But when the pandemic became part of a novel and important characters like Mir Nihal, Ashgar and Bilqueece personally suffer, it comes down from the domain of collective and larger danger to that of individual and personal risk. There is no repression, cultural concealment and ignorance about this pandemic in the novel. Everything was totally exposed. The pandemic seemed no more alien, far-fetched or something that could never reach us. With literature, the forgotten pandemic made more sense.

Conclusion

Realism for Ali was more than just a writing style. For Ali and the PWA members, this meant a new thinking of a free nation. Though debates continue to grow to determine the nature of this realism – critical realism, socialist realism, catastrophic realism, etc. – the selection of realism as a stylistic component was definitely radical and revolutionary. The realist narratives hover around the boundaries of Western Avant-garde movements and Marxism, and the intention was always to create something revolutionary. The selection of realism therefore served twin purposes for Ali. First, it helped him to break from the tradition of mythology and pastoralism of nationalist practices, and then the narrative became a suitable vehicle to incorporate the history of 1918 Influenza flu, the impact of which would never be achieved if treated with the traditional Nationalist practice. In nationalist practice, histories of illness and death by a virus hardly fit. Looking back to a pandemic for Ali was not just analogous to the transition of Delhi and the suffering of the common people during that transition, and it was also a colonial reminder which is not just a history of India but history of India under colonization that needs to change. The intention was also to react to the nationalist history writing hierarchy that eliminates mass death because that was not of noble cause for the country's liberation. The narratives of suffering, oppression, administrative callousness, racial and communal discrepancies which are steeped in the novel demand a new and independent India which the Progressive Movement envisioned. The new narrative crafted the new vision of India where people and art complement each other where the suffering of the common is equally an important matter as suffering for national cause.

Ali's looking back to the pandemic in the novel criticized the nationalist practice of looking back at a glorious past and being happy about it. It offered an alternative troubling historiography of a time, shadowed by the prevalence of Gandhi, Nationalism and liberation, of this otherwise "proud" nation, to act, fight and change for Independence. The consideration and acknowledgement of these alternative accounts also offer a continuous reminder to decolonize the understanding of the national history, dominated by the "grand" narratives of the nation.

Works Cited

Ali, Ahmed. "Progressive View of Art." *Marxist Cultural Movement in India*, edited by Sudhi Pradhan. National Book Agency Pvt. Ltd., 1960.
———. *Twilight in Delhi*. New Directions Publishing, 1994.
Anderson, Mark D. *Disaster Writing: The Cultural Politics of Catastrophe in Latin America*. U of Virginia P, 2011.
Arnold, David. "Death and the Modern Empire: The 1918–19 Influenza Pandemic in India." *Transactions of the Royal Historical Society*, vol. 29, Dec. 2019, pp. 181–200, doi:10.1017/S0080440119000082. Accessed 20 Oct. 2021.
Beck, Ulrich. *Risk Society: Towards a New Modernity*. Translated by Mark Ritter, Sage, 1992.
Bhattacharya, Sourit. *Postcolonial Modernity and the Indian Novel: On Catastrophic Realism*. Palgrave Macmillan, 2020.
Blanchot, Maurice. *The Writing of the Disaster*. Translated by Ann Smock. U of Nebraska P, 1995.
Coppola, Carlo, editor. *Marxist Influences and South Asian Literature*, vol. 1, South Asia Series Occasional Paper No. 23. Asian Studies Centre, Michigan State UP, Winter 1974.

Gopal, Priyamvada. *Literary Radicalism in India: Gender, Nation and the Transition to Independence*. Routledge, 2005.

Hovanec, Caroline. *The 1918 Influenza Pandemic in Literature and Memory*. Vanderbilt U. MA dissertation, 2009. Accessed 20 October 2021.

Morton-Jack, George. *Shells, Songs and Bombs: How Indians Experienced World War I in the Home Front*. https://scroll.in/article/902246/shells-songs-and-bombs-how-indians-experienced-world-war-i-on-the-home-front. Accessed 20 Oct. 2021.

Mukherjee, Pablo. *Famine, Fevers, and Other Epidemics in Victorian India*. Palgrave Macmillan, 2013.

Nixon, Rob. *Slow Violence and the Environmentalism of the Poor*. Harvard UP, 2011.

Outka, Elizabeth. *Viral Modernism: The Influenza Pandemic and Interwar Literature*. Columbia UP, 2020.

Paine, Robert. "Danger and the No-Risk Thesis." *Catastrophe and Culture: The Anthropology of Disaster*, edited by Susanna M. Hoffman and Anthony Oliver-Smith. School of American Research Press, 2002.

Pradhan, Sudhi, editor. *Marxist Cultural Movement in India*. National Book Agency Pvt. Ltd., 1960.

Singh, Madhu. "Bombay Fever/Spanish Flu: Public Health and Native Press in Colonial Bombay 1918–19." *South Asia Research*, vol. 41, no. 1, 2021, pp. 35–52. doi:10.1177/0262728020966096. Accessed 20 Oct. 2021.

Weber, Thomas, and Dennis Dalton. "Gandhi and the Pandemic." *Economic and Political Weekly*, vol. 55, no. 25, 20 June 2020. Accessed 20 Oct. 2021.

Zaheer, Sajjad. "A Note on Progressive Writers' Association, 1936." *Marxist Cultural Movement in India*, edited by Sudhi Pradhan. National Book Agency Pvt. Ltd., 1960.

Zaman, Mukhtar. "Professor Ahmed Ali, The Rebel That Was." *The Journal of Indian Writing in English*, vol. 23, no. 1&2, 1995, pp. 19–26. Accessed 18 Sept. 2021.

13

PANDEMIC FEAR

Death and the Ruin of Civilization in Jack London's *The Scarlet Plague*

Paramita Dutta

"Of all base passions, fear is most accursed".
– *William Shakespeare,* Henry, VI,
Part I *(Act V Scene II, ll. 18).*

"Ay, but to die, and go we know not where;
To lie in cold obstruction and to rot;
. . .
The weariest and most loathed worldly life
That age, ache, penury and imprisonment
Can lay on nature is a paradise
To what we fear of death".
– *William Shakespeare,* Measure for Measure,
(Act III Scene I, ll. 129–30; 140–43)

Jack London's post-apocalyptic novel *The Scarlet Plague*, first published serially in London Magazine in 1912, captures accurately the scope of this "base passion", the "fear of death" that Shakespeare expresses with such poetic exquisiteness in the aforementioned quotations and is a harrowing testimony of how this fundamental and universal emotion is not only associated with death and ruin of civilization in the horrific events that unfold in the novel but also plays an important role in the survival of humans as a species in their continuous struggle for existence.

The Scarlet Plague is set in wild and savage America, in the future in 2073, 60 years after the spread of the Scarlet Death, an uncontainable epidemic that spread like wildfire and depopulated and destroyed the human civilization in 2013. It opens with an old man and a 12-year-old boy walking through the wilderness on the site of an erstwhile railroad where they are almost attacked by a grizzly bear. We soon find out that this primeval forest is none other than what used to be the San

DOI: 10.4324/9781003294436-18

Francisco Bay Area. The doddering old man is James Howard Smith, who used to be Professor of English, at the University of California, Berkeley, before the scarlet plague or red death struck and annihilated most of the people in the world. As one of the few lucky survivors, James Howard Smith or "Granser", recounts to his disbelieving near-savage grandsons, Edwin, Hare-lip and Hoo-Hoo, how the infectious plague spread like quickfire in the world and describes vividly the fear, the violence, the social destruction and ruin of civilization that followed the contagion. The world has regressed to a primitive and wild way of life post the pandemic, the crude grandsons, who are hunter-gatherers, do not comprehend most of what their "Granser" says and don't take his ruminations and recollections any more seriously than geriatric convoluted rigmarole.

This dystopian novel was written by Jack London before the Spanish influenza pandemic of 1918 which caused the death of millions of persons worldwide, but the gamut of emotions described by those suffering the pandemic hold true to this age, when the human race is struggling to overcome COVID-19 pandemic that unleashed itself on the unsuspecting world in 2020. *The Scarlet Plague* especially feels contemporary in spite of being published a century ago, as it allows modern readers to reflect on the worldwide fear of pandemics, contagion, death and social disruption, fears that have become a part of life since 2020. This chapter proposes to study this "base passion", the fear of the pandemic and death, important in generating the survival instinct, along with the corresponding ruin of civilization in London's novel. It reflects on and reveals the deeply entrenched fault lines in society as portrayed in this fictional narrative which also provides a framework to contextualize some of the events surrounding the current dread of the COVID-19 pandemic.

Literary Tradition of the Plague

Riva, Benedetti and Cesana have pointed out that by exploring the motif of the plague, London has followed a very well-developed literary tradition that reflected on the primal fear that humans had of infectious diseases. Since ancestral times, plagues and other calamities were feared especially as they had no known cure. Furthermore, the belief that pandemics were the result of unknown supernatural causes was deep-rooted. It has been seen that in the Bible (e.g. Exodus 9:14, Numbers 11:33, 1 Samuel 4:8, Psalms 89:23, Isaiah 9:13), the plague was often seen as a divine punishment for sins. Likewise, the Greek literary texts, such as Homer's *Iliad* and Sophocles' *Oedipus the King*, also underlined the causal relationship between contagion and sin.

On the contrary, they correctly note that writers like the Greek historian Thucydides (c. 460–395) in his *History of the Peloponnesian War*, and the Latin poet Lucretius (c. 99–55), in his *De Rerum Natura*, focused more on the uncontrolled fear of infection that the contagion brought about with the accompanying loss of social conventions and rise of the evils of self-absorbing avarice, and debunked a supernatural origin of the disease. Medieval works, like *The Decameron* by Giovanni Boccaccio (1313–1375) and *The Canterbury Tales* by Geoffrey Chaucer (1343–1400), emphasized human behaviour: the fear of contagion that generated vices such as covetousness, and corruption, which paradoxically led to infection and thus to not only physical but also moral death.

Much later, *A Journal of the Plague Year*, by Daniel Defoe (1659–1731), which was an eyewitness account[1] of the Great Plague of London 1665, also focused on the human responses to the plague in this detailed narrative. In the twentieth century, the English novelist Mary Shelley (1797–1851) wrote *The Last Man* (1826) which was one of the first apocalyptic novels, describing a future world that had been devastated by a plague. Only a handful of persons appear to be immune and isolate themselves. The concept of immunization in this book demonstrates that Mary Shelley, most famous for the novel *Frankenstein*, had a deep understanding of concurrent theories about the nature of contagion (1753).

Jack London's post-apocalyptic work of fiction definitely borrows from this tradition of stressing not on supernatural causes or sin as the cause of the plague but describes the modern condition of increased population and diseases as contributing to the spread of infection. It too focuses on the fear, violence and corruption that is generated in the common populace by the spread of the deadly infection and touches upon the concept of immunization through vaccination, the "serum" that was being created by Germany, as we shall see later.

Absence of Fear to Abject Fear in *The Scarlet Plague*

Thomas S. Langner in *Choices for Living: Coping with Fear of Dying* has correctly affirmed that the most common emotion engendered by death is fear (1). He goes on to delineate Gardner Murphy's list of seven "attitudes toward death", six of which are fears which include the "fear of losing consciousness (loss of control or mastery)", "fear of loneliness (separation from loved ones)", "fear of the unknown", "fear of punishment (hellfire, mutilation, disintegration)", "fear of what might happen to loved ones left behind, especially dependents" and "fear of failure (unfulfilled lives, tasks left undone, regrets)" (3). Apart from these six fears, another attitude towards death is when it is regarded as final acceptance. According to Langner, another helpful addition of "fear of individuality" can be made to this list which could act as a subcategory of the fear of loneliness, and it would be the solitariness and finality of dying as an individual, whereas there is a scope of living on in the group if one dies as part of a group (Ibid.).

Before we go on to discuss the attitudes towards death and the kind of fears inspired by the pandemic described in this dystopic novel by Jack London, I would also like to add the instinct of self-preservation or survival instinct that is engendered in human beings at the thought of immediacy of death as another attitude towards death to the ones mentioned earlier.

In *The Scarlet Plague*, when "Granser" or Smith starts recounting how the plague started in 2013, when he was a young man of 27, what is remarkable is the initial absence of fear among the people, and how they were not really alarmed by the thought of this pestilence. He describes, "Nobody thought anything about the news. It was only a small thing. There had been only a few deaths". Even when deaths began to be reported in Chicago and it was found that London had already been fighting the plague for 2 weeks shrouded in secrecy, and the public came to know that "the trouble was the astonishing quickness with which this germ destroyed human beings, and the fact that it inevitably killed any human body it entered. No one ever recovered", the people were still not paralysed by fear and instead had immense faith in the power of science or in the bacteriologists, who were expected to cure this scourge:

> We were sure that the bacteriologists would find a way to overcome this new germ, just as they had overcome other germs in the past.
>
> *(Chapter III)*

The description of this plague steadily becomes frightening as it is seen to kill swiftly, within fifteen minutes to an hour of contracting the contagion. Granser recounts vividly the horrific developments from the moment of a person's being infected by the infection:

> The heart began to beat faster and the heat of the body to increase. Then came the scarlet rash, spreading like wildfire over the face and body. Most persons never noticed the increase in heat and heart – beat, and the first they knew was when the scarlet rash came out. Usually, they had convulsions at the time of the appearance of the rash. But these convulsions did not last long and were not very severe. If one lived through them, he became perfectly quiet, and only did he feel a numbness swiftly creeping up his body from the feet. The heels became numb first, then the legs, and hips, and when the numbness reached as high as his heart he died. They did not rave or sleep. Their minds always remained cool and calm up to the moment their heart numbed and stopped. And another strange thing was the rapidity of decomposition. No sooner was a person dead than the body seemed to fall to pieces, to fly apart, to melt away even as you looked at it. That was one of the reasons the plague spread so rapidly. All the billions of germs in a corpse were so immediately released.
>
> *(Ibid.)*

London describes how the men of science, the bacteriologists, failed to combat this infection and themselves ironically and heroically succumbed to it in the laboratories. Numerous drugs and antidotes were tried to no avail. Finally, it is said:

> They tried to fight it with other germs, to put into the body of a sick man germs that were the enemies of the plague germs.
>
> *(Ibid.)*

The antidote described is what we would today call vaccination, which has been a source of immense controversy in the context of the current COVID-19, polarized by its supporters who believe it protects against the virus and its detractors/anti-vaxxers who believe it is more harmful than useful or preventive. In the time of the Scarlet Death too, as is in the context of COVID-19, this vaccination is not 100% efficacious.

The first description of public fear of the pandemic is seen after one of Smith's students Ms. Collbran gets infected and dies within fifteen minutes of manifesting the symptoms of the contagious Scarlet Death. Smith recounts, "the first fear of the plague was already on all of us and we knew that it had come" (Ibid.). What we see in the rest of her classmates and other students of the university as the news spreads like wildfire, along with the President of Faculty, President Hoag to whom Smith reports, is a combination of Murphy's fear of the unknown that Langner mentions in his book and what I added as the attitude towards immediacy of death – the instinct of self-preservation or survival instinct. In this case, this fearful attitude releases the flight response as a coping mechanism and everyone flees the victim along with those who have been exposed to the Scarlet Death. The screams of his housekeeper and cook, who too desert him resonate in his ears as Smith ruefully recounts,

> we did not act in this way when ordinary diseases smote us. We were always calm over such things, and sent for the doctors and nurses who knew just what to do. But this was different. It struck so suddenly, and killed so swiftly, and never missed a stroke.
>
> *(Ibid.)*

The trajectory from faith in science and absence of fear to loss of trust in science and abject pandemic fear of death had been spanned in no time in Smith's world of 2013. The world turns topsy-turvy and the serum of the plague that is reported as being discovered by Hoffmeyer, a bacteriologist of the Metchnikoff School in Germany, never reaches the shores of America and nothing more is heard of it.

The attitude of fear of the unknown, fear of losing consciousness (loss of control or mastery), and the attitude of the instinct of self-preservation, as mentioned earlier, are seen in the events that follow as Smith and his colleagues and their families take refuge in the Chemistry building of the university, whereas riots, shooting and looting break out in the cities. Some workingmen are seen to band together out of the city in groups to keep attackers at bay, and there we see instances of the attitudes of death as final acceptance coupled with self-sacrifice, when people who are infected in the group, voluntarily and without remonstrance leave the group to die alone of the plague.

There are also a few redeeming instances of love as superior to the attitude of self-preservation as depicted by some characters like Doctor Swinton, who chooses to be with his wife, Mrs. Swinton, when the contagion strikes her, to take care of her, in full knowledge that he too will contract the infection from her and both will not live to tell their story.

Pandemic Fear and the Ruin of Civilization

Commenting on the ubiquity of the idea of civilization in the contemporary world, Andrew Linklater mentions that in the nineteenth century, notions of civilization were fundamental to the personal and collective identities of the group as a whole. They were of paramount significance to the "social habitus" which included rules governing daily comportment and the related forms of emotion management that bound people together as a whole. This self-representation at the same time considers the "lower orders" to lack polish and refinement who therefore are considered inferiors (2). Additionally, according to him,

> the central coordinates of civilization included basic manners and rules of etiquette as well as hostility to barbaric forms of punishment and repugnance towards the violent resolution of disputes within advanced societies.
>
> *(Ibid.)*

One of the foremost things that the pandemic fear causes in *The Scarlet Plague* is the crumbling of this idea of civilization and exposure of the raw hostility and selfish self-preservation underneath the veneer of social cohesion of the people in this community. In the chaos following the spread of the pandemic, Smith speaks of how the grocer's store was attacked and set on fire in front of his eyes, and how he did not rush to help,

> I did not go to the groceryman's assistance. The time for such acts had already passed. Civilization was crumbling, and it was each for himself.
>
> *(Chapter III)*

He also narrates how he avoided helping the man he recognized on the street as the poet he admired when the latter was shot dead by hooligans (Chapter IV) and we understand that the "base passion" of fear of his own death and the instinct of self-preservation had kicked in to prompt his flight response. As rioting and shooting becomes rampant, Smith recollects ruefully,

> In the midst of our civilization, down in our slums and labor – ghettos, we had bred a race of barbarians, of savages; and now, in the time of our calamity, they turned upon us like the wild beasts they were and destroyed us. And they destroyed themselves as well.
>
> *(Chapter IV)*

This is a fault line in the concept of civilization itself as pointed out by Linklater, of the way the lower orders are perceived, and often the racialized terms used for the disadvantaged; and when the pandemic destroys the social fabric, all such imposed order and civil and community cohesion is turned upside down. Furthermore, Smith links the scope of the plague with human progress and modernity by stating,

> Long and long and long ago, when there were only a few men in the world, there were few diseases. But as men increased and lived closely together in great cities and civilizations, new diseases arose, new kinds of germs entered their bodies. Thus were countless millions and billions of human beings killed. And the more thickly men packed together, the more terrible were the new diseases that came to be.
>
> *(Chapter II)*

This implies that the idea of modern progress and civilization embodies within itself the idea of disorder and death arising from conditions such as excessive population and rise of diseases that proliferate easily among the people.

Wylie Lenz has shown how London's plague functions apocalyptically and not only depopulates the world but also causes social levelling in socio-economic terms. The rich are not immune to the plague, and the survivors are the ones who have a better immune system, be it Smith the professor or the man known as Chauffeur from his previous occupation (3–4). Smith rues the passing away of "hundreds of millions, yea, billions, of better men" while men like Bill, the Chauffeur, survived. The latter who is an uncouth man of dubious moral fabric gloats over the new-found possibilities that the plague has offered him, by erasing all social differences between his erstwhile master's wife Vesta and him, whereby he can possess her and treat her as his chattel and take his revenge on the upper social class that had oppressed him before the pandemic. He refuses to let her go with Smith and triumphantly declares,

> "You had your day before the plague", he said; "but this is my day, and a damned good day it is. I wouldn't trade back to the old times for anything".
>
> *(Chapter V)*

In the light of the systematic oppression that the lower orders have suffered in the hands of the higher social orders in the pre-plague days when civilization and modernity were at its prime, the Scarlet Death and corresponding ruin of civilization have given people like Bill, the Chauffeur, however ghoulish he may be in Smith's opinion, liberation and the right to live on their own dictated terms. He makes his train of thought even more explicit when he explains that "we're up against a regular Garden-of-Eden proposition" (Ibid.). Lenz correctly mentions that "In the neo-tribal order that develops among scattered groups of survivors along the California coast after an anarchic interregnum, a former laboring ghoul might very well thrive", and he does prosper and the tribe he creates remains until the day the novel is set in 2073 is called the Chauffeur Tribe. For Smith, as Lenz correctly asserts, the union of the base Chauffeur and lady Vesta is representative of unacceptable miscegenation, and he explains to his grandsons that "in the days before the plague, the slightest contact with such as he would have been pollution", thereby conflating racial mixing/"pollution" with the pandemic infection (4).

It is also to be noted that it is only Smith, representative of the educated upper class before the plague, who finds the Chauffeur uncouth, but the other characters, his grandsons, Edwin, Hare-Lip and Hoo-Hoo, who do not have the concept of civilization to fall back on having been born long after the plague in the primordial wilderness, appreciate him in their own ways. Hare-Lip describes him to be a "corker" and "son of a gun" admiringly (Chapter V) and considers him to be more manly and powerful than their grandfather who is pitied as being senile.

With the coming of the Scarlet Death the world fell apart, absolutely, irreversibly. Ten thousand years of culture and civilization passed in the blink of an eye, "lapsed like foam" (Chapter I). Not only was the world depopulated, leaving a handful of people from scattered groups surviving; the land enveloped by wild vegetation with all signs of buildings and other symbols of modernity erased, but it also destroyed language to a large degree. What the grandsons speak in 2073 is described to be a hardly comprehensible remnant of what used to be the English language in all its glory. Jack London describes, "They spoke in monosyllables and short jerky sentences that was more a gibberish than a language" (Chapter I). Moreover, the regression was so severe that there was no longer any concept of money in the post-pandemic world and neither did the grandsons have any idea of numbers.

Smith narrates how food in its infinite abundance and variety was a great achievement of his civilization. While talking about the people who produced food in their society, he lays bare the social inequalities between the producers and consumers of the same food in his society:

> Our food – getters were called freemen. This was a joke. We of the ruling classes owned all the land, all the machines, everything. These food – getters were our slaves. We took almost all the food they got, and left them a little so that they might eat, and work, and get us more food.
>
> *(Chapter I)*

In the post-pandemic primitive society, the Granser and his grandsons are hunter-gatherers and the latter do not comprehend the concept of well-cooked gourmet meals and the idea of any "toothsome delicacy" that their grandfather speaks of with such relish and nostalgia.

Furthermore, the grandsons also do not understand the meaning of "education" and what Smith considers to be a noble profession, being a Professor of English Literature at the University of California, Berkeley, is immediately reduced to nothingness by Hoo-Hoo when he exclaims after hearing that his grandfather used to deliver lectures:

> "Was that all you did? – just talk, talk, talk?" Hoo – Hoo demanded. "Who hunted your meat for you? and milked the goats? and caught the fish?"
>
> *(Chapter II)*

Life after the pandemic is stripped of any sophistication, of any cultural superiority, etiquette and manners that we associate with civilization, and is reduced to its basic functions that are necessary for survival in the natural environment. Although Smith has stored his books in a cave on Telegraph Hill with a key to the alphabet so that the knowledge of the ancients can be saved for the future, it does not seem that it will easily happen, given that he has himself not been able to successfully pass the knowledge on to either his children or grandsons who are not able to read and speak what is described as "gabble".

The role that media plays in this work of dystopic fiction is also very meaningful and has far-reaching even if indirect contribution to the ruin of civilization. Smith describes the heroic endeavours of the wireless operator and the newspaperman in transmitting the latest updates on the plague situation, including the development of the serum in Germany, and the news of the widespread conflagrations in Chapter II. Once the men responsible for transmitting the messages die, and there are no more newspapers produced and distributed, there is no further dissemination of what is happening across the world, and essentially the world shrinks as the different places are alienated from each other through the breakdown of communication.

The Scarlet Plague and the COVID-19 Pandemic

Although the COVID-19 pandemic has struck us a little more than a century after Jack London wrote his novel, and even though it predates its setting of 2073 by 50 years, the human behavioural responses to the plague/pandemic are comparable on many counts. In both, we see the trajectory of not taking the pandemic seriously to developing a fear psychosis of the infection. The attitude of the fear of unknown, that of the fear of infection contributing to the attitude of self-preservation that we see in the novel, is seen during the initial stages of the COVID-19 pandemic when people started hoarding food and North America also started suffering from something as ridiculous as a toilet paper crisis because of excessive hoarding! The media played a crucial role in the 2020 pandemic, by spreading information as well as sometimes misinformation causing panic. At the same time, social media and virtual communication have played a pivotal role in keeping people connected when physically they had to be distanced and cities underwent lockdown all over the world. It may be the world after the COVID-19 pandemic of 2020 has not regressed to a primitive and isolated way of life as in London's novel, but we are living in a "new normal" with more emphasis on virtual communication and digital and technological innovation for work and education, to the extent that people are ceasing to have interactions in person and getting isolated in their own bubbles.

Conclusion

According to Elana Gomel, "Post apocalypse, however, is a discourse not so much of radical transformation as of 'aftermaths and remainders' (Berger xii). . . . If the apocalypse promises glorious rebirth, post apocalypse is enmeshed in the backward-looking narrative of trauma" (408). The post-apocalyptic *The Scarlet Plague* is similarly enmeshed in Smith's "backward-looking narrative of trauma" that begins with the pandemic and vividly captures the pandemic fear of death and the ruin of civilization that this plague brings about. At the same time as Joe Matthews says, "this old little novel retains considerable power as a warning about the vulnerability of our state and civilization", especially in the light of the COVID-19 pandemic. Fear of death is universal and it is not impossible for even advanced societies to disintegrate, and Jack London seems to remind us that present-day horrors were not really unthinkable when he was writing, and that we should always be on our guard to protect our civilization and our future.

Note

1   There is a controversy surrounding its status as a work of nonfiction eyewitness account as Daniel Defoe was 5 years of age at the time the bubonic plague occurred in London.

Works Cited

Berger, James. *After the End: Representations of Post-Apocalypse.* U of Minnesota 1999, p. xii. Quoted in Gomel, Elana. "The Plague of Utopias: Pestilence and the Apocalyptic Body." *Literature and Apocalypse,* special issue of *Twentieth Century Literature,* vol. 46, no. 4, 2000, pp. 405–33. JSTOR. www.jstor.org/stable/827840.

Gomel, Elana. "The Plague of Utopias: Pestilence and the Apocalyptic Body." *Literature and Apocalypse,* special issue of *Twentieth Century Literature,* vol. 46, no. 4, 2000, pp. 405–33. JSTOR. www.jstor.org/stable/827840.

Langner, Thomas S. *Choices for Living: Coping with Fear of Dying.* Kluwer Academic Publishers, 2002.

Lenz, Wylie. "Toward a Genealogy of the American Zombie Novel: From Jack London to Colson Whitehead." *Contemporary Literary Criticism,* edited by Jennifer Stock, vol. 477. Gale, 2021. Gale Literature Resource Center. www.link.gale.com/apps/doc/H1100 129493/LitRC?u=rpu_main&sid=summon&xid=b735bfb1 (Originally published in *The Written Dead,* edited by Kyle William Bishop and Angela Tenga. McFarland, 2017, pp. 98–119).

Linklater, Andrew. *The Idea of Civilization and the Making of the Global Order.* Bristol UP, 2021.

London, Jack. *The Scarlet Plague.* Project Gutenberg, 29 June 2007. www.gutenberg.org/ebooks/21970.

Matthews, Joe. "The 21st Century California Plague That Jack London Saw Coming." *Fox &Hounds.* Granada Hills, 2020. Project Muse, blog. http://ezproxy.lib.ryerson.ca/login?url=www.proquest.com/blogs-podcastswebsites/21st-century-california-plague-that-jack-london/docview/2388710897/se-2?accountid=13631.

Riva, Michele Augusto, et al. "Pandemic Fear and Literature: Observations from Jack London's *The Scarlet Plague.*" *Emerging Infectious Diseases,* vol. 20, no. 10, pp. 1753–57. doi:10.3201/eid2010.130278.

Wells, Stanley, and Gary Taylor, general editors. *William Shakespeare: The Complete Works.* 2nd ed. Clarendon Press, 2005.

14

PANDEMIC AND THE END OF THE WORLD IN MARGARET ATWOOD'S *ORYX AND CRAKE*

Sayan Aich Bhowmik

> I' th' commonwealth I would by all contraries
> Execute all things; for no kind of traffic
> Would I admit; no name of magistrate;.
> Letters should not be known; riches poverty,
> And use of service, none . . .
>
> *(Shakespeare 35)*

Gonzalo in *The Tempest* talks of setting up a utopian regime, where there will be no "traffic", "magistrate" or even "occupation", where men would be free from political and ideological repressions. Human society, however, in its endeavour to create such a state, invariably ends up suppressing and marginalizing one of its factions. What we then realize is that there is a very fine dividing line between an idealized and utopian space and that space degenerating into a claustrophobic dystopian vision for the silenced and sub-alterned, revealing chinks in the dominant discursive framework. Dystopic spaces are sometimes characterized as anti-utopian, but this clear-cut binary is problematized. Surveillance, political and social, as well as erasure of subaltern history and culture, which leads to an ethnic cleansing all come together to create dissonant voices in the model commonwealth. Class revolts, armed rebellions later, societies are but a rotten carcass of its conceptual dream. As Claire Curtis remarks,

> Such events by their very character are understood to destroy functional government, food distribution, organized medical care and the infrastructure on which we rely for most of what we do.
>
> *(Curtis 4)*

DOI: 10.4324/9781003294436-19

The Premise

A pandemic, as one would be forced to agree, is an event which not only alters perceptions about life and every aspect associated with it but also redraws boundaries and borders, temporarily closing some while permanently shutting others. The reason why I began this chapter by talking of utopian dreams and dystopic spaces is to stress the trope found in post-apocalyptic films and fiction of humans trying to reach a more advanced stage of human existence and in their endeavour to do so, violating the fine dividing line that I spoke of earlier, turning the world as we know it into a wasteland. This spatial reconfiguration is matched by its temporal counterpart – with respect to the outbreak of the COVID-19 virus, terms like Pre-COVID Era and Post-COVID Era have entered the common parlance and lexicon. What we also find fascinating is how death and mayhem surrounding the pandemic are treated in popular imagination and culture. The twentieth-century Spanish flu which led to the death of millions hardly found a voice in the literature of the period, even though those years were the glory years of High Modernism. Also intriguing is the way in which the pandemic has been used as a metaphor for the developing political scenario in the world, especially the US foreign policy during the Cold War.

It is from this aspect that I would like to analyse Margaret Atwood's *Oryx and Crake* which presents a post-apocalyptic world after a pandemic has wiped out the entire civilization leaving, literally and metaphorically, "the last man standing". The novel presents a vision of a world, driven by a desire for betterment, even at the cost of independence and choice. The class divides, the carnivorous consumer culture typical of US mainstream society are scathingly attacked and man pays the ultimate price of trying to play God. The apocalyptic vision too is significant. The virus that has caused the plague was actually meant to create a more intelligent species constituting of the best in humanity. My analysis would also bring in the US foreign policy in Afghanistan and its repercussions and reaching its fateful climax in 9/11, the destruction of the twin towers.

The Russian invasion of Afghanistan saw an immediate response from America in the early 1980s and what followed was the policy of arming the Indigenous tribes with arms and training them so as to set them as an antagonistic force to the Russians. But when the Russians left in the early 1990s, these same tribes and factions came under the rubric of Islamic Fundamentalist forces, to be led by Osama Bin Laden, and would come to haunt the United States, culminating in the Jihad and the US war on terror and the subsequent invasion of Afghanistan and Iraq. In a way, this is the classic case of Frankenstein meeting his match in his own creation, and my argument in this chapter is along these same lines – how literature and films dealing with the pandemic and the end of the world are a metaphor and extension of the way the US foreign policy panned out and the resultant conflict with the Taliban/Al-Qaeda.

Neo-Colonialism and the New Empire

Debates have ranged over the past few decades regarding whether the "empire" as we knew it in the nineteenth and twentieth centuries has ceased to exist. The years following the World War II saw a host of countries achieve independence after a long, protracted and in most cases a bloody anti-colonial struggle. And yet the way the world markets have opened up, resulting in Multinational Companies looking for and finding cheap labour in the so-called developing Third World Nations, resulting in the creation of a really expendable workforce, one begins to question whether these countries, despite being politically free, are free from the tentacles of the world market and the apparent "Macdonaldisation" of the economy.

(Colas 2)

What this does is to make us re-evaluate our understanding of colonialism and come to the conclusion that many independent nations are just renewed and refurbished versions of their colonial masters. With Britain and France losing their colonies and the revenue that they would generate, the United States and USSR emerged as the main players in the 1950s. But the United States was an empire with a difference:

> It was premised not on the relentless expansion of territorial frontiers and the deprivation of political sovereignty for subject peoples, but on the proliferation of competing centers of political authority and the promotion of formal territorial sovereignty for peoples previously subject to European, Japanese and indeed U.S imperialism.
>
> (Colas 2)

The Cold War and the Power Block

A large chunk of the second half of the twentieth century was spent in the political tug of war and manoeuverings between the two superpowers trying to outdo each other, pushing the world onto the brink of a nuclear war every time political tension escalated. It is to be noted that for the United States, every time they felt that their quest for a capitalist world order/hegemony was under threat, Washington stepped into the scene in the role of the saviour of the people, a role that had been sanctioned upon themselves, a twentieth-century version of the burden of the white man. Hall Gardner succinctly and ironically describes the United States as the modern-day Hercules, which engages itself in unending "labors", to provide stability and support to governments across the world every time it senses an opportunity or an economic market which could be later tapped (Gardener 4). The imposing and coercive global economic power and arm flexing was used to strengthen state authority and ensure that the capitalist market remain opened for investment and exploitation. USSR's presence was an important factor as Colas and Saull observe:

> The Soviet Block was a key external source for encouraging political and economic cooperation amongst the major capitalist states under U.S political hegemony and military protection.
>
> *(Colas and Saull 12)*

This was most evident in the last decades before the fall of the Soviet Union in Central Asia and in Afghanistan. What followed was the arming of the local/ tribal Afghans and not only providing them with ammunition and training but also recognizing them as the only possible and final resort of resistance against the Russians. This was not restricted to Afghanistan alone, as Gardner points out in his extensive study of the US foreign policy in the region,

> Concurrently, the U.S. backed "radical" Sunni Moslem, as well as *Wahabist* and *Deobandi*, movements against the Soviet Union in Afghanistan and Sunni/secular Iraq against pan- Shi'ite Iran, which was regarded as the greater of the two evils. By 1982–83, the U.S along with Saudi Arabia, fully supported Saddam Hussein's war with Ayatollah Khomeini, which was instigated in reaction to Iranian support for Shi'a and Kurdish factions in Iraq.
>
> *(Gardener 113)*

One is curiously reminded of the end credits of the film *Rambo III*, where it is explicitly stated that the film is a homage to the gallant people of Afghanistan, the *Mujahedeens*. Ironically, the same faction would come to haunt America in just over a decade's time with Al-Qaeda destroying the World Trade Centre in what is only the second case of a foreign attack on American soil after the Pearl Harbour bombings. It is important to remember that the Al-Qaeda turned on the United States the moment the former felt that the United States had abandoned its pan-Islamic cause (Gardener 115). I would like to argue that this support and creation of right-wing fundamentalist forces under diplomatic cover to counter an ideological and political threat of Communist Russia is the archetypal Frankenstein syndrome and texts like *Oryx and Crake* can be seen as a reworking of this myth/syndrome under the rubric of a post-apocalyptic tale of a society which has been reduced to a wasteland by the very agents of development and scientific advancement which was supposed to take it forward.

Margaret Atwood and Speculative Fiction

Margaret Atwood has, for a very long time, resisted and protested against her works being labelled as "science fiction". Rather, she prefers the term "Speculative Fiction" and does so with the firm belief that the latter is at a higher pedestal than

Science Fiction, since science fiction seeks only to entertain, whereas speculative fiction attempts to make the reader take a cognitive and objective view on the world around them by comparing it to the fictional setting as presented in the novel/short story. As Katherine Snyder notes,

> The reader of such fiction must sustain a kind of double consciousness with respect both to the fictionality of the world portrayed and to its potential as our own world's future.
>
> *(Snyder 470)*

The world of *Oryx and Crake* is one which is a remnant of the world we once knew after a deadly pandemic has wiped out the entire populace. The post-apocalyptic world has its genesis in a dream of a better future and society, one which is not spiritually dead. But Crake, the over-reaching scientist, born and bred in a society which supports and sponsors such dreams, is responsible for the experiment horribly going wrong. The narrative rides on the description of the only human survivor, Snowman, who is the one entrusted with looking after the new species *Crakers* delineate the sense of loss all around. Above all, it is man's desire to play God and control, not only human lives and politics but rather Nature itself that is the root of this collapse of apocalyptic proportions. The fact that Atwood is not narrating a fantastical tale but rather one which is realistic and identifiable is evident from the epigraph of the novel,

> I could perhaps like others have astonished you with strange improbable tales; but I rather choose to relate plain matter of fact in the simplest manner and style; because my principle design was to inform you, and not to amuse you.
>
> *(Atwood 1)*

The setting of *Oryx and Crake* has elements that are all too familiar to most of us. The social elite lives inside gated communities, while the not so fortunate and on the lower rungs of the social and economic order are pushed inside urban jungles called *pleeblands*. Snyder further remarks,

> The futurist setting of the novel suggests that we are at risk of coming to such a pass, though some readers may feel that this is already substantially, if not literally, the way we live now.
>
> *(Snyder 471)*

The world of *Oryx and Crake*, before the man-made pandemic set in, is one which promotes a commercialization of life, commodification of women and rampant pornography and widening the chasm between the rich and the poor. The entire society is obsessed with science and technology, and the novel examines the ethical consequences of this dependence and obsession.

But does Atwood's post-apocalyptic vision work in the culmination of trends in politics, and military invasion whose seeds have been sown in the twentieth and the twenty-first centuries? The novel deals with the creation of the virus which would help in the establishment of a better race, and yet, it is the cause of the end of civilization as we know it. The issue is how has the monster turned on Frankenstein the creator. If the Arab world turned against their Western counterpart, they did so using the latter's machinery. The militant fundamentalists see themselves as the warriors of god, a David taking on a Goliath, but this time with Goliath's own aeroplanes and bombs, in their own heartland. The technology of the most advanced civilization on earth had been used as daggers on its own back.

Crake's desire to do some good for the society leads to the release of the deadly virus that leads to the almost total extinction of the human race. This trope is found in numerous movies of the late 1990s and early 2000s, the most famous being *I Am Legend*. The novel can be read as a parable of the typically American foreign policy, something that has been discussed in the previous sections. *Oryx and Crake* is a tale of man playing God with dangerous consequences. Crake's intellectual arrogance leads him to play with the human race as though it were a computer game. He had the possibilities of violence, religion and racism erased from the DNA of his creation but all this at the cost of the deadly pandemic that he himself has brought upon the world.

The novel ends on a note which leaves questions unanswered and the readers hanging on the edge. The Snowman has decided, "It is time to go" (Atwood 323), but the readers cannot be sure as to what this means. Is there a flicker of hope for mankind or is the Snowman about to give himself up to the unsuspecting group of human survivors? We are provided with no clear-cut answer which is symptomatic of the entire novel, which throws up more questions than solutions.

Works Cited

Atwood, Margaret. *Oryx and Crake*. Bloomsbury, 2003.

Colas, A., and R. Saull, editors. *The War on Terror and the American Empire After the Cold War*. Routledge, 2006.

Curtis, Claire. *Post-Apocalyptic Fiction and the Social Contract*. Lexington, 2010.

Gardener, Hall. *American Global Strategy and the War on Terrorism*. Ashgate, 2001.

Lundstad, Geir. "The Empire by Invitation: United States and Western Europe, 1945–1952." *Journal of Peace Research*, vol. 23, no. 3, 1986, pp. 263–77.

Shakespeare, William. *The Tempest*. Arden, 2000.

Snyder, Katherine. "The Post Apocalyptic and the Post-Traumatic in Margaret Atwood's *Oryx and Crake*." *Studies in the Novel, University of North Texas*, vol. 43, no. 4, 2011, pp. 470–89.

V

COVID-19, Public Health and Social Justice

15

POWER AND THE PANDEMIC THROUGH TWO GOTHIC TROPES

Tabish Khair

It is difficult to talk of vampire or zombie films in Indian cinema, though theorists, film critics and, above all, market agents commonly use these convenient generic demarcations. As I noted in a paper on the vampire in South Asia, various cultural factors – such as the relative absence of a universal Devil/Satan in Indian mythologies, common belief in rebirth and the dominant Hindu practice of cremation – militate against any easy translation of the vampire figure.[1] I had also pointed out that the general impression that the vampire has a longer Indian heritage is a case of colonial mistranslation, largely because the folk tales known as *Baital Paichasi*, usually sourced as eleventh-century Sanskrit recensions in the collection of stories known as *Kathâ-Sarit-Sâgara* (Ocean of the Stream of Stories), appeared in English in 1870 as Sir Richard Francis Burton's *Vikram and the Vampire: or Tales of Hindu Devilry*.

The Zombie and Indian Cinema

Burton's translation of Baital – also pronounced Vetaal and Betaal – as "vampire" was of course performed in a decade when, prior to Bram Stoker's consolidation of the vampire in the European imagination, the term "vampire" itself had looser connotations. Baitaal, vetaal and betaal can be translated in many other ways, and have been. For instance, in Hindi, Phantom, the Ghost who Walks, appears as Vetaal in comic books. And a recent Indian Netflix series, considered a zombie adaptation, is titled *Betaal*.

Actually, very often both quasi-vampire and quasi-zombie adaptations in Indian cinema are overlaid by a very Indian sub-genre, one that can be called "spirit possession". This element, for instance, is shared by both the popular 1979 Bombay "vampire-film", *Jaani Dushman*, and the recent three-part Indian "zombie series", *Ghoul*. Both, while slanting towards the two Western genres, are essentially about

DOI: 10.4324/9781003294436-21

a spirit or a "being" who, in different ways and for very different reasons, takes possession of its victims, in the case of *Ghoul* assuming their identity after partly cannibalizing them. Reflecting the social concerns of the decades, across half a century, when they were produced, while *Jaani Dushman* is set in a rural, semi-feudal backdrop, *Ghoul* is set in the future, where a fascist state is fighting a xenophobic war against real and imagined terror.

Actually, I can think of only two Indian films that tally closely with Western zombie expectations. Arguably, *Miruthan*, a 2016 Indian Tamil-language film written and directed by Shakti Soundar Rajan, is a zombie film, as the zombies in it are the consequence of chemical pollution and not a case of spirit possession or magical practices (as in *Ghoul*). Not surprisingly, the title of the film, *Miruthham*, is a neologism, combining the Tamil word that means "animal" with the word that means "man", and hence obtaining a word for "zombie" in the language. Another largely zombie film is the 2013 Bollywood production, *Go Goa Gone*, which however has a "Western" backdrop, featuring drug raves, the Russian mafia and tourists.

As such, when I claim, as I do here, that Indian cinema has largely moved from proto-vampire horror to proto-zombie horror, I can be faulted for not parsing the differences between Western meanings of both vampire and zombie and their Indian adaptations. However, I will make that point, also because I think that it connects to a global shift in which the vampire has largely disappeared as a figure of horror (surviving sometimes in romanticized dark hero forms) while the zombie, with minor exceptions, remains a figure of horror and shock. All the above, zombie films in India have been produced over the past few years, and both *Go Goa Gone* and *Mirugam* have sequels on the way. For significant vampire horror adaptations, one needs to look further back.

COVID-19 – Fear and Vulnerability

In this chapter, I make the point – not original – that the zombie expresses our repressed fears more than the vampire today, and I go on to read it in the light of the pandemic. But let me say a few things about the vampire first. Karl Marx's reference to capital as "vampire-like" is legendary. This was developed in the early work of Franco Moretti, who essentially examined the vampire (in Bram Stoker's *Dracula*) as a hoarder who then invests in and from the international metropolitan world, aspiring to a kind of monopoly; creates an army of workers and subservient beings; lives by sucking their lifeblood ("surplus value" in Marxist terms); and maintains a strict class hierarchy. Such a vampire can also become invisible, but both he and the nature of his exploitation are thoroughly embodied, even "rooted" in the soil. As Moretti indicates, this tallies with our experience of classical capitalism, especially if one looks at it from the left, and particularly if one applies various Marxist perspectives.

But are we still living in a world where, as both Adam Smith and Karl Marx said, wealth is created by human labour? Whatever the ethics of capital, until recently it was assumed, and not just by leftists, that wealth needs human labour to come into being, and that the relationships of capitalism, whether exploitative or beneficial, involve production and trade. This is no longer the case. Thomas Picketty and others make similar points but in extended technical terms, however, I will use a single, relatively pithy, quotation from a book by the economist Samir Amin.

> Goods and services transactions [of world GDP] represented 3 percent of the monetary and financial transactions conducted in 2002; transactions concerning international trade amounted to hardly 2 percent of the foreign exchange transactions; settlements of purchase and sales of shares and bonds in organised markets (operations considered as being constituents by excellence to capital markets) amounted to only 3.4 percent of all monetary settlements! It is transactions in hedging products – designed to cover the operator's risks – which have literally exploded! . . . The ratio between hedging operations [on the one side] and production and international trading [on the other] was 28:1 in 2002 – a disproportion that has been constantly growing for about the last twenty years and which has never been witnessed in the entire history of capitalism.[2]

What Amin is stressing about in 2002, and commenting on as a novel feature of capitalism, one that evolved in the 1980s and has grown since then, is this: Both Adam Smith and Karl Marx were partly wrong in assuming that capitalism is a relationship, beneficial or exploitative, between capital, labour and goods. It looks like both labour and goods – as production or trade – are no longer necessary to becoming rich. Capital, which was always suspected by Marxists of a tendency towards self-perpetuation, can now multiply without production or trade – and, hence, without human labour.

This has been borne out during and by the current pandemic. Even with industries shutting down and workers and employees getting laid off by the millions, the richest of the rich have made mind-boggling profits.

> A report by Swiss bank UBS found that billionaires increased their wealth by more than a quarter (27.5%) at the height of the crisis from April to July 2020, just as millions of people around the world lost their jobs or were struggling to get by on government schemes.[3]

The situation was similar in India, where the wealth of the super-rich is estimated to have risen by 35% in roughly the same period.[4] This trend has continued into 2021, as more recent figures indicate.

While some of this rise has to do with the financial ability of the super-rich to continue to buy or retain dropping shares, a lot also has to do with the structure that I have highlighted: the fact that wealth need not be put back and increased through human labour – as production or trade. It can be increased through sheer play of numbers, mostly digitized. The blood of human labour that Marx accused the vampire of capital of sucking is no longer inevitable. The worker – also as a middle-class employee – is no longer necessary for capital to increase.

It is in this situation, with the pandemic raging and with recalcitrant nations finally announcing lockdowns, that we encountered a very zombie-like situation in India. On 25 March 2020, the Prime Minister of India, Mr. Narendra Modi, ordered a "folk curfew" and a nation-wide lockdown, with an advance notice of four hours. With large and petty industries shutting down and even middle-class Indians, worried about their own safety, laying off their servants, the vast "informal economy" of India was suddenly pitched on the roads. Asked to "stay home", and with no income to pay for their food or accommodation, the millions of "migrant workers" that keep Indian cities running became desperate to return to their village homes – where they could be "safe" and manage to subsist. This was not possible using public and private transports, as the road and railway services had been discontinued or were severely curtailed. In due course, millions of these workers started trekking back to their villages, which were sometimes eight or nine hundred kilometres away. Even as some official help was later organized, what was witnessed – and mostly under-reported by the mainstream media, which sometimes portrayed these workers as pests and "super-spreaders" – was a mass migration that rivalled those during the independence and partition of India in 1947.[5]

The few scenes of this forced labour migration captured on film are reminiscent of zombie apocalypses as imagined by Hollywood. Streams of dazed people, including children and women, carrying the few possessions they have managed to assemble, trudging along the sides of roads and highways. There were hundreds of deaths: by illness, starvation and accident. It was a process that continued for months.

Note that the tragic migrations of 1947 were marked and driven by conflicts between communities, not this image of an obdurate, mechanical trek to escape – but escape what, escape where? The virus that your companion might be carrying, or that the next stranger could contaminate you with?

My choice of "zombie" is not anecdotal: it stresses the reality of these workers. They are no longer necessary to the vampire of capital, as Marx, rightly or wrongly, saw it. They are superfluous, like zombies, well past their expiry date as workers, as humans. Their choices are limited too: no industrial sabotage and no garlic, no strikes and no crucifix. All they can do is trek away, fleeing from something that they cannot even hope to escape. No wonder zombie films and narratives, despite all their distortions, fascinate us, in India and elsewhere, far more than vampire ones. No wonder the vampire has assumed nostalgic shapes, for at least the vampire still denoted a mutual relationship. If the vampire was the undead, it needed those who were alive. That is not the case with the worker today – or with the zombie. The vampire was the fear of classical capitalism. The zombie is the horror of neoliberalism.

It is to be noted that neoliberalism is buoyed up by the myth of voluntary work, working from home, millions of start-ups, etc. Capital in neoliberalism has become fully abstract numbers, and is ideally accessible to everyone: the treasure hoard of

Dracula's castle is not necessary to start Dracula off in London. Capital, as digitized numbers, breeds on its own, invisibly. No one seems to exploit anyone else under neoliberalism; we exploit ourselves, some, like Elon Musk, are just supposed to be better at exploiting themselves. A general agreement among us – also leading to political populism – is considered not just essential, but unavoidable: "There is no better option". The zombie is "non-hierarchical"; all of us just turn into zombies. Who is to blame: well, there is no top vampire to point our fingers at. A zombie is hugely communal: even populist. The "infection" in a zombie is entirely invisible, like capital as numbers. Nothing really to produce: zombies are their own production.

With these factors in mind, it is possible to "understand" the official response to the pandemic – as well as discussion of the virus – in India. It essentially echoed the discourse of zombification: invisible infection, caste-like untouchability, banging plates as a united "one" nation from balconies, armies of dazed unemployed useless workers trekking back home through the hinterland, etc. And yes, of course, the zombie can be allowed to die. The vampire needs its victims, but the zombie is useless. No wonder so many governments around the world essentially failed to protect their citizens from the Novel Coronavirus. In this, India was not an exception. The old people's homes that were turned into death traps in the United Kingdom; the COVID-19 denialism in places like the United States and Brazil that caused many avoidable deaths, there is a long list of bad or mixed management in the face of a pandemic which, despite media obfuscation, was not a mystery once China traced and published the genetic code of the virus. Of course, India had its own version of this failure. It just adopted the zombie reality, as Indian films adapt the zombie genre, with some cultural modifications.

Increasing Xenophobia

Actually, in my 2016 book, *The New Xenophobia*, I had sadly predicted this as an increasing aspect of xenophobia in the neoliberal age: not targeted genocides as much as overlooked, evaded ones; not people herded into gas chambers, but people allowed to die.[6] I suspect that when, and if, an objective history of the pandemic is written, this is what will astound historians: the ability of various governments, governments to the left, middle and right of the political spectrum, to allow "superfluous" sections of their society (manual labourers, old citizens, etc.) to suffer and die, when much of it could have been avoided. The zombie, as a trope, is not just a figure of threat, as is the vampire, but a figure of superfluity: it remains today, in our phase of "neoliberal capitalism", the best encapsulation of what has happened to millions of human beings who, as superannuated workers inside and outside national borders, have fallen through the cracks in the floor of globalization. They exist, for their material existence cannot be denied, but they exist as a struggling, amorphous, incoherent mass – not really as specific workers, with particular kinds of training, with faces and hands, with lifeblood.

This was always an element of late capitalist unemployment, as Tony Harrison's "skinhead" saw it way back in 1985 in the long poem "V", when he ranted against his dead "forefathers", all of whom with jobs for life until they retired and still identified as "butcher", etc. on their tombstones. The skinhead noted that his generation would be buried under tombstones that say that the "cunts who lieth'ere wor unemployed?"[7] This undifferentiated living on the "dole" all one's life, as against the specific jobs of the skinhead's ancestors in the capitalist–industrial phase, is an aspect of zombification. Harrison identified it early, actually in the first decade of the ascendency of neoliberalism.

As the jobs disappear, not only are workers laid off but an entire undifferentiated class comes into being that is thoroughly identical in its endless and growing precarity. It poses a threat, in its monstrous physicality, but it is at the same time highly expendable. The vampire's victims were not expendable. Even the death of a vampire, at least until that figure itself was often zombified from the 1990s onwards, was an event. It required meticulous planning, often a ceremony. It was not a genocide, but a precisely planned activity. The death of zombies is nothing like that. They can be mowed down by the hundreds. They can be allowed to die endlessly, in massive numbers, because they are finally superfluous to power. It is not a coincidence that the images that come to the forefront when one thinks of the COVID-19 pandemic are not those of the vampire, or its victims, but that of the zombie.

Notes

1   Khair, "The Man-Eating Tiger", 105–20.
2   Amin, *From Capitalism to Civilization*, 97–98.
3   www.theguardian.com/business/2020/oct/07/covid-19-crisis-boosts-the-fortunes-of-worlds-billionaires.
4   www.theleaflet.in/in-pandemic-indias-super-rich-get-richer-by-35-while-common-people-suffer-the-most/#.
5   https://slate.com/news-and-politics/2020/05/indias-coronavirus-lockdown-created-a-mass-migration.html.
6   Khair, *The New Xenophobia*.
7   www.lrb.co.uk/the-paper/v07/n01/tony-harrison/v.

Works cited

Amin, Samir. *From Capitalism to Civilization: Reconstructing the Socialist Perspective*. Tulika Books, 2010.

Harrison, Tony. *V*. www.lrb.co.uk/the-paper/v07/n01/tony-harrison/v.

Khair, Tabish. "The Man-Eating Tiger and the Vampire in South Asia." *Transnational and Postcolonial Vampires*, edited by Tabish Khair and Johan Höglund. Palgrave, 2013, pp. 105–20.

———. *The New Xenophobia*. Oxford UP, 2016.

Neate, Rupert. *Billionaires' Wealth Rises to $10.2 Trillion Amid Covid Crisis*, 7 Oct. 2020. www.theguardian.com/business/2020/oct/07/covid-19-crisis-boosts-the-fortunes-of-worlds-billionaires.

Pahwa, Nitish. *India's Stay-at-Home Order Created a Migration Crisis.* https://slate.com/news-and-politics/2020/05/indias-coronavirus-lockdown-created-a-mass-migration.html.

Patnaik, Prabhat. *In Pandemic, India's Super Rich Get Richer by 35% While Common People Suffer the Most.* www.theleaflet.in/in-pandemic-indias-super-rich-get-richer-by-35-while-common-people-suffer-the-most/.

16

FOLLOWING THE DEAD

Digital Obituaries as Rituals of Selective Remembrance During the COVID-19 Pandemic

Yash Gupta

Obituaries as Literary Texts

Leslie Leake was 75, Enekee Leake was 45 and John Leake Jr. was 44 when they passed away within a span of 2 weeks due to the Coronavirus. Soon, their collective obituary became a part of CNN's *We Remember*, a compilation of 105 pandemic obituaries posted by American families. The same was submitted by Shanta Leake-Cherry, recounting Leslie Leake, her mother, as "the one that exemplified love", her sister Enekee Leake as a "social butterfly", and her brother John Leake Jr. as "just a joy" (Leake-Cherry). The Leakes' experience is typical of mourning practices in a context restrictive of human collectivity and crisscrossed with digital affordances. Indeed, Walter et. al note that humans have been engaging with the internet as a space for mourning since the 1990s (282). Yet the upending of "normalcy" in the way we process death during the pandemic has re-emphasized the role of the digital, especially virtual mortuary texts like obituaries, in transacting posthumous identities.

This chapter draws from these parameters, evaluating digital American obituaries during the COVID-19 pandemic, considering them as contemporary literary rituals of selective memorialization. While doing so, I treat the obituaries as "mediatized rituals", whereby due to the "interconnection of human communication with media and the resulting social and cultural changes" (Thimm and Nehls 328), obituaries "have the ability to create a shared experience" (Harju 141) and restore social order. According to Durkheim, rituals consist of repeated core symbols that unify individuals based on shared norms and guidelines (Pantti and Sumiala 122). Similarly, Fowler suggests that obituaries serve an ideological role, emphasizing normative codes of that good life and good death (*Mapping the Obituary*148). Thus, this chapter contends that owing to the seclusionary context of the pandemic, normative discourses generated within obituary pages reproduce ritualistic functions.

DOI: 10.4324/9781003294436-22

Parallelly, I also maintain that obituary pages are dynamic, both fostering and contesting normative expectations.

Following Kluckhohn, I take internal and external repetitions to be at the core of an obituary's ritualistic function (66), basing my analysis on the split between function (external repetition) and form (internal repetition). The first part of this chapter aims to establish the literary basis and context of the obituary, following which the second part explores how the online obituary negotiates its form in relation to social scripts. The third and final part evaluates the ritualistic paralleling of the obituary at the intersections of its digital and temporal context. In approaching the obituaries, I adopt critical and thematic discourse analysis, informed by a social constructivist lens. As a framework, critical discourse analysis evaluates implicit sentiments expressed in a text as ideological inferences (Harju 134). This is bolstered by thematic analysis, whereby recurring patterns in speech are viewed as structural choices revelatory of social norms (Hume and Bressers 260). Furthermore, the analysis, while taking into account several obituary pages such as *Time's The Lives Lost to Coronavirus* and *NBC's The Loss*, focuses on the aforementioned *We Remember* hosted by CNN, to maintain unity of theme and content. Thus, in exploring digital obituaries during the pandemic, I take into account not only normativity but also the potential of functional novelty.

Obituaries as Kernels of Narrative

Mortuary texts have been constant to grieving rituals, with their digital variations representing a new link in a year-long chain of death reportage. Fowler traces the origin point of the form to John Aubrey's *Brief Lives*, a collection of biographies penned from 1669 to 1696. The obituary, as a form, was later popularized in the eighteenth century, with the rise of biographies as a literary genre, especially through *The Gentleman's Magazine* (*Obituary as Collective Memory* 4). Yet, as life narratives, obituaries maintain a tenuous relationship with the biographical genre, negotiating expectations of length, audience and authorship. However, following Shield, I pose that "obituaries. . . carry, like genes packed tight in their separate chromosomes, tiny kernels of narrative" (Shields in McNeill 187). As pieces that reduce the expectations of life into small columns, obituaries foster both the journalistic imperative towards truth, and the literary maintenance of form (Fowler, *Mapping the Obituary* 149).

Online obituaries represent a techno-spiritual and spatio-temporal evolution of the form, allowing one to engage with their emotions, before, during and after the end of ceremonial time frames. The pandemic obituary pages in consideration can be viewed as public journalistic cemeteries evident from imagery such as burning candles and muted tones on the websites. COVID-19 deaths assume a central position within these sites, as any deaths unrelated to the pandemic escape mentioned. This, it can be argued, is because digital discourses are often context-oriented, and since other deaths fail to meet the mould, their mentions take lesser precedence.

Furthermore, unlike newspaper obituaries, digital obituary pages are defined by elasticity of expression transacted through text, audios, videos and images. Of the obituaries analyzed, 38.10% were textual, 11.43% were audio-based, 16.19% were a combination of text and audio, and 34.29% were an amalgamation of text and video, with all submissions hosting images of the deceased.[1] The flexibility of media not only allows the next of kin to project their own conception of the departed but also offers the readers a pictorial opportunity to acquaint themselves with the dead. This can act as a source of affect for both the authors and readers, allowing "People (to) face into their grief, to the point where family members sometimes hug the monitor when a video is played" (*The Washington Post* qtd. in Hume and Brasser 258).

However, while images can sustain affect and closure, they also centre, what Hallam and Hockey call, "publicly visible faces" (qtd. in McNeill 191). Specifically, since obituaries are born out of selection rooted in public acceptance, they act as grounds for gauging moments and characteristics deemed vital in one's life. Obituary images are, thus, often the "idealized" version of those being remembered, in their prime, as healthy individuals. They serve as instances of contradictory idealization, for while the past-oriented images aim at the erasure of illness, the placement of the entry on pandemic death pages undermines the same.

Furthermore, it is the aforementioned audience of the obituary that creates a drive towards idealization. Spectatorship in digital obituary pages remains ever-present, illustrated through the use of third-person pronouns that describe the deceased to an assumed group of individuals. Similar to a printed obituary, the consumers of a digital obituary actively engage with the life narratives of their private/public contemporaries. Through the process of reading, the audience creates a community around the narrative of shared characteristics, experiences, values, norms and trajectories (McNeill 187). The casting of the deceased in social moulds (mother, father, sibling or friends) acts to universalize the text, serving an audience that would harbour expectations in link with similar labels. Obituaries, therefore, can be marked as journalistic micro-life narrative/assessments which, through the process of multi-layered selection, both reify specific cultural ideals and link the individual with the collective.

Internal Repetition and Norm

For Fowler, contemporary obituaries offer sociodicies or justification of society, its norms and its processes (*Obituaries as Collective Memory* 18). Similarly, within the framework adopted in this chapter, digital obituaries act as a means of establishing collectivity based on normatively shared ideals. They are ritualistic in so far that their repetition, both internal and external works to alleviate the anxiety of death by offering predictable forms of grieving (Kluckhohn 57). Hume and Bressers parallelly argue that since obituaries are idealized texts geared towards public consumption, they should be evaluated in light of public memory (258). The genre of obituaries and its assumed audience exists in a cycle of influence. Cultural scripts sanction specific forms of memorialization, with the individual obituaries negotiating structural hierarchies to legitimize their claim to public memory. To recapitulate, the form of the obituary rests upon the need to represent the deceased as a productive member of society, especially one "worth remembering" in the public domain. Thus, as manifestations of collective beliefs, obituaries relay, through the acts of exclusion/inclusion or remembering/forgetting, the "cultural politics of canonization" (Fowler, *Mapping the Obituary*162).

Noting the recurrence of specific patterns, online obituaries can be deemed "intertextual" for they create a cohesive web with other entries present on a specific page. The formation of generic scripts that centre name, age, occupation, affiliations, reference to survivors and social contributions occurs specifically since the wider audience remains unaware of the deceased's intimate personality traits. Consequently, obituarists take recourse to the known norms of the "good life" and "good death" to create public meaning within the life of the deceased. Thus, for instance, digital obituary pages reconcile gendered expectations by reproducing normative gender roles in the narratives they present. Central to this conclusion was Kastenbaun, Peyton and Kastenbaum's 1977 argument, "dominant male-preferring value system of the United States would carry over the threshold from life to death" (qtd. In Moremen and Cradduck 242). Demonstratively, of the obituaries analyzed on CNN's COVID-19 obituary page, only 31.42% were dedicated to "women". Indeed, within the obituaries of *We Remember*, gender, regardless of its complexity, was treated in a binary, illustrated through the sole usage of she/her/hers and he/him/his pronouns in relation to conventional gender presentation. This was compounded by the absence of sexual identities in the obituaries analyzed. The stake here is not whether the deceased identified non-heteronormatively, but rather how these absences constitute illocutionary silences.

Austin, in his proposal of speech-act theory, suggests that speech constitutes illocutionary acts, prompting a response or perlocutionary consequence. Sauntson draws from this, suggesting that the illocutionary silencing of non-normative identities results in heteronormative assumption, where a body is perceived normative until proven otherwise (Depalma 6–7). Following this, my mentions of *men, male, women* and *female* in the following paragraphs are cognizant of the deep complexity of gender, yet are repeated to reproduce the gendered distinctions established on the obituary pages.

Thus, Islam Uddin Khan's obituary is illustrative of the characteristics idealized among male-presenting individuals. Rija Khan, his daughter, remembers him as, "a good leader, a role model – a patriarch of the family" (Khan). Similarly, Dr. Wethington's obituary mentions his service, "as a county medical examiner for 25 years . . . (helping) establish a missionary medical clinic in Guatemala" (Wethington et al.). Indeed, subjectivities concerning profession and male leadership have for a long time been the focus of formal newspaper obituaries, revealing a male bias in the commemoration of the past.

Here, it is essential to consider obituaries as documents of history, ensuring the survival of generational narratives. Hence, obituaries such as those dedicated to

John "Jack" Hennigan who "survived the Vietnam War, suffering lung damage as a result of Agent Orange" (Hennigan), are indicative of not only male ideals but also the gendering of the American public memory. Hume notes that dominantly male national experiences continue to serve as strong symbols of American public memory, often centering on events such as the Vietnam War, or the World Wars (17). Consequently, while 11.11% of all male obituaries analyzed mention veteran status, no female obituaries mention military involvement, reflecting how specific forms of engagements are read prominently in specific gendered contexts. Therefore, internal repetitions in male obituaries suggest that the most valuable components of the normative patriarch remain in service and economic success in different sectors.

Yet, male obituaries, particularly the ones dedicated to younger generations, simultaneously offer a wide range of expression, especially when compared to obituaries dedicated to women. Digital spaces act as a space for negotiating and constructing personal notions of identity monikers such as masculinity. Accordingly, male obituaries also take into account the deceased's familial roles, personal traits, involvement in the arts, religious affiliations and married life, among other themes. In contrast, female obituaries present constricted narratives centering on the roles of devoted and selfless caretakers, mothers and wives. To this point, "Angela White was '*destined*' to be the mother of four girls", acting as a "kind of a mom to so many people . . . (acting as) one of my best friends, confidant, cheerleader and anything a mom would be" (Kay, *emphasis mine*). Female obituaries play an integral role in the reproduction of social hierarchies, disseminating the characteristics of proper remembrance to the next generation of assumed mothers and wives.

Moremen and Cradduck further this, suggesting that female-presenting individuals are often confined to specific occupational categories, being overrepresented in service and clerical roles (252). Correspondingly, only 33% of the female obituaries analyzed, mentioned professional engagement, out of which 63.64% of the deceased were involved in care-based professions (nursing and education). The heightened emphasis on normatively feminine economic roles, regardless of the myriad ways women function within the economic sphere, reflects the sanctioning of select subjectivities online. Contrarily, outliers such as Arlene Stringer-Cuevas, who "was the first woman to represent the neighborhood of Washington Heights on the New York City Council", were made socially legible by distinctly marking them as "single mother(s)" (Stringer), wives and daughters.

Digital obituary spaces, thus, are contested zones of identity affirmation, representation and remembrance, constantly negotiating boundaries of acceptance. For instance, though the internet has proved more inclusive of "deviant deaths"[2] and disenfranchised grief, they are often sequestered on websites solely dedicated to them (Walter et al 286). The provision of space on the internet does not always translate into the acceptance of a given expression. Similarly, while immigrants or individuals within a diaspora occupy a comparatively high 13.34% of all obituary mentions, they remain locked in the paradigms of the "hardworking male immigrant" and the "culturally stagnant female immigrant". Hence, Leonardo Guzman who "immigrated to the US from Colombia in the 1980s . . . worked really, really hard for our family to have better opportunities" (Uribe). By the same token, Ann Marie Robain who "was born in Trinidad and moved to America in 1973 . . . was known for making traditional Trinidad dishes, such as roti, black cake and pastelles" (Fontaine). Non-dominant bodies play an essential role in deconstructing and negotiating the genre through mentions constituted as difference, yet they do so by both assimilating with and subverting normative expectations. Decisively, online obituary pages are marked by a drive towards restrictive diversification, where increasing representation is tempered by normative consistency.

Inquiring Consistency

The consistency in conservative structures between the online and the offline, Taussig notes, can be traced to the re-establishment of print standards in the digital realm (203). This partially arises since alteration in grieving processes can be viewed as disrespectful of the deceased. The pandemic has made this relationship even more tenuous, especially since physical means of grief alleviation have proved inefficient during isolation. Furthermore, besides being regulated by the funeral industry, the discourse on respect remains so scantily broached, that opposition to the status quo is often dismissed. Thus, the increased importance of the obituary as an outlet for grief, coupled with the stagnant discourse surrounding it, has created an aversion to change.

Furthermore, obituarists often follow known codes defined by digital guidebooks, since virtual gravesites hold the discretion to refuse the publication of submissions deemed "inappropriate". The same is also reinstated in several how-to pages that guide the obituarist to follow offline formats concerned with age, professions and social roles. For example, *The Remembrance Process*, a website that specializes in conveying end-of-life information, mentions,

> We begin with the name, age, and place of residence of the deceased . . . a recounting of the most important events, qualities, contributions and connections in a person's life . . . date and place of marriage, birth name of spouse, education, work, and military service.
>
> *("How To Write An Obituary – A Step-by-Step Guide")*

Thus, online obituaries rely heavily upon the perceived stability of the genre and, regardless of the innovative freedom constituted by audio messages or flexible lengths, become another platform for staging traditional cultural performances.

Moreover, I contend that cultural scripts act as a means of stifling the offensiveness of memory. By offensiveness, I refer to the totality of memory that engages and often disturbs culturally constructed notions of posthumous respect. Normative guidelines allow authors to erase traits that may undermine claims to public memory. Within biographical mortuary texts, events that are to be highlighted fall, rather complexly, into categories of the respectful, and the offensive. While not a concrete distinction, memories deemed respectful find easy acceptance in digital obituary pages, while offensive events may either be rejected, become a part of personal remembrance, or be assimilated in "negative" or "ironic" obituaries (Fowler, *Obituary as Collective Memory*18–21).

Online obituaries, therefore, act as rituals of selective remembrance. As a ritual, they provide "a sense of finality while celebrating the deceased's noteworthy attributes, preserving and legitimizing these important characteristics of Americans throughout the nation's history" (Hume 20). Concurrently, the tunnelling of culturally readable subjectivities, regardless of their social costs, plays an important role in constructing known affectual channels of grief and alleviation of cultural anxieties. By limiting the variations that mortuary texts can take, cultural scripts manifest obituaries with predictability, thereby materializing the immaterial nature of death (Kluckhohn 58).

External Repetition and Obituaries as Rituals of Selective Remembrance

For Amato, death "causes people to tell stories" that are "shaped by moral judgment, fashioned for the sake of argument, made buoyant by metaphor, or given meaning by the rituals of culture and the promise of religion" (qtd. in Hume 15–16). Certainly, obituaries as "stories" of the dead are more secular than other forms of rituals; yet, they maintain a degree of authority in legitimizing social norms. Similarly, within a virtual landscape, obituaries do more than just mediate rituals, rather "performatively enacting" (Pantti and Sumiala 120), altering and adopting modes of processing grief. Situating death in a memory landscape, and thereby including the deceased in the present, is integral to death rituals. Recognizing this, Fowler calls an obituary a "secularized *rite de passage*" (*Collective Memory* 61) at the intersection of ethics and politics. Mediatized mourning allows grievers to not only revisit "gravesites" but also integrate the dead through individual engagement, thereby acting as everyday rituals.

Mediatized rituals are indicative of the expansion and alteration of our affective landscapes. I draw from Granovetter in suggesting that digital media enables communities to be established on "weak ties". According to them, strong ties consist of relations comprising family and friends, and are characterized by emotional support; on the other hand, weak ties consist of broader social circles, defined by social capital and wider geographies (Walter et al. 278). Consequently, the affordances provided by the internet have allowed mourners to build community trans-spatially and atemporally.

A central claim of this chapter is that considering the physical constrictions on mourning, digital obituaries during the COVID-19 pandemic have been fulfilling, if only partly, the roles of a death ritual. I cite Durkheim again in considering that in the act of coming together, a group of individuals renew the legitimacy of their collective values (Pantti and Sumiala 122). Parallelly, journalistic pieces also assume an audience of shared values, "telling stories and creating characters who stand for something larger than themselves, something that is cultural and historical rather than personal and momentary" (Kitchand Hume qtd. in Taussig 6).

Rituals aid in making comprehensible and recognizable the contradictory nature of life, and by extension, death. However, during the pandemic, digital obituaries have acted as one of the sole public recognitions of the process. Since the public announcement and recognition of death is a traditional requirement for several grieving processes, online obituaries enact a communal behavioural change by announcing the need for an appropriate response. Indeed, Wolfelt suggests that the primary function of a ritual lies in its ability to label an individual as a mourner. This is most evident within social media platforms, where comments such as "miss you" or "RIP" work to define the posters as communal mourners. Similarly, on virtual obituary pages, the mentions of authors and the " 'survived by" act establish the living as grievers.

However, the invocation of community also surfaces concerns of belief systems which can create both connections and cleavages (Wolfelt). Rituals are, if not always religious, connected to different belief systems. This function is not specific to the online obituary, for print media has for long engaged with pictorial symbols and textual references. However, the mention of ideology online has allowed for a wider representation of non-majoritarian belief systems, especially in pages dedicated to specific forms of death. On CNN's *We Remember*, Christianity emerged as the biggest affiliation, exemplified in Doris Sander's obituary. Her daughter, Sonja Sanders described her as "a woman of deep faith . . . (who) On their last phone call . . . asked for a pastor's prayer" (Sanders). On the other hand, while politicization of the virus was not a dominant theme on CNN's page owing to the lack of a comments section, it was constant in digital mortuary discourse surrounding the pandemic. For instance, a post on MyDeathSpace's Facebook page focused on, "Karen Kolb Sehlke (~45) (who) died from COVID-19 after ranting about the virus being a hoax three weeks prior" (MyDeathSpace). Weeks earlier, Sehlke had expressed, "You don't need hand sanitizer, toilet paper, and Lysol. You need common sense, a sense of direction, (and) faith" (MyDeathSpace). While the validity of the post remains ambiguous due to the deactivation of Sehlke's profile after her death, several comments soon flooded the post. One commenter wrote, "I would feel sorry for Karen and her family but I don't . . . Were the body bags in the NYC hospital part of the hoax?" (MyDeathSpace). In response another individual commented, "I'm looking at these comments and I now know why Donald Trump will be reelected in November. The left is just gross" (MyDeathSpace). The platform thus transformed into a space for opposing discussions upon the reality of the pandemic, conflated with the larger political scenario in the United States of America. Ideology or belief was integral to both scenarios, as the life narrative of the deceased was used to affirm/destabilize contesting thought systems.

Indeed, Walter in *A new model of grief: bereavement and biography* argues that the contextualization of the biographies of both the living and the dead lies at the core of bereavement (9). The multiple authors of a digital obituary act collectively to create the deceased's biography through multiple lenses. For example, Edna

Addams' obituary recounts several key moments from her life as perceived by the authors,

> She lived through the 1918 flu pandemic, women's suffrage, the Great Depression and two world wars . . . moving into a nursing home after her 100th birthday . . . becoming the District of Columbia's oldest coronavirus victim.
>
> *(Lang)*

The shared construction of a biography is a self-reflexive process that both marks the deceased as "worth remembering" and justifies the sharer's emotion towards the dead. Within the offline world, transitional rituals like wakes and funerals aid the living in adopting a new status as the "survived by". Similarly, obituaries, through the cyclical affirmation of the living, aid individuals to transition through social roles on a public stage (Wolfelt). The same could be gleaned through the collective obituary of the Leakes, where Leslie Leake as the "survived by" not only engaged in the process of biographic creation of the deceased but also partook in the construction of her own "relational identity", or her sense of self that arose out of her roles to others (Walter 20–21). To witness, as a griever, Leslie Leake was simultaneously involved in establishing herself as the "sister and daughter" of the deceased.

Yet, central to the different functions of a death ritual is to make the memory of the dead continuous with the living, through the internalization, individualization and immortalization of the deceased (Walter 7). However, for several, the pandemic has been a homogenizing tragedy, instigated by the saturation of death in public discourse. As a recourse, one of the primary means to individuate the deceased has been through the uniqueness of the obituaries. An offshoot of the same has been the creation of the "Heroes of the Pandemic", silent citizens who perished while serving their communities. Bill Mantell's obituary, for example, mentions his service as the owner of

> a small community pharmacy. . . (which) stayed open even as the community was hit hard by the coronavirus pandemic. . .He said, 'I own a pharmacy and people need their medication'.
>
> *(The Mantell Family)*

By marking one as a "martyr", this subcategory creates not only another venue of worth for the deceased but also a hierarchy of acknowledgement and permanent remembrance. These obituaries emphasize role over totality, mourning the loss of archetypes represented by the deceased. Accordingly, Leilani Jordan's obituary centers on the role of a "good Samaritan" and a "caretaker", who regardless of her "cerebral palsy . . . insisted on going to work to help the store's elderly customers" (Shepard andCharles). Not only this but highlighting the exceptional contribution of private citizens evolves to American social history by placing the individual in the public, thereby defining ideal "Americanness" (McNeill 199). Situating one's death in the vicinity of a temporal event such as the pandemic makes simultaneous one's death with the general history.

However, it is also important to highlight that mediatized memorialization is a deeply contested sphere. Unlike a structured physical gathering, online biography creation is open to wider contestation due to the involvement of several subjectivities. Here, "shared" does not translate into cooperative, since mourners might be confronted with alternative narratives or mourning patterns that they do not identify with (such as radical religiosity or offensive phraseology) (Walter et al. 291). This is specifically so since digital media might bring survivors from different social spheres in contact, bringing into proximity different perceptions of the deceased. Further disagreements may arise during the cyclical creation of the biographical self, as the mourners may feel the need to create a justificatory stake in the deceased's life narrative. Online obituary spaces, therefore, may transform into complex negotiations between several biographical processes. Thus, even when rituals can be considered a means of creating community, Pantti and Sumiala caution against equating the effect of ritual with "a we-feeling" (121). Obituaries as rituals occur in and affirm specific cultural contexts. The publication of an obituary is not solely a simple act of remembrance, but one where memory is strung and made cohesive with an already existing web of expectations.

Conclusion

Rolando "Sonny" Aravena was only 44 when he passed away on his twin daughters' 10th birthday. In the video dedicated to him, his wife Melody Aravena describes him as a "selfless man . . . (who) loved everyone" (Aravena). Regardless of the several works that will eventually concern the pandemic, it is easy to lose sight of the individual tragedies that mark this period. Obituaries, as a *rite de passage*, hold important lessons for the readers: believe in God, help each other, respect familial relations and stick together. For several trapped inside, death has migrated to brightly lit screens. While affirming norms, they also teach us how to process grief, how to respond with "RIP(s)", congregate around images of candles and audios of the mourners, and remember the dead (Kitchand Hume qtd. in Hume and Bressers 259). These spaces convey a lot more than information, aiding with biography creation, continuing relations with the dead and grieving with weak ties.

Digital obituaries during the pandemic negotiate constantly the constancy of the genre and the heft of function. McNeill aptly summarizes the same when they suggest that,

> Within this conservative genre (of obituaries), the possibilities for auto/biographical constructions are continuously foreclosed by the formulae and expectations of the genre and the culture it both creates and is created by.

(189)

However, organized forgetting often accompanies public remembrance (Fowler, *Mapping The Obituary* 149). Societies carry memories that go beyond the personal and are often a reflection of the past distilled in the present. To allow the individual to be memorialized publicly, they must be made readable through cultural scripts; consequently requiring that the everyday life be made to fit in the mould of legible biographical obituaries. For those who fail to conform to the script, like non-English-speaking public, those unable to access the internet, individuals without families, criminals and outliers, the rituals of collective auto/biography are selective.

The genre regulates boundaries of acceptance, for considering the thousands of COVID-19-related deaths each day, only a hundred or so have made it to these compilation pages. Obituaries thus serve to construct institutional history in their assessment of the good dead that fulfilled their roles as good citizens, family members and providers. In memorializing the dead, the living are equally implicated, creating texts that are often much more alive than the people they are dedicated to.

Notes

1   The percentages have been rounded off to the nearest hundreds. Furthermore, while videos and audios were taken into consideration, the focus of the analysis is on the textual aspects of the obituaries.
2   Deviant or marginalized deaths are characteristically unnatural and culturally stigmatized. This involves deaths and the dead that do not parallel our hegemonic notions of a good life/death such as suicide victims, or individuals who succumb to conflated reasons such as HIV, among others.

Works Cited

Aravena, Melody. "Rolando 'Sonny' Aravena." *We Remember, CNN*, 2020.www.edition.cnn. com/interactive/2020/health/coronavirus-victims-memories/.

DePalma, Renée. "Gay Penguins, Sissy Ducklings . . . and Beyond? Exploring Gender andSexuality Diversity Through Children's Literature." *Discourse: Studies in the Cultural Politics of Education*, vol. 34, no. 6, 2016, pp. 1–18.Taylor & Francis.doi:10.4324/978 1315122762-3.

Fontaine, Alexis. "AnnMarie Thelma Robain." *We Remember, CNN*, 2020.www.edition. cnn.com/interactive/2020/health/coronavirus-victims-memories/.

Fowler, Bridget. "Mapping the Obituary: Notes Towards a Bourdieusian Interpretation." *The Sociological Review*, 2004, pp. 148–71.doi:10.1111/j.1467-954x.2005.00529.x.

———."Collective Memory and Forgetting: Components for a Study of Obituaries." *Theory Culture Society*, vol. 22, no. 53, 2005, pp. 53–72. doi:10.1177/0263276405059414.

———. *The Obituary as Collective Memory*. Routledge, 2009.

Harju, Anu. "Socially Shared Mourning: Construction and Consumption of Collective Memory." *New Review of Hypermedia and Multimedia*, vol. 21, no. 1–2, 2014, pp. 123–45. doi:10.1080/13614568.2014.983562.

Hennigan. Karen. "John 'Jack' Hennigan." *We Remember, CNN*, 2020.www.edition.cnn. com/interactive/2020/health/coronavirus-victims-memories/.

"How to Write an Obituary – a Step-by-Step Guide." *The Remembrance Process: From Grieving to Remembrance*, 2020. www.remembranceprocess.com/capturing-a-life-in-words/guide-to-writing-an-obituary/.

Hume, Janice. *Obituaries in American Culture.* UP of Mississippi, 2000.

Hume, Janice, and Bonnie Bressers. "Obituaries Online: New Connections with the Living – and the Dead." *OMEGA – Journal of Death and Dying*, vol. 60, no. 3, 2010, pp. 255–71. doi:10.2190/om.60.3.d.

Kay, Hope. "Angela White." *We Remember, CNN*, 2020. edition.cnn.com/interactive/2020/health/coronavirus-victims-memories/.

Khan, Rija. "Islam Uddin Khan." *We Remember, CNN*, 2020.www.edition.cnn.com/interactive/2020/health/coronavirus-victims-memories/.

Kluckhohn, Clyde. "Myths and Rituals: A General Theory." *Harvard Theological Review*, vol. 35, no. 1, 1942, pp. 45–79. doi:10.1017/s0017816000005150.

Lang, M.J. "Edna Addams." *Faces of the Dead, Washington Post*, 16 Mar. 2020. www.washingtonpost.com/health/2020/04/24/coronavirus-dead-victims-stories/?arc404=true-Edna Adams.

Leake-Cherry, Shanta. "Leslie Leake, Enekee Leake and John Leake Jr." *We Remember, CNN*, 2020.www.edition.cnn.com/interactive/2020/health/coronavirus-victims-memories/.

The Mantell Family. "Bill Mantell." *We Remember, CNN*, 2020.www.edition.cnn.com/interactive/2020/health/coronavirus-victims-memories/.

McNeill, Laurie. "Writing Lives in Death: Canadian Death Notices as Auto/Biography." *Auto/Biography in Canada Critical Directions*, edited by Julie Rak. Wilfrid Laurier UP, 2005, pp. 187–206.

"MyDeathSpace." *Facebook*, 4 Apr. 2020. www.facebook.com/MyDeathSpace/posts/not-to-get-political-but-sometimes-the-universe-works-in-mysterious-ways-karen-k/10157123249601497/.

Moremen, Robin D., and Cathy Cradduck. "'How Will You Be Remembered After You Die?' Gender Discrimination After Death Twenty Years Later." *OMEGA – Journal of Death and Dying*, vol. 38, no. 4, 1999, pp. 241–54.doi:10.2190/0ky0-p54v-kfdb-9vcr.

Pantti, Mervi, and Johanna Sumiala. "Till Death Do Us Join: Media, Mourning Rituals and the Sacred Centre of the Society." *Media, Culture & Society*, vol. 31, no. 1, 2009, pp. 119–35.doi:10.1177/0163443708098251.

Sanders, Sonja. "Doris Granderson Jr." *We Remember, CNN*, 2020. www.edition.cnn.com/interactive/2020/health/coronavirus-victims-memories/.

Shepard, Zenobia, and S. Charles. "Leilani Jordan." *We Remember, CNN*, 2020.www.edition.cnn.com/interactive/2020/health/coronavirus-victims-memories/.

Stringer, Scott. "Arlene Stringer-Cuevas." *We Remember, CNN*, 2020.www.edition.cnn.com/interactive/2020/health/coronavirus-victims-memories/.

Taussig, Doron. "Your Story Is Our Story: Collective Memory in Obituaries of US Military Veterans." *Memory Studies*, vol. 10, no. 4, 2016, pp. 459–73. doi:10.1177/1750698016653441.

Thimm, Caja, and Patrick Nehls. "Sharing Grief and Mourning on Instagram: Digital Patterns of Family Memories." *Communications*, vol. 42, no. 3, 2017, pp. 327–49.doi:10.1515/commun-2017-0035.

Uribe, Ericka. "Leonardo Guzman." *We Remember, CNN*, 2020.www.edition.cnn.com/interactive/2020/health/coronavirus-victims-memories/.

Walter, Tony. "A New Model of Grief: Bereavement and Biography." *Mortality*, vol. 1, no. 1, 1996, pp. 7–25. doi:10.1080/713685822.

Walter, Tony, et al. "Does the Internet Change How We Die and Mourn? Overview and Analysis." *OMEGA – Journal of Death and Dying*, vol. 64, no. 4, 2012, pp. 275–302. doi:10.2190/om.64.4.a.

Wethington, Joseph Francis, et al. "Dr. Joseph Francis Wethington." *We Remember, CNN*, 2020.www.edition.cnn.com/interactive/2020/health/coronavirus-victims-memories/.

Wolfelt, Alan. "Why Is the Funeral Ritual Important?" *Center for Loss & Life Transition*, 16 Dec. 2016.www.centerforloss.com/2016/12/funeral-ritual-important/.

INDEX